James MacGregor Burns

★★★★★★★★★★★★★★★★★★★★

★★★★★★★★★★★★★★★★★★★★★★

JOHN KENNEDY

A Political Profile

Illustrated

AVON BOOK DIVISION
The Hearst Corporation
959 Eighth Avenue
New York 19, N. Y.

For My Mother

"To John Kennedy"

... But if, as I'm informéd weel,
Ye hate as ill's the vera Deil
The flinty heart that canna feel—
    Come, sir, here's tae you!
Hae, there's my han', I wiss you weel,
    An' Gude be wi' you!

       Robert Burns, 1786

CONTENTS

Inauguration 1961—A Foreword

In the long sweep of history the decisive mark of the man entering the White House in 1961 will not be his age, or his religion, or his Senatorial background, or the other matters so much discussed this past year. What will be crucial is that once again America has a political craftsman as President.

Born of a political family in one of the most political of cities, Kennedy has spent all his adult life, aside from the war years, in the scuffle of legislative and electoral combat. The key difference between the outgoing and incoming Presidents is that Dwight D. Eisenhower dislikes this kind of politics and that John F. Kennedy likes it. Kennedy considers it indispensable to the operation of a great democracy, even inevitable. "No President," he says, "can escape politics."

The great test of Kennedy's Presidency will be the test he, himself, would be the first to apply: not whether he will be a politician—he will—but what kind of politician he will be, and whether his kind of political craftsmanship will be enough for the staggering job ahead. What are the prospects? The answer turns on the nature of the Presidential office and on the nature of the new incumbent.

Most of the time, the Presidency is not a command post from which clear and concerted orders are issued to troops waiting to spring into action. Most of the time, it is a fulcrum of maneuver and bargaining, with the President seeking to convert a limited amount of power into governmental action.

It is a place where he must deal with hundreds of other powerful men and their separate sources of power in and outside the government. Most of the time, the Presidency calls less for a master leader than for a master broker.

By experience and by temperament, Kennedy should qualify as a master broker. The Boston brand of politics in which he was schooled is a kind of institute of advanced training in political manipulation. For fourteen years in the congressional labyrinth, he has learned to negotiate with proud legislative leaders and party factions. In addition, in two years of preconvention delegate hunting, he had to bargain with state officials and city bosses whose political interests were far different from those of a junior Senator on the make.

Like a good poker player, a master broker must be cool-headed and clear-minded, utterly realistic about his own hand and that of his opponents unflustered and unwilling to be hurried. These, too, are keynotes of Kennedy's political style. Observers have noted again and again his detached attitude toward himself, his cold insight into the balance of power, and his capacity to move quickly or slowly as conditions demanded. His Cabinet-making was a case in point. Despite pressures to hurry on with the job, he took his time as he sorted and measured and cut to fit.

Skill in bargaining is vital not only in negotiation with foot-dragging congressmen and governors. A President must also bargain with Cabinet members and agency heads "supposedly" under him. "I sit here all day trying to persuade people to do the things they ought to have sense enough to do without my persuading them," Harry S. Truman said. "That is all the powers of the President amount to." A new President soon finds that the neat lines of authority on the organization chart are actually snarled and broken by the political tempests that rage around the White House.

"When it comes to power," says Professor Richard E. Neustadt, of Columbia, a former Truman aide, "nobody is expert but the President; if he, too, acts as layman, it goes hard with him." Kennedy can be rated as a professional in the care and nourishment of political power. A President, he said to a visitor recently, must be careful not to use up his credit too quickly. He needs the best people around him, but in the end he must depend upon himself. And, he added, he has only four years to make good.

To be effective, a master broker must operate at the center of the political cobweb. He must see to it that lines of influence focus in him and radiate from him. We hear much of a President being his "own Secretary of State," but in this sense he also must be his own Secretary of the Treasury and Attorney General and all the rest. He must be a silent partner in every office in his administration.

That the new President will operate through a network of personal control, rather than along the stiff lines of an organization chart, was made clear in the way he built his administration. In several cases he selected subordinate officials before he chose the department head; obviously these officials will be as much beholden to him as to their immediate superiors.

As an administrator, Kennedy may remind us of Franklin D. Roosevelt, who used to bypass eminent secretaries like Cordell Hull in order to deal directly with second-level men like Sumner Welles. Roosevelt joyously drove a team of spirited horses kept in harness mainly by his own vigor and *élan*. The result—a disorderly but productive administration—may be duplicated in the days ahead.

It is essential in this kind of personal administration for the President to have all the reins in his hands. He cannot delegate much of the job of persuading and bargaining because success turns so heavily on his personal participation. Representative Joseph W. Martin, former Republican majority leader, has complained that Mr. Eisenhower dealt with congressional leaders through subordinates, "telling them 'the chief wants this' or 'the chief wants that.'" Congressmen "would like to hear it from the Chief himself once in a while," Martin said. President Kennedy would not make this mistake.

To maximize his bargaining power, a President must have a kind of built-in computer that weighs his personal influence and channels it in the right direction. Recent visitors to Georgetown and Palm Beach have been surprised by the absence of harried staff aides and thick piles of documents. Kennedy seems to hold all the data in his head. So far, top decision-making has been a solo performance. It is not likely to be very different even in the heavily institutionalized White House.

To be a good broker, a President must also be highly accessible to men and ideas. He can never become the prisoner of a tight little staff. Kennedy has reached out over his immediate entourage to hire men whom he had never known. In a manner reminiscent of FDR, he has deliberately set up task forces that will supply him with ideas that may conflict with those of new department heads. He has appointed to staff positions men who may work at cross-purposes, but out of whose arguments new ideas may be heated up. He, himself, makes a point of reading hostile editorials and columns (and he is easily irritated by them).

Only a man confident of his political capacity could run a personal, loose-jointed operation, and Kennedy is such a person. Where does he get his self-confidence? In part from a well-developed competitive sense; he simply feels that he is more effective politically than most of his rivals. In part, too, from his recent political successes, especially during the past year. Recently, while stretched out on a deck chair under a hot Florida sun, he was asked whether he really felt as relaxed amid all the pressure as he seemed. He answered that after the crises of the 1960 campaign, which he named one after another—the Wisconsin and West Virginia primaries, the preconvention opposition of powerful party leaders like Truman, the Houston answer to criticism by Protestant leaders, the debates with Nixon—he was ready for anything.

"That was a long year and a tough campaign," he said with a wry smile, "and I survived it."

Outwardly, Kennedy does not seem scarred by battle. These days, he appears relaxed, composed, and unhurried; his talk runs easily from foreign-policy problems to the latest political shenanigans in Massachusetts. His face is fuller and stronger than it was two years ago, but still unlined. Men who fight their way to the top often take on a grave mien and ponderous ways; but not so Kennedy. He carries none of the weighty trappings of authority. He is still simple, direct, unaffected, and surprisingly candid about his views and plans. Perhaps he feels that he need not look like a man holding authority; he need simply embody it.

Yet, he is very much the product of political combat. He can be wary about mens' intentions and cautious about playing out his own political hand. He has dealt so long with intractable problems that he resists sweeping judgments and doctrinaire solutions. His thinking is literal and specific; he personalizes social and political forces, seeing them in terms of individual leaders—an editor, a senator, a union chief—who are hostile or friendly and who can be resisted or bargained with. He has been called ruthless and cold, and doubtless he can be on occasion; more often he is flexible, fast-moving, resourceful, and wily. To him, politics is the art of the possible.

Kennedy is a pragmatist, acting directly in the tradition not only of all our great Presidents since Washington, but of the "near-great" such as Polk and Hayes and McKinley. These latter lacked genius, but because each in his own way was a craftsman, they were effective Presidents. Kennedy's political skill almost guarantees that he will measure up to this company.

But will political craftsmanship be enough in the 1960s? The great lesson of the Presidency is that the man in the White House must be more than a politician and a hard bargainer and a shrewd broker. He must be a leader—a party leader, a legislative leader, a moral leader. In Machiavelli's old analogy, he must be a lion as well as a fox.

A great leader must do more than negotiate with men; he must know how to command them. Instead of trying to unravel the tangled threads of politics and administration, he must sometimes cut through them with a decisive stroke. He may have to jettison some of his allies for the sake of an overriding goal. He must sound a note of national purpose to galvanize lesser men into action and sacrifice for ends that they do not wholly perceive. "History is a preceptor of prudence," wrote Edmund Burke, one of Kennedy's favorite oracles. But history also teaches that at great turning points and in supreme crises prudence is dangerous, and the leader must boldly throw his whole weight into the balance. And he must do so sometimes when the fog of battle is heavy, when experience offers little help, when the usual guide lines are lacking and ordinary men are terrified of the unknown. "In case of doubt," Henry Stimson used to say, "march toward the guns."

It is this quality more than any other that has separated the great Presidents from the merely able ones. During the Civil War, men around Lincoln could think of many reasons for a prudent approach to the complexities of freeing the slaves in the South; but Lincoln finally rose above the doubts and proclaimed emancipation. In 1940, there were many considerations of national defense and foreign relations that counseled against helping Britain; but Roosevelt sent the destroyers. In 1951, there were plenty of ways Truman could have glossed over his differences with General MacArthur, but Truman dismissed him because, right or wrong, the President must be boss.

What about John Kennedy on this score? A year ago, many close observers were skeptical that he had this kind of quality, for he seemed so dispassionate, so levelheaded, indeed so disdainful of dramatics and grandiloquence. His speeches were fact-filled, logical; his numbered arguments were well marshaled, but his speeches had little of Wilson's golden rhetoric. Often he seemed to drain the sentiment out of situations, in contrast to the first Roosevelt's showmanship and the second Roosevelt's ability to make even the mixing of cocktails in his study a dramatic performance.

A year later, it is by no means so clear that Kennedy lacks commitment. To be sure, he still dislikes histrionics and sentimentality, and he does not consider himself bound to deliver on every promise in the party platform within the first few months. And his commitment may be less to a rigid party program than to the changing needs of the less privileged, especially the urban masses and minority groups. But this past year has shown that crises produce in him a zest for action, an intensity of effort, and an instinct for the telling blow, that seem to stem from a strong political and intellectual, if not emotional, commitment to deeply felt goals. Just as Franklin Roosevelt, despite the zigzag routes he seemed to delight in, always came back to a "little left of center," as he described it, so Kennedy's convictions seem no less solid because he presents them without sentiment or emotion. His coolness and self-possession apparently do not reflect neutralism at the core.

The campaign proved all this. At the very outset of it, Kennedy declared that "the American Presidency will demand more than ringing manifestos issued from the rear of battle. It will demand that the President place himself in the very thick of the fight, that he care passionately about the fate of the people he leads, that he be willing to serve them at the risk of incurring their momentary displeasure."

He campaigned for the Presidency in the spirit of those words. When it would have seemed prudent to ignore the issue of religion in the Presidential primary in heavily Protestant West Virginia, he met the question directly in every section of the state. When the religious issue was raised again during the campaign, he confronted Protestant ministers on their own home grounds with a point-by-point rebuttal. When he was under pressure to play down civil rights in order to win Southern support, he took the symbolic step of publicly expressing sympathy to Mrs. Martin Luther King. When there was the serious question of whether the voters were responding to his warnings of sacrifice ahead, he insistently repeated that he would ask more from the people than he would offer them. These were not the acts of a volatile, uncommitted man.

But if Kennedy will be just as resolute and strong-willed in his way as earlier Presidents were in theirs, we must not forget that it will still be *Kennedy's* way. He has his own political style; he will not change it to please a popular image of strong Presidents based on very different men. If he displays little of Lincoln's anguish or Theodore Roosevelt's magnetism or Wilson's rhetoric or Franklin Roosevelt's buoyant charm, he is likely to demonstrate his own special qualities, which will be as relevent to our times as the earlier Presidents' images were to theirs.

Still we must ask the question: Will even these qualities be enough? Granted Kennedy's political skill, and assuming an underlying commitment and conviction, will the Presidency during the 1960s call for a further capacity that no previous President has displayed? In my judgment, it will.

There is a striking difference, I think, between the major task facing earlier liberal Democratic Presidents in this century and that facing Kennedy. Both Wilson and Franklin Roosevelt had to frame and push through Congress some badly needed and long-overdue measures of reform and reconstruction—for example, Wilson's Federal Reserve Act and Roosevelt's Social Security program. Once their bills were passed, the two Presidents needed mainly to perfect and defend them, until they each faced a whole new set of problems caused by war abroad. Kennedy's big job, on the other hand, is not simply to put through some new measures, such as medical aid under Social Security. It is to mobilize, day after day and month after month, America's economic, military, scientific, and moral power. To do this systematically will call for a continuous and consistent exercise of Presidential power rather than for simply the kind of brilliant and staccato political stroke that marked the early years of Wilson's and Roosevelt's Presidencies.

Unhappily, consistently strong Presidential leadership is precisely what our system of government is designed to thwart. It is one thing to utter golden words and to pressure a momentous bill through Congress while the nation watches. It is something else to steer a continuous flow of legislation, especially fiscal measures, through congressional committees, around potent congressional leaders, against aroused interests, amid popular apathy. Even outside of Congress our fiscal machinery is not organized for fast and concerted action. Yet President Kennedy will have to provide economic leadership throughout his years in office, for fiscal policy is framed largely on an annual basis.

But this is only part of the problem. The biggest task facing Kennedy, if, as he has promised, he wants to provide a "thousand days of action" instead of just a hundred, will be to strengthen the whole machinery of government. Some governmental reforms have long been urged and are widely accepted today: curbing the filibuster and other obstructionist devices in Congress, reinforcing the President's executive power over his administration, recruiting and holding on to the ablest men in government. Others are less known but coming into greater prominence; among them, reconstruction of the regulatory agencies and unifying the Pentagon. Still others are both formidable and controversial; for example, strengthening and perhaps realigning the two national parties.

Whatever the precise nature of the changes, it seems inevitable that the machinery of government must be strengthened if Presidential leadership is to result in sustained action. What can we expect from President Kennedy on this score?

In recent weeks, beset by a hundred pressing problems, he has had little time to think about long-term needs. On structural and Constitutional aspects of government, moreover, he has always been something of a traditionalist; for example, he has been cool to proposals for changing the seniority rule in Congress, and he seems wary of intervening to alter the filibuster rule.

But the main reason Kennedy will go slow in initiating basic governmental changes is his success in operating the present machinery. Like Roosevelt, he is likely to extract the last ounce of energy from it by hard bargaining, and this may little dispose him to junk it. Then, too, the greater his use of the present machinery, the greater becomes his commitment to it. For example, the more he bargains with the senior members of Congress, the more he must offer them political advantages—such as patronage—that they can use to bolster their own independent positions. The more he recognizes existing party leaders and organizations, the more he alienates the reform element that might serve as the basis for a stronger Democratic party.

On the other hand, the new President is history-minded and, as a historian, he knows that in the long run the bargaining power of even the strongest and ablest President has run out. Presidential authority is not limitless—and the claims on it in the years ahead will be extraordinary. This was the experience of all the strong Presidents and most of the others. Wilson managed the machinery of government brilliantly during his first term, only to be thwarted by it during his second. Roosevelt had the same experience; then he made a desperate effort to reform his party, and the executive branch, and the judiciary, and he failed.

Kennedy may, of course, use the Rooseveltian technique of exploiting crisis in order to replenish his reservoir of political and moral authority. But another cardinal difference between the 1930s and the 1960s may be this: It was enough for Roosevelt to cope with crises, but it will be essential for Kennedy to head them off. And to head them off he must act early, systematically, and continuously through the whole machinery of government.

Viewed in these terms, the Presidency in the 1960s will demand as a minimum that Kennedy act with skill and craft. It will doubtless demand much more. Whether the new President must simply rise above the vast give and take that represents the machinery of government, or whether he will have to go much farther and reconstruct the machinery even while he manipulates it, it is certain that he must act with valor and even audacity. Daring in the face of great odds is the single quality that John F. Kennedy has always most admired. Does he still? He must, for the nation will settle for no less than a glowing new profile in courage.

—JAMES MACGREGOR BURNS
WILLIAMSTOWN, MASS., 1961

PREFACE

As a venture in contemporary biography in a year of controversy, this book raises problems that I can best present by describing the background of the book.

In 1958, I was the Democratic candidate for Congress in the westernmost district of Massachusetts. During the campaign I maintained a friendly working relationship with Senator Kennedy, who was a candidate for re-election, as I had done personally and politically for some years before. Following his re-election and my defeat, Senator Kennedy offered me a responsible position his office, which I declined because I felt that, despite my affection and admiration for him, I did not know enough about his presidential qualifications to make the complete commitment that such a job required.

When Harcourt, Brace subsequently suggested that I write a biography of the Senator, I was responsive for two reasons: doing so would satisfy my own curiosity about his presidential potential; and, more important, it would give me a chance to write about a man before the voters might have to pass judgment on him. It has always seemed to me unfortunate that we learn most about our politicians after they have died and become statesmen. I was also impressed by a remark of James Reston of the New York *Times* that "it was of immense importance that the press in its widest sense, by which I mean magazines, books, and all the rest of the newspapers, concentrate upon digging into the pasts of these men, not in the sense of trying to do an improper personal exposé, but in terms of trying to find out ahead of time what the qualities of these men are."

But attempting such a biography raised an urgent question: Could I get full and authentic information on a candidate running for high office? I put this question to Senator Kennedy late in 1958. I said that I would like to do as honest a study of his life as I would try to do if he were indeed a dead statesman. Such an attempt would require his and his family's willingness to be interviewed extensively, assistance from his office and aides, and complete and unrestricted access to his official and personal files. I made it clear that I was not interested simply in documents and letters that he would make available; I wanted independent access to the records. To all this he agreed, and with such an understanding, I wrote this book.

Senator Kennedy has fully honored this understanding. I have talked extensively with him, recording our conversations on tape, I have interviewed his wife and parents and others members of his family, his teachers, assistants, political supporters and political opponents, and many others; and I have traveled with him during his campaigning. Most important, I have had full access to past and current files of correspondence, legislative records, family records, and the like, as the bibliographical notes explain in greater detail. This book is based largely on these records.

Then a second problem arose. The more I accumulated information on Kennedy's career, especially his later years, the more it became clear to me that he must be taken with the utmost seriousness as a presidential candidate, that he has displayed impressive legislative competence and political judgment as a national leader, and that he has far more intellectual depth and steadfastness than many supposed. I had some misgivings—the most important is raised in the last pages of this book—but I came to feel that Senator Kennedy was of high presidential quality and promise.

Some advised me that this was all very well, but that if I wanted this book to be taken seriously as an independent study, I should have to enter a neutral judgment—four or five pro-Kennedy conclusions balanced neatly against an equal number of conclusions against him. Otherwise, I was told, the book would be taken simply as another campaign biography. But this course seemed to me the most dishonest of all, because it would entail coming to an artificial neutrality for appearance's sake—as though objectivity always required neutrality. So I have decided against that kind of neutrality. Since others may look at the same set of facts and come to different conclusions, however, I have felt that my first responsibility was to present as full a factual account of Senator Kennedy's career as time and space permitted. This I have tried to do.

The book, in short, is neither an authorized biography nor a campaign biography, but an attempt to supply needed information, a measure of analysis, and a few judgments on one of the best-known and least-understood of American political leaders at a crucial point in his country's, and his own, history.

My debts are numerous. I wish to thank Mildred C. Baxter and Winthrop F. Sheerin, Jr., for indispensable help in conducting research; Professor Kermit Gordon, of Williams College, and Dr. Alexander Preston for valued counsel on a number of matters; Senator Kennedy, Mrs. Evelyn Lincoln, Timothy J. Reardon, Theodore Sorensen, and other members of the Senator's staff for many courtesies graciously extended despite the press of affairs in the office; Duane and Linda Lockhart for helpful comments on the manuscript; the staff of the Boston Athenaeum, the Boston Public Library, Widener Library, the Boston *Globe*, the Boston *Herald*, the Williams College library, and the Roper Public Opinion Center at Williams College for assistance in acquiring information; and the many persons who consented to be interviewed. Especially, I express my deep appreciation to my wife, Janet Thompson Burns, who helped with the usual editorial chores and who made suggestions on the basis of her own wide observations in Massachusetts politics.

                                                    J. M. B.

November 1959

1 ★ ROOM AT THE TOP

On a magnificent height rising steeply from the Blackwater River in southern Ireland stands Lismore Castle, built eight centuries ago by King John. Here in 1185 the archbishops and bishops of Ireland paid allegiance to the English invaders. Three centuries later, the castle passed into the hands of Sir Walter Raleigh, and, more recently, surviving fire and siege, came into the possession of the Dukes of Devonshire.

One August morning in 1947, a wealthy and engaging young American congressman, son of the former Ambassador to the Court of St. James's, drove off from Lismore Castle on an exploration back into time. He carried with him a letter from an aunt in America giving directions to the old family home in New Ross, fifty miles east of Lismore. At his side in his American station wagon sat an English lady from the company at the castle. Through the soft green countryside along the southeastern coast of Ireland and across the bottom tip of Kilkenny County they motored on to the market town of New Ross, settled on the banks of the Barrow River.

An Irishman standing on the road into town knew where the Kennedys lived—"just up the way a hundred yards and turn to the right." And there it was—an ordinary farm cottage with thatch roof, whitewashed walls, and dirt floor. They found a farmer and his wife and their half-dozen bright, towheaded children.

"I'm John Kennedy from Boston," the young congressman said, sticking out his hand. "I believe this is the old Kennedy homestead." The farmer and his wife greeted him cordially while the children stared at the gleaming station wagon. The New Ross Kennedys knew little, it seemed, about their American cousins. But they remembered a Patrick Kennedy from Boston—John Kennedy's grandfather—who had visited them some thirty-five years before.

"It sounded from their conversation as if all the Kennedys had emigrated," Kennedy said later. "I spent about an hour there surrounded by chickens and pigs, and left in a flow of nostalgia and sentiment. This was not punctured by the English lady turning to me as we drove off and saying, 'That was just like Tobacco Road!' She had not understood at all the magic of the afternoon. . . ."

They drove back to the castle where Kennedy and his sister, the widowed Marchioness of Hartington, daughter-in-law of the Duke of Devonshire, were host and hostess to an aristocratic company that included Anthony Eden, later prime minister, Mrs. Randolph Churchill, the Earl of Roselyn, and various political and literary figures.

For Kennedy, the trip back to Lismore Castle that day took hardly two hours. For his family, that trip had taken a hundred years. First there had been a long journey across the Atlantic. Then had come the hardest and longest move of all —inching up the rungs of the American class ladder until the Kennedys stood near the top and could look as equals on the dukes and earls whose ancestors had ruled their native land.

To the Land of the Shanties

A century before, New Ross had been a place of troubles. During the early 1840's, the Irish were depending more than ever on their potato crop, which at best barely tided the cottiers' families from one year to another. But something was wrong with the all-important potato—a blight that rotted the tubers in the ground and even seemed to reach them in the storehouse. In 1845 Ireland lost almost half its potato crop. "If the next crop fails us," a peasant said, "it will be the end of the world for us." The crop did fail. The blight rotted the potatoes with terrifying speed—in a single night, some said. A priest traveling from Cork to Dublin one day rejoiced at the rich harvest in the making; returning a week later he saw "one wide waste of putrefying vegetation."

Misery lay on the land like a pall. Some families took to the road, wandering from blighted field to blighted field, leaving the old and the young dying in the ditches. Others waited quietly in their cottages to die. Some survived near-starvation to perish of typhus, which was spreading through the drifting population. Others had only one dream—to leave this land on which God seemed to have laid a curse and escape to another country, to America, land of gold and milk and honey. Men fished their last sovereigns from the secret places in the thatch; women pawned their pewter and plate; families loaded their belongings into carts and trundled down to crowded quays to wait for the next steamer. Even their priests were urging them to go. Some farmers had no choice; the landlords' bailiffs, encouraged by the harsh Poor Law, evicted them and knocked down their cottages with crowbars so they could not creep back.

When the flight from famine was at its peak, young Patrick Kennedy deserted his thatch-roofed home in New Ross and joined the great migration of the hungry and the helpless. Doubtless he boarded a Cunarder at Cork or Liverpool and crossed the Atlantic in the crowded steerage. He was lucky to be able to raise the fare—$20, including provisions—and lucky, too, to avoid the epidemics that sometimes decimated the shiploads of immigrants on the long passage.

Years before, the Cunard Line had fixed its western terminus at Noddle's Island in East Boston, lying across a narrow arm of Boston Harbor. On this island Pat Kennedy settled about 1850. It was a busy, noisy place; Cunard was building piers and warehouses; Irish laborers and stevedores were flocking in to look for work; a steam ferry plowed across the bay every five minutes and brought ten or more thousand passengers a day for a two-cent fare. Soon Pat had found a job as a cooper.

Pat Kennedy was in Boston to stay, but many an Irishman took one look at the city and wanted to catch the next Cunarder back to the old sod. Immigrant Boston was a forbidding land. If they could find a place to lay their heads at all, the newcomers were crowded in with the old; often they lived in cellars flooded from backed-up drains, or in garrets only three feet high. About the time Pat Kennedy came to Boston, hundreds of basements housed five to fifteen persons each, with at least one holding thirty-nine every night. One sink might serve a house, one privy a neighborhood. Filth spread through courts and alleys, and with it tuberculosis, cholera, and smallpox, which thrived most in the poorest districts where the Irish lived.

To be sure, by working on the docks or elevators or freight yards, a man could make a quicker dollar here than back home. But prices were high, too, and families could not keep a pig or cow or garden in tenement Boston. And work was hard—usually fifteen hours a day seven days a week, with no Sabbath and none of the pastoral pleasures of farm life.

The Irish were the lowest of the low, lower than the Germans or Scandinavians or Jews, or even the Negroes, who had come earlier and edged a bit up the economic ladder. Irishmen were lucky if they could find part-time work on the dock or in the ditch; Irish girls hoped at best to get work as maids in hotels or in big houses on Beacon Hill. Around 1850, Irish transient paupers outnumbered the sum of all other nationalities. The people from Ireland were a proletariat without machine skills or capital. Their sections of Boston were the land of the shanty Irish.

The only defense the Irish had was the classic weapon of oppressed people—solidarity. Tighter and tighter they bound themselves with the thongs of their national identity. Thrown back on their families and neighborhoods, on their priests and wakes and churches, on their memories of life in Ireland, they grew fiercely independent of the Yankees and the others around them. "Unable to participate in the normal associational affairs of the community," says Oscar Handlin, the foremost historian of Boston's immigrants, "the Irish felt obliged to erect a society within a society, to act together in their own way. In every contact therefore the group . . . became intensely aware of its peculiar and exclusive identity." Everything conspired to make this process easy—the brogue, the church, oppression in Ireland, and shared hardships in the migration and in the congested alleys of Boston.

As the newcomers solidified their loyal ranks, so did the other blocs. Tension deepened between the Irish and the skilled workmen of older national groups, as Germans, Scots, Englishmen, and Canadians saw their own wages cut by the new proletarians. John Kennedy was to say many years later: "Each wave disliked and distrusted the next. The English said the Irish 'kept the Sabbath and everything else they could lay their hands on'. The English and the Irish distrusted the Germans who 'worked too hard'. The English and the Irish and the Germans disliked the Italians; and the Italians joined their predecessors in disparaging the Slavs. . . ."

One might have expected the Irish and Italians and other immigrants to unite against the Yankees, and to some extent they did. But coalition was not easy because of economic and social tensions between national groupings. They fought for jobs and for political recognition. The anti-Semitism of the Boston Irish stemmed from economic as well as from religious and cultural sources. Joseph Kennedy himself often made remarks that sounded anti-Semitic; they were the result of the fierce economic tensions of groups trying to work their way upward. The origin of this prejudice was suggested by the fact that the next generation of Kennedys—John's and Bob's generation—was free of such bias.

No group was more determined to maintain a wall between the Irish and itself than the Yankees. Apprehensive, soon to be outnumbered by the immigrants, the old stock withdrew increasingly into its own world and turned to the Protestant Brahmins for leadership.

On Noddle's Island, Pat Kennedy probably had little time to worry about such remote matters; he was busy making his way in this tight little community of longshoremen, laborers, and servants. Irishmen dominated the cooper's trade, doubtless because so many barrels of liquor ended up in Irishmen's saloons. Pat prospered a bit, married an Irish girl, and sired four children. The last, born in January 1862, was named Patrick J. Kennedy, and he was to become John Kennedy's grandfather. Soon after his birth, the father died, perhaps in one of the epidemics that still swept Boston.

Behind the Lace Curtain

How does a man break his way out of the world of the shanty Irish? One way was to sell things to his fellow Irishmen, build up a little capital, and perhaps open a shop or a saloon. Another way was to capture their votes and thus store up influence to trade in the political arena. Young Patrick J. Kennedy did both.

Things were hard at first. His mother had to go to work in a shop, leaving him at home with his three older sisters. For a time, Patrick attended a nearby school taught by the Sisters of Notre Dame and helped his mother at the store. But he soon turned to the Boston liquor trade, perhaps because his father had made contacts there. He started a saloon, and later branched out into the retail liquor business. Located across from an East Boston shipyard, the saloon attracted thirsty laborers on their way home from work. At night, Irishmen fled their dingy tenements and crowded into Pat Kennedy's bar, singing, joking, carousing, sometimes going out for a short bout of the fists.

Pat was a popular saloonkeeper, and he looked the part, with his stocky build and black handlebar mustaches. Standing behind the bar, he listened patiently to the latest gossip and complaints. Everyone knew Pat and he knew everyone. Loyal and generous to his kind, he helped many a fellow Irishman who was down on his luck. Increasingly he won the respect of the community. He was a soft-spoken man who never swore; the worst he had ever been heard to say about a man was, "He's a no-good loafer." He was a bit austere, too; he rarely lifted a glass himself, and he kept his blue eyes cocked on the bar to see that no one got noisily drunk in his establishment. Although he had never finished grammar school, he loved to read, and friends would often find him after hours, his glasses pushed up on his forehead, a book—usually an American history book—in his hands.

It was only natural that an Irish saloonkeeper like Pat would go into politics, just as "Big Tim" Sullivan did so successfully in the Bowery of New York and "Hinky Dink" Kenna in Chicago. For the main thing a man needed to rise in Boston politics was a big, devoted personal following. East Boston politics was a network of family, neighborhood, and religious ties, all bound together in loyalty to the party and the party leader. Pat's saloon became a rallying place, a caucus room, and a campaign headquarters.

Slowly during the early 1880's, Pat Kennedy built his influence throughout his ward. Like most city bosses, he stayed in the background and worked with his lieutenants in the back room. Even while campaigning for office, he rarely made speeches. He did not need to. Five years in a row in the late 1880's, he ran for state representative and won every time; then he moved up to the state senate. After that, he held various city jobs: fire commissioner, street commissioner, election commissioner. But Pat's chief concern was not holding office, but wielding power and the patronage that went with it. He wanted to run his ward—and he did. As the years passed, he became a member of the unofficial "Board of Strategy," a coalition of bosses who picked Democratic candidates and ran city affairs from the old Quincy House on Brattle Street. The most noted member of the Board of Strategy was Martin Lomasney, boss of famed Ward Eight, and a brilliant political organizer.

The '80's and '90's were the ideal time for Pat to enter politics, for the Irish were capturing almost complete control of the city government. Unlike most immigrant groups, they adapted themselves easily to urban politics. Most of them spoke English; they had learned the mechanics of politics in the old country; the democratic politics in America gave them the one road to power that the Yankees could not block. But beyond this the Irish simply loved city politics—the derby-hatted politicos and their blarney, the fast deals and double deals, the singing and fighting and laughing, the simmering hatreds and glowing friendships. At wakes and weddings, after mass or on the back stoop, the Irish endlessly played the intricate game of politics.

On the Board of Strategy, Pat came to know another young politician, John F. Fitzgerald, whose daughter one day would marry Pat's son. Fitzgerald had been born in 1863, not far from the Old North Church. He was raised in an eight-family tenement on lower Hanover Street. The third oldest of a brood of nine, he had, like Pat Kennedy, found life hard at first, for he had lost both parents by the time he was sixteen and had to help raise the younger members of the family. He secured a clerkship in the customhouse under the Brahmin blue blood Leverett Saltonstall, grandfather of Senator Saltonstall, and soon thereafter started running for office —for councilman, alderman, state legislator, United States congressman, and, finally, mayor of Boston.

In the ever-shifting kaleidoscope of Boston's Democratic factions, Kennedy and Fitzgerald were sometimes allies and sometimes foes, but they became good friends. They made a sharply contrasted pair. Pat was quiet, cautious, even a little severe, and not too much in the public eye; Fitzgerald was merry, ebullient, talkative, and usually willing to take a political dare.

Everywhere Fitzgerald went he filled the political life of Boston with fun and gusto. He loved to sing, and Bostonians would never forget "Honey Fitz" standing amid his cronies, his eyes sparkling, his florid face turned heavenward, his full cheeks puffed out, his sandy hair parted down the middle like an old-time vaudeville actor, singing his political theme song, "Sweet Adeline." He was the only man who could sing that song sober and get away with it, the Republican Boston *Herald* said. He loved to attend wedding parties, attired in top hat and morning coat, even if he had to crash them. Short, bouncy, quick, he was a master of political showmanship and techniques, adept, for example, at the "Irish switch," which consisted of pumping one person's hand while talking volubly to another, but he even improved on it by gazing fondly all the time at yet a third.

Bostonians loved Fitzgerald, whom they usually called "John F.," or "Fitz" or "Honey Fitz" (this last he professed to dislike). He had many political rivals but few personal enemies. One of the latter, though, was James Michael Curley, a man of harder mien, aggressive, pushing, ruthless, vindictive. Sometimes Fitz outwitted Curley. On one occasion —it was the final game of the 1914 World Series, won by the Boston Braves—Curley, then mayor, was about to address the crowd when Fitz paraded by in a high hat leading the Royal Rooters. As his archenemy rose to speak, Fitz lifted his arms, started up his band, and drowned out the oration.

But Honey Fitz had the defects of his virtues, some Bostonians said. Aside from his implacable opposition to Prohibition, he had few strong convictions on national issues. During the '90's, for example, he shilly-shallied on the free-silver issue until political expediency forced him to take a stand in favor of it. His only intense loyalty was to his own city, which he never tired of promoting as a "Bigger, Better, Busier Boston." Cheered on by his friends, he would plunge into a political campaign, only to pull out unexpectedly if the going got too rough. He could not act the part of the tough boss; it was hard for him to follow the routine procedure of firing his political foes when he entered city office. He was too affable and easygoing to stand up for long against rough-and-tumble fighters like Curley. And much as he liked to help people, he would never do what Curley did— take a civil-service examination for a friend who could not pass it and sign his friend's name, for which Curley went to jail and emerged to Boston Irishmen a hero.

John F.'s upbringing had been more genteel than Pat's, but both men advanced far up into the ranks of middle-class respectability. They were now "lace-curtain" Irish, or, as Curley called them mockingly, "cut-glass" or the "F.I.F.'s" ("First Irish Families"). Both men married socially a notch above themselves—Pat a Hickey and John a Hannon from Lexington. But the acid test of respectability in East Boston was a man's standing in his church, and both politicians were devout and loyal members of their parishes. The church in turn favored the more upright politicians in its flock. Once, William Cardinal O'Connell asked Curley to withdraw from a race against Fitzgerald, but Curley flatly refused.

In 1910, Fitz staged a lively campaign to become mayor of Boston. He was the first native-born son of Irish parents to win that office. At the same time, Pat's reign in East Boston was stronger than ever. To be sure, the shanty districts were filling up with a new proletariat of Italians, Poles, and Slavs, but the newcomers needed help from the Irish bosses in getting housing, jobs, and licenses as peddlers or junk dealers. The Irish "organized and disciplined the inrushing immigrant masses," and the influx boosted them higher up the social ladder. Indeed, even Fitz joined the migration of some of the lace-curtain Irish out to the suburbs, and lived for a time in the pleasant fashionable suburb of Concord, of Yankee "minuteman" fame.

But there always seemed to be a limit, both politically and socially, beyond which a successful Irish politico could not go. Several times Fitz ran for statewide office, including the governorship, but the things that made him so popular in Boston did not go over so well in the suburbs or on the South Shore or in the staid Republican towns like Northampton or Greenfield or in the rural Berkshires. Yankee Protestantism may have lost out in Boston but it still controlled the state. Fitzgerald's most daring plunge was for United States Senator against the mighty Henry Cabot Lodge in 1916, but to no avail. It was maddening that so many Irish would vote for Lodge simply because he was a Brahmin who would tip his hat in the St. Patrick's Day parade, throw them a few favors, and tweak the British lion's tail. To make matters worse, Fitz was not very friendly with the Wilson administration, and the national and state Democratic tickets did little to help each other. And there was always the danger that the shanty Irish, rallying around men like Curley, or the fanatical Sinn Feiners, with their demands of independence for Ireland, could cut him from the other side.

To win statewide office, an Irishman needed the support of liberals and reformers who, like the Democratic bosses, had no use for the standpat Republicans usually in control of state affairs. But support was rarely forthcoming from those quarters. The reason throws light on a vital strand of the state's political history and makes more understandable the attitude of Pat's and Fitz's grandson toward McCarthyism a half-century later. The background is this: Aside from their distaste for the Republican Old Guard, the Democratic bosses and the liberals had no basis for joint political action. The bosses were concerned with immediate economic and social needs—jobs, wages, housing, workmen's compensation —needs that they could provide directly or through the government. Yankee liberalism was remote from all this; indeed, to some prescient Irishmen, the more remote the problem, the more aroused these reformers seemed to become. For decades, the reformers had been agitating about far-off problems—slavery, suppression of liberal movements in Europe, the rights of minorities, the plight of distant peoples. And the reformers' more domestic interests seemed just as strange and repugnant to Irish leaders; women's rights, public-school education, rights for Negroes (who competed for Irish laborers' jobs), religious liberty, curbs on gambling, temperance, and even Prohibition. The Roman Catholic Church, frowning on many of these reforms, helped cut the Irish off from the Protestant reformers, and from the whole Western liberal heritage of civil liberty, tolerance, intellectual freedom, social equality, and philosophical rationalism and pragmatism.

Socially, too, the Yankees presented closed ranks. Retreating politically and economically in Boston before the rising immigrant pressures, they could still hold out in their clubs and cotillions and to some extent in their college—Harvard, of course—and in certain banks and businesses. They were gracious to Fitz but it was a graciousness tinged with a mutual recognition of Yankee superiority. "What this city needs is a lunch club where the blue bloods will lunch with the rest of us!" Fitzgerald said. On occasion, Yankee snobbishness caused him to lose his good humor.

"You have plenty of Irish depositors—why don't you have some Irishmen on your board of directors?" he suddenly demanded of a bank president one day.

"Well, a couple of the tellers are Irish Catholic," the president said.

"Yes," snapped Fitzgerald, "and I suppose the charwomen are, too." And he turned on his heel.

Still, a well-liked Irishman could forget these matters back in the bosom of his family. Both Pat and Fitz had a goodly number of children. And in 1914 the two families were united by marriage.

Upward Bound

Some East Bostonians raised their eyebrows when they heard that Pat's eldest boy, Joseph Patrick Kennedy, had won the hand of Rose Fitzgerald, the mayor's daughter, one of the most eligible Catholic girls in town. This was pretty good for the son of a ward boss and saloonkeeper. But those who knew Joe Kennedy were not surprised. He was a go-getter in everything he tried, they said, and he would be a good husband and a good provider.

They were right. Only nine years after his birth in 1888, Joe had sold peanuts and candy on Boston excursion boats, and a few years later had worked as office boy in a bank. He attended parochial school until seventh grade, then shifted to Boston Latin, the famed school where Benjamin Franklin and Henry Adams had been students. This meant getting up early to catch the North Ferry every morning, at a penny a trip, but it was worth it, for at Boston Latin Joe mixed with youths from elite Back Bay and the West End and not just East Boston. He was a popular boy and a fine athlete. His favorite sport was baseball, which he played so well that he won the mayor's cup, presented by his future father-in-law, the great John F. himself.

His mother, ambitious for her son, wanted Joe to go to Harvard, and he entered with the class of 1912. He made the baseball team his junior year. His popularity and athletic prowess helped him get elected to the undergraduate societies Dicky, Delta Upsilon, and Hasty Pudding, but he never made the so-called best clubs. His grades were only mediocre; once when the baseball captain warned him that he was dangerously low in an economics course, he switched to music. But he revered some of the great teachers at Harvard—men like Bliss Perry and Charles Copeland—and he felt flattered when "Copey" dropped by his room and invited him to his famous readings.

Looking at the American scene through his calm, appraising eyes, Joe could see that sports and politics and literature were fun, but money really talked. During the summer vacations he and a partner earned several thousand dollars by running a sight-seeing bus to historic Lexington. He vowed to make a million by the time he was thirty-five, and he did, probably several times over. After he graduated from Harvard in 1912, he got a job as a bank examiner and learned the practical side of finance. When a small East Boston bank, owned in part by members of his family, was about to be taken over by another bank, Joe rounded up some capital and proxies and, with the help of his family, was elected bank president at the age of twenty-five, reportedly the youngest in the country.

By then he was courting Rose Fitzgerald, and the two were married in the private chapel of Cardinal O'Connell in Boston in October 1914. With her dark hair and rosy cheeks, the bride had her father's good looks and charm, but she also showed something of her mother's dignity and serenity. She had gone to parochial and public schools and studied music in Europe; she was popular and a good student. The couple settled down in a $6,500 house in a respectable, lower-middle-class neighborhood in Brookline. The groom, in debt at the time as a result of buying the bank stock, had to borrow money to make the down payment. But he was soon solvent. Children came rapidly: the first, Joe, Jr., within a year of the marriage, followed by another boy, John F., in 1917, then five girls and a son—Rosemary, Kathleen, Eunice, Patricia, Jean, and Robert F.—during the 1920's, and finally another son, Edward, in 1932.

With the coming of World War I in 1917, Kennedy resigned from the bank and became assistant general manager of Bethlehem Steel's huge shipyards in Quincy. After the war he moved swiftly toward his first million. Boston finance was still controlled by conservative Yankees not very sympathetic to aggressive Irishmen, but Kennedy, acting on the old political maxim "If you can't lick 'em, join 'em," deliberately studied the habits of Boston financiers, even to the point of taking a seat near them on the train. One of these, Galen Stone, was so impressed that he hired him as head of his investment banking house, Hayden, Stone and Company, and in this job Kennedy learned market operations and began to speculate on his own. He took some hard losses, recouped them, and then, with a group of Bostonians, bought control of a chain of thirty-one small movie theaters scattered throughout New England.

But many a Yankee banker still could not wholly accept Joe Kennedy. It was all right for Irishmen to run little East Boston banks and handle immigrants' remittances, they felt, but not to crash the central citadels of finance. So Kennedy, disgusted, began to operate more and more in New York and Hollywood. During the mid-1920's, he moved in on the booming, turbulent movie industry, won control of several motion-picture companies, reshuffled them, and sold out at a huge profit. Independently, he produced two features starring Gloria Swanson, who had become a close family friend, but one was so vivid, involving a seduction scene of a convent girl, that he refused to exhibit it.

By this time Kennedy was a business legend and a man of mystery. Long after he quit the movies in the late '20's, people were arguing about whether he had left behind him a string of strengthened companies or heaps of wreckage. When he deserted Hollywood and began to speculate in the bull market, his operations became even more obscure. "He moved in the intense, secretive circles of operators in the wildest stock market in history," *Fortune* later commented, "with routine plots and pools, inside information and wild guesses." But Kennedy came out of the bull market with many millions, made more in the crash, and even more by shrewd speculation in liquor importing, real estate, and numerous other enterprises joined together in a financial labyrinth that probably only the financier himself understood. "The legend of Joe Kennedy," said *Fortune* in its painstaking and admiring profile, "made him at once the hero of a Frank Merriwell captain-of-the-nine adventure, a Horatio Alger success story, an E. Phillips Oppenheim tale of intrigue, and a John Dos Passos disillusioning report on the search for the big money. The truth makes him the central character of a picaresque novel of a sort not yet written."

Kennedy had been raised in a heavily political atmosphere; he says today that one of his first memories was of two men coming to his father and reporting in a matter-of-fact way, "Pat, we voted 128 times today." But Boston politics, with its petty intrigues and backbiting, bored him. Having made his millions, he moved up through politics, as Pat and Honey Fitz had done, but on a national scale. In 1932 he supported Roosevelt before the convention and gave $15,000 to the Democratic campaign fund, lent it $50,000 more, and probably contributed many more thousands indirectly. In 1934 the President made him first head of the new Securities and Exchange Commission—to the consternation of some—and, later, head of the Maritime Commission. Two years later, in 1936, Kennedy wrote a ringing endorsement of the Democratic nominee in a book called *I'm for Roosevelt*, and he gave the Democrats another big campaign donation.

His book made a forceful case for the main New Deal policies except for a few—notably Roosevelt's 1936 tax bill—that Kennedy admitted he disliked. Although he hoped his book would help restore "temperate discussion of issues," he himself ignored his own advice in discussing the attitude of some fashionable and wealthy circles—"an unreasoning, fanatical, blind, irrational prejudice"—against the President. He scored the "privileged aristocrats," the "ungrateful rich," and the "modern Bourbons" in phrases that might have been struck off by Roosevelt himself. Some people were annoyed that Kennedy, a speculator himself, could criticize the rich so sharply; but perhaps this was not so hard for a businessman who had never been wholly accepted in certain circles of the business world. On one occasion, indeed, he pleased Roosevelt by quoting a Frenchman as saying that the President had exploded one of the most popular concepts in America in dissociating the concept of wealth from the concept of virtue.

The President thought the book "splendid" and a help not only in the campaign but in the "sane education" of the country. Those who read the book carefully might have noticed that its support for the New Deal, while vigorous, was narrowly based. Kennedy liked the New Deal for its emphasis on welfare and security, for its bread-and-butter liberalism. He knew of "no higher duty or more noble function of the state," he said, "than caring for the needy among our citizens," and he quoted in his support the famous encyclical of Pope Leo XIII on the condition of the working classes. The noneconomic elements of liberalism—the relation of the New Deal to individual freedom—he laid aside scornfully as "question begging abstractions." What matters a vote to a hungry man? he demanded.

He was away from home often during the late summer of 1936 setting up businessmen's organizations for Roosevelt and looking for men in finance and business who would support the New Deal. But during the late '30's he became disenchanted with the direction of the New Deal. He said little publicly, and he remained on friendly personal terms with Roosevelt, but the radical fiscal policies he had begun to oppose in the first term disturbed him even more during the second.

Now in his late forties, Kennedy had become a national figure—a big, intense man, with sandy hair thinning a bit over a freckled forehead and horn-rimmed glasses that gave him a slightly owlish look. But he always remained something of an enigma to the public. For one thing, it was hard to place him. A strong Roosevelt man, he was yet so repugnant to liberals that they had greeted his SEC appointment as "grotesque," "appalling," "literally incredible"—a big-pool operator regulating his fellow sharks. Generally he had been conservative politically, but he had supported the La Follette–Wheeler Progressive ticket in 1924. He had made money out of movies in their pre-Legion of Decency days but he was a devout Catholic and a friend of Cardinal Pacelli, later Pope Pius XII. Then, too, his friends seemed a curious collection—William Randolph Hearst, Father Coughlin, but also, when he won their confidence by his direction of the SEC, New Dealers like James Landis, Ben Cohen, and Tom Corcoran. The man himself was unpredictable, one moment overcoming you with his blarney, the next moment hard as steel, sometimes endlessly patient, then suddenly blowing up in a real Irish temper. And where did he live, anyway—Boston, New York, Hollywood, Washington, Palm Beach? He seemed to have homes everywhere.

Appearances were not too deceiving; Kennedy was indeed a lone wolf whom very few men knew. He never stayed in one job or enterprise very long; the moment he stepped in he seemed to be planning when he wanted to get out. He was never wholly accepted by either the business community or the liberals. The respectable rich looked on him as a political opportunist, the liberals as a Wall Street plunger. And of course there was the old problem of the Yankees. Kennedy left Boston primarily because he considered their attitude frigid and aloof. People were more tolerant in New York and Hollywood. But everywhere he went, he was labeled as an Irishman.

"I was born here," he exploded one day. "My children were born here. What the hell do I have to do to be an American?"

No Terrors at Home

Joe Kennedy's great consolation in these strenuous years was his family. Indeed, he justified his feverish money-making largely as a way of ensuring his nine children's security in the years to come. Explaining to visitors why he could go on despite suspicion and criticism, he liked to quote a senator's reply to an angry voter who threatened to drive him out of office: "Home holds no terrors for me."

He was often away from home. Once, he spent seven straight weeks juggling stock in a room in the old Waldorf Astoria. He woke up one morning, exhausted, and realized that his new baby, Patricia, was almost a month old and he had not even seen her. He tried, however, to get home weekends whenever it was possible. When the children were small, he pulled them around the snowy streets of Brookline in a homemade soapbox sled. According to a family story, once he almost lost his oldest son. While Joe, Sr. was thinking about far-off matters, Joe, Jr. toppled off the sled and was not found until later, playing merrily in the snow. As the children grew older, their father plunged into their games and contests with gusto—tennis, swimming, softball, sailing, golf—and he was usually able to hold his own.

Even among his family, however, Kennedy could not escape from the press of finance and politics; perhaps he did not try. At home he was pursued by telegrams and long-distance calls, and the house was full of aides, politicians, financiers. Visitors would find him happily stretched out on the big porch at Hyannisport, a stock-market ticker chattering away at his side.

Actually, Kennedy had no wish to seal his children off from the outside world. They might as well know at the start that it was harshly competitive. "Every single kid," a close friend of the family told a reporter, "was raised to think, First, what shall I do about this problem? Second, what will Dad say about my solution of it?" When he was home he encouraged talk at the dinner table about American government and politics, but money matters could not be raised. "I have never discussed money with my wife and family," Kennedy said years later, "and I never will."

The father wanted his children to be competitive with one another, and they vied among themselves fiercely in parlor games and sports. Sometimes the girls would leave the tennis courts sobbing after being bested by their brothers. Touch football games were almost fratricidal. "They are the most competitive and at the same time the most cohesive family I've ever seen," said another long-time family friend some years after. "They fight each other, yet they feed on each other. They stimulate each other. Their minds strike sparks. Each of them has warm friends. But none they like and admire so much as they like and admire their own brothers and sisters."

He wanted his children, however competitive they might be with one another, to present a united front against the outside world. Consciously or not, he was copying the ways of his father and the Democratic bosses of old, who allowed fighting among the district leaders between elections but not on the day when they had to beat Republicans. The fierce loyalty of the Kennedys to each other exists to this day and has been especially helpful to John Kennedy in his political campaigns.

During Kennedy's long absences, Joe, Jr. increasingly assumed his father's family responsibilities. He taught the others how to sail and swim with something of Joe, Sr.'s perfectionism. Indeed, he was much like his father—generous, considerate, and loving, and, at the same time, driving, domineering, and hot-tempered.

But the main steadying element in this boisterous household was Rose Kennedy. Even as a young woman, she impressed her friends with her scrupulous sense of duty and her devotion to the church. What she lacked in intellectual brilliance she made up in her intense love for her family. Love and a sense of duty were needed in the Kennedy home. The children were so numerous that she had to keep records of their vaccinations, illnesses, food problems, and the like, on file cards, but she was still able to give each child some individual attention. Somehow she survived and even thrived, keeping her face unlined and her figure as modish as ever. Years later, on meeting this mother of nine still looking so young, a gallant gentleman took her hand and exclaimed, "At last—I believe in the stork!"

In her husband's absence, she would even work up current-events topics and guide the discussion of them by the children at the table—her husband would have expected it. With him away so often and for so long, the daily routine, despite household help, was not simple, certainly not so easy as it later seemed to some of the family. Occasionally—and more often as the children went off to school—she got out from under her big family by taking vacations with her husband in Florida or Europe. She also devoted herself increasingly to the church. "She was terribly religious," Kennedy says. "She was a little removed, and still is, which I think is the only way to survive when you have nine children. I thought she was a very model mother for a big family."

2 ★ THE GREEN BLOODS

John Fitzgerald Kennedy was born on May 29, 1917, in Brookline, a suburb of Boston. America had just entered the war, and about this time his father left to take his post at the Fore River shipyards. For several years the family lived at 83 Beals Street, in a large frame house set back a bit from the sidewalk on a small plot. It was a quiet, lower-middle-class area, the other side of town from East Boston. Here Jack spent his early childhood—years that he hardly remembers today.

As his father became more prosperous, the family moved to higher-class houses and neighborhoods, pursuing the Yankee blue bloods, who still outdistanced them in social prestige. The next stop on the way was on the corner of Naples and Abbotsford Roads in Brookline, in a bigger house with a dozen rooms for the rapidly growing Kennedy family. Here Jack and his older brother, Joe, romped on the long porch that stretched halfway around the house, read picture books in front of the fireplaces in the old-fashioned, high-ceilinged living room and parlor, raced each other under the shade trees outside. Here, too, Jack first went to grade school. Dexter School, about six blocks from the Kennedy home, was a private academy, but not a parochial school; Joe and Jack may have been at the time its only Catholic students.

Sometimes Grandpa Fitz, still a booster of Boston, would pick the boys up and take them to a Red Sox game or to the swan boats in Boston's Public Garden or to some other favorite haunt. One of Jack's earliest memories is of touring the wards with his grandfather when Fitz was running for governor in 1922. Fitz even tried out some of his speeches with the six-year-old boy as an audience of one. Rose took the older children on historical pilgrimages—to the Yankee landmarks of Plymouth Rock, Concord Bridge, and Bunker Hill—strengthening their allegiance to the family's adopted land. Sundays the family drove over to spend the afternoon with old Pat Kennedy, who was now in his sixties and less active in politics. To the children, Grandfather Kennedy was a kind but somewhat awesome figure. "On those Sunday afternoon visits he wouldn't let us cut up or even wink in his presence," Kennedy recalls.

But the pleasant Boston days were soon over. Joseph Kennedy had outgrown his native city, and he settled his family near the center of his New York financial empire, first in Riverdale and then in Bronxville. The Bronxville house has since been torn down and the lot subdivided, but it was a rather affluent place surrounded by broad lawns where the children played baseball and football. Jack went to fourth, fifth, and sixth grades at nearby Riverdale School; the teachers remembered him later as a rather slight boy, polite, industrious, and likable, with a special interest in English history—and a hot temper. His mother came to school often to check solicitously on her son's progress; his father sometimes invited the teachers to the house to see private showings of the latest movies.

Looking back today, Kennedy cannot remember any unhappy times during his childhood. It was an easy, prosperous life, supervised by maids and nurses, with more and more younger sisters to boss and to play with. Closest to him in age was Rosemary, but she was a sweet, rather withdrawn girl, not up to the children's competitive life. Jack's favorite among them was the second oldest girl, Kathleen, nicknamed "Kick." She loved games and sports and often could hold her own with her older brother.

Even as a boy, Jack showed some of the skill at persuasion that would mark his political career later. He addressed a strategic "Plea for a raise" to his father (with a slight Biblical overtone—I Corinthians 13):

"My recent allowance is 40¢," the petition began. "This I used for aeroplanes and other playthings of childhood but now I am a scout and I put away my childish things. Before I would spend 20¢ of my 40¢ allowance and in five minutes I would have empty pockets and nothing to gain and 20¢ to lose. When I am a scout I have to buy canteens, haversacks, blankets, searchligcs, poncho things that will last for years and I can always use it while I can't use chocolate marshmallow sunday ice cream and so I put in my plea for a raise of thirty cents for me to buy schut things and pay my own way around. . . ." There is no record of the effect of the petition on his father.

Canterbury and Choate

At thirteen, Jack left his Bronxville home for boarding school. For a year he went to Canterbury School in New Milford, Connecticut, the only Catholic school he ever attended. After an initial bout with homesickness—"I felt pretty homesick but it's O.K. now"—he settled easily into the life of the school. "We have chapel every morning and evening," he wrote to his mother, "and I will be quite pius I guess when I get home." (For years he had trouble with his spelling; "I learnt how to play baggamon to-day," he wrote from Canterbury, and he had gone out for "football pracite.") He showed early a trait that baffles his office staff today—an almost photographic memory for correspondence, conversations, and historical fact, but an almost total absent-mindedness about where he has mislaid speeches, books, and clothing. "We are reading Ivanhoe in English," he wrote to his father from school, "and though I may not be able to remember material things such as tickets, gloves and so on I can remember things like Ivanhoe and the last time we had an exam on it I got a ninety eight." Always a ready competitor, he tried out for football, baseball, and other sports, with fair success. He reported that he could swim fifty yards in thirty seconds; this swimming skill would save his life many years later.

By the fall of 1930, the Depression was on, and Jack, hearing fragments in between school activities, followed the distant news from the outside world. "Please send me the Litary Digest," he wrote his father, "because I did not know about the Market Slump until a long time after, or a paper. Please send me some golf balls. . . ." His studies at Canterbury went only moderately well. His main trouble was Latin; one month his Latin marks averaged 55. "He can do better than this," his teacher reported. The year at Canterbury was cut short at Easter by a severe attack of appendicitis, and Jack never returned.

The next fall he shifted to Choate, a rather select private school with a strong Episcopal flavor, in Wallingford, Connecticut, where Adlai Stevenson and Chester Bowles had been students years before. Joe, Jr. was there, making out well. The boys' father chose Choate because he wanted them to mix and compete with a greater variety of boys than in a Catholic school. Here they could meet the sons of upper-class Yankees on their own ground. Kennedy today can recall no evidence of feeling against him at Choate because of his Catholicism. On his part he dutifully lived up to his religious obligations as he knew his mother would want him to do. "I received Communion this morning and am going to Church on tuesday," he wrote his parents his first winter at Choate. "I received the prayer-book and would you please send me a puff because it is very cold. . . ."

The Choate campus was typically New England, with its spacious lawns, shaded walks, and lofty elms. Jack lived in an old frame house, in a large room next to the housemaster's apartment. It was a bit trying to be under a master's eye, but it seemed worthwhile on Sunday nights when the house-master's wife made her famous waffles. The housemaster served as football coach also and enforced discipline by chasing the boys with a paddle. Years later, Kennedy returned to Choate as its alumnus-of-the-year and reminded his old coach gleefully, "You never could catch me with that paddle, could you?"

Occasionally Jack took part in rough-housing or throwing food out of windows, but he did not seem to resent authority. Both his teachers and fellows liked him. He sent home a barrage of request for clothes, victrola records, golf balls, and "choclate pie with whipt cream in the middle." As at Canterbury, he went out for a half-dozen sports, but failed to make the varsity. Coaches found him an eager, scrappy player in intramural games yet reluctant to apply himself in practice. In his studies his Latin was still low, his French not much better, his English and history only fair. To some teachers he seemed content to coast along as a "gentleman C scholar." He graduated sixty-fourth in a class of 112. But to his class-mates, if not to his teachers, he must have shown some glimpse of his potential ability and later drive, for they voted him "the most likely to succeed."

As his father's riches piled up in the 1920's, Jack spent many winter vacations at the family's new resort home at Palm Beach and summers at another home at Hyannisport, on Cape Cod. He especially loved Hyannisport, and still does. The big house there looked out over a long beach, a tennis court, and a well-tended lawn handy for softball and other family games. Jutting out from the beach was a break-water shielding the yachts of the summer folk. Jack's competitive instinct showed up early—he named his first sail-boat "Victura," which he explained was Latin "meaning something about winning."

But life was not always a victory. Wherever he was, at school or at home, Jack was conscious of his father's incessant concern that he do better, especially in his studies. His letters home were full of defensive, self-belittling remarks about his grades and his athletic skill. He offered excuses for his poor showing, at the same time denying that these were alibis.

"If it were not for Latin," he wrote his mother, "I would probably lead the lower school but I am flunking that by ten points." In a letter to his father his second spring at Choate, he listed the high points of a recent vacation and concluded: "I hope my marks go up because I guess that is the best way to say thanks for the trip." "Maybe Dad thinks I am alibing but I am not," he wrote on another occasion. "I have also been doing a little worrying about my studies because what he said about me starting of[f] great and then going down sunk in." Clearly Jack realized that what his father wanted above all was that he excel in his studies, as a prelude to competition in later life.

In his senior year at Choate, he wrote his father that he and LeMoyne Billings, his best friend, had been talking about their poor work, "and we have definitely decided to stop fooling around. I really do realize how important it is that I get a good job done this year, if I want to go to England. I really feel, now that I think it over, that I have been bluffing myself about how much real work I have been doing." From Washington, where Kennedy, Sr. had just taken the SEC chairmanship, he wrote back with "great satisfaction" about this "forthrightness and directness that you are usually lacking," also about his improved penmanship.

"Now Jack, I don't want to give the impression that I am a nagger, for goodness knows I think that is the worst thing any parent can be," the father wrote. "After long experience in sizing up people I definitely know you have the goods and you can go a long way. Now aren't you foolish not to get all there is out of what God has given you. . . . After all, I would be lacking even as a friend if I did not urge you to take advantage of the qualities you have. It is very difficult to make up fundamentals that you have neglected when you were very young and that is why I am always urging you to do the best you can. I am not expecting too much and I will not be disappointed if you don't turn out to be a real genius, but I think you can be a really worthwhile citizen with good judgment and good understanding. . . ."

If failure aroused parental frowns, achievement was recognized in a very material way. A sailboat, a pony, a trip to England were rewards for better grades. When Eddie Moore, his father's aide and confidant and once secretary to Mayor Fitz, stopped in at school and found the boy underweight, he offered him money to gain weight, beginning at a dollar a pound. Jack had a checking account and a modest allowance at Choate, but like any other boy he often went through the money quickly and he depended on the extra help that approval could bring.

For Jack, competition was not some abstract thing that his father wanted. It was right in the family and its name was "Joe." In their father's long absences, Jack's big brother ruled the roost. Joe was bigger and heavier, more boisterous and outgoing than Jack. He demanded absolute obedience from the younger children in exchange for his brotherly help. Even today when asked whether anything really bothered him as a child, Kennedy can think only of his big brother: "He had a pugnacious personality. Later on it smoothed out but it was a problem in my boyhood."

Jack was the only rival to Joe's throne; the next in line were girls and the other boys were too young to serve as more than nuisances. The two oldest boys often fought, and Jack always seemed to come off second. When the two boys raced around the block on their bicycles in opposite directions and collided head on, it was Jack who had to have twenty-eight stitches and Joe who emerged unscathed. Joe would throw a boy overboard for sloppy sailing in a race, and he would lie in wait to catch a rebellious brother—usually Jack—coming in off the breakwater. Bobby Kennedy to this day remembers cowering with his sisters upstairs while his older brothers fought furiously on the first floor.

The boys' father knew about the rivalry but it did not bother him, except when it got out of hand. He wanted competition in the family as long as the children stuck together in dealing with the world outside. He knew, too, that Joe Jr. made up for his bullying ways in generosity and kindness to his young brothers and sisters. Jack, too, for all his troubles at the hands of his older brother, feels today that Joe's overbearing ways, when later smoothed out, were one reason for his own success in school and in the war.

The family competition was not just physical. The father encouraged political argument at the dinner table, especially among himself and the older boys. He asserted his own views strongly, but, though Jack says today that his father was sometimes rather harsh, he did not force his views on Joe, Jr. or on Jack. The boys could not help being influenced, however, by their father's opinions, for he was forceful, knowledgeable, and articulate. At this point in their lives, any influence he had on his sons of a political nature must have been in a liberal direction, using that term here to mean support for governmental restrictions on business excesses and more economic welfare and social security for the underprivileged, for by the mid-1930's, when Jack was finishing Choate, Joseph Kennedy, Sr., was an outspoken New Dealer. In his 1936 book, *I'm for Roosevelt,* he wrote: "I have no political ambitions for myself or my children, and I put down these few thoughts about our President, conscious only of my concern as a father for the future of his family and my anxiety as a citizen that the facts about the President's philosophy be not lost in a fog of unworthy emotions."

There is no evidence that Jack was especially interested in that campaign himself. Though he certainly favored Roosevelt over Alfred Landon, he showed no indication that the President was a hero in his eyes. He became an omnivorous reader during these school years, but history and stories of famous men, rather than current affairs, were his favorites.

Less intellectual impulses evidently were stirring, too. "Jack was a very naughty boy when he was home," Jean, the youngest sister, wrote indignantly to her father at Palm Beach. "He kissed Betty Young under the mistletoe down in the front hall. He had a temperature of 102° one night, too, and Miss Cahill couldn't make him mind." Jean recommended a good spanking.

Harvard

At eighteen, when he graduated from Choate, Jack Kennedy was a tall, thin, wiry boy with a narrow face, an almost snub nose, and a mop of hair that he tried unsuccessfully to control with hair tonic. He was good-looking but not as husky or as handsome as Joe, who had a square, open face, radiating Irish charm. Joe had gone on to Harvard after winning athletic and scholarly honors at Choate that Jack could not equal. Partly because many of his classmates were going, partly perhaps because he wanted to get out from under Joe, Jack chose Princeton instead of his father's and his brother's alma mater.

His father, determined that Jack should make good use of the summer before college, packed him off to the London School of Economics to study under the noted Socialist professor Harold J. Laski, whom he knew through Felix Frankfurter from the old Boston days. He wanted Jack to rub shoulders with the polyglot population of British Laborites, European refugees, radicals from the colonies, Indian civil servants, and others at the school. Joe, Jr. had already studied under Laski, who had come to love the eager, zestful boy even though, as Laski wrote later, "his mind was only just beginning to discover the enchantment of thought." Laski said also that Joe, Jr. had been determined to be President. Jack had little contact with Laski, for he fell ill with jaundice in London, left the London School, but was not well enough to enter Princeton until several weeks after classes began. His career at Princeton was cut short at Christmas by a recurrence of jaundice, so he took the rest of the year off. Then he decided to go to Harvard rather than return to Princeton.

In the fall of 1936, Jack came back to Boston, after almost ten years' absence. Grandpa Kennedy had died in 1929, but Grandpa Fitz was still very much alive, still active in politics, and delighted that he now had Jack as well as Joe to swoop down on and take to a ball game. Jack's first two years at Harvard were in some ways a duplicate of his life at Choate. Sports still excited him far more than studies. During his freshman year he tried out for football, swimming, and golf, and crowded in some softball, too. As he had at Choate, he played furiously but his drive was greater than his athletic skill. He was fearless and willing to fight until the game was over. He was plagued by illness, however, and he also injured his back at football, an injury that has followed him into adulthood.

Swimming was his passion and his best sport. A classmate recalls one occasion when Jack was hospitalized with a bad case of grippe just before he was to try out for a spot on the swimming squad that was to face Yale. Jack feared that the infirmary diet would leave him too weak to do well, so he persuaded his roommate to smuggle in steaks and chocolate malted milks. He sneaked out of the infirmary, swam furiously—and lost.

As a freshman, Jack took English, French, history, and economics, and got C's in all except economics, where he earned a B. At the end of the year he was in the second lowest group of passing students. He did no better his sophomore year, receiving four C's, one D, and one B, though he concentrated in history and government and still read a good deal on his own, especially American history and biography. To his teachers he was a pleasant, bright, easygoing student.

What young Kennedy did *not* do at Harvard was more significant than what he did do. The Harvard campus, like other college campuses, was boiling with ideas, fads, stunts —a ferment of protest against parents, deans, and, more in the 1930's than ever before, politics and the world situation.

Students huddled around the radio listening to Roosevelt's fireside chats or trying to interpret Hitler's frenzied diatribes at Nürnberg; they read avidly the *Nation* and *New Republic* and *New Masses;* they picketed factories, tried to organize university janitors and cafeteria workers, burned Hitler and the other dictators in effigy, formed the Veterans of Future Wars, paraded to demonstrate their indignation with the state of things, and sometimes landed in jail for disturbing the peace. Little clubs of radicals, liberals, socialists, pacifists, and communists grew up everywhere, their members arguing passionately far into the night.

But Jack Kennedy had no part of this. He was moderately active in extracurricular affairs; he joined Winthrop House, won a berth on the Harvard *Crimson*, belonged to St. Paul's Catholic Club, was chosen a member of the Spee Club and Hasty Pudding, to which his father had belonged. But the Harvard Liberal Union, the Young Democrats, and the others left him cold. Stranger still, practical politics did not interest him very much, nor, evidently, did the New Deal. A Harvard government professor remembers that Kennedy, in doing an outside paper, became absorbed in the study of a politician, but the politician was no glamorous New Deal leader and not even a Democrat—it was Bertrand Snell, a conservative Republican from upper New York State who devoted much of his official life to a fight against public power.

In his junior year, Kennedy began to come into his own. For one thing, Joe, Jr. graduated, bequeathing to Jack, incidentally, George Taylor, "gentleman's gentleman". Joe, Jr., more charming than ever, a born leader, gregarious, had played varsity football, won election to class offices, graduated with honors. True, he was now in Harvard Law School, but at least Jack was not completely in his shadow. Then, too, Jack particularly enjoyed rooming with Torbert Macdonald, a well-known Harvard football star.

Perhaps the most decisive step was Kennedy's trip with his friend Les Billings to France, Spain, and Italy in the summer of 1937. He had traveled a good deal, but never as observantly as now. He had an audience with the Pope, and with Cardinal Pacelli, who inquired cordially after his father ("He is quite a fellow," Kennedy wrote home about the Cardinal); he saw a bullfight, climbed Vesuvius, and somehow talked his way into Monte Carlo with his bad French. "Played with my 5 fr. chips next to a woman who was playing $40.00 chips and she was quite upset by my winning 1.20 while she lost about $500.00," he reported to his father triumphantly. He talked with hitchhikers, reporters, diplomats. He found himself an admirer of the fascist corporate system in Italy, "as everyone seemed to like it in Italy." From Spain he wrote his father a dispassionate analysis of Britain's strategic stake in a victory for the Loyalists.

One thing that impressed him, his letter said, was "the almost complete ignorance 95% of the people in the U.S. have about situations as a whole here. For example, most people in the U.S. are for Franco, and while I felt that perhaps it would be far better for Spain if Franco should win—as he would strengthen and unite Spain—yet at the beginning the government was in the right morally speaking as its program was similar to the New Deal. . . . Their attitude towards the Church *was* just a reaction to the strength of the Jesuits who had become much too powerful—the affiliation between church and state being much to close." In America, he added, everyone was too prejudiced to get an impartial opinion. "Peoples' financial status seem to form their political opinions, and even the newspapermen, at least the foreign ones are all prejudiced, due to the peculiar position of the press as party instruments over here."

Jack wrote his father that it was not so much what he learned abroad but the incentive it gave him to study when he got back that was important. If this was true, the incentive took more than a year to show up in his work at Harvard. But his grades did improve in his junior year; he became much more involved in his studies, probably because they were now more directly related to the events he had seen in Europe. He was majoring in government, with emphasis on international relations. He read extensively in political theory —nationalism, fascism, and colonialism. He followed the newspapers closely; it was a time when political philosophers' doubts about the goodness of man and the future of the race seemed confirmed in the morning papers.

Solid, sound, earnest, but not brilliant—this is how his professors of government summed him up. "Kennedy is surprisingly able when he gets down to work," one of them noted. "His preparation may be spotty, but his general ability should bolster him up. A commendable fellow." He was affectionate, generous, and loyal to those who broke through his reserve, a reserve that was sometimes disguised as cockiness, sometimes as coolness.

Alone at the Top

At the end of 1937, when Jack was still in his sophomore year, President Roosevelt had suddenly appointed Joseph Kennedy ambassador to Britain. Many Boston aristocrats were aghast. Joe Kennedy, an Irishman and a Catholic, the envoy to the Court of St. James's? The President must be mad. But, after all, they added bitterly, what could you expect of a man who had deserted his class? And in East Boston the Irish were wondering, too. Imagine Pat Kennedy's boy all dressed up in satin knickers bowing before King George!

The most prized of all the diplomatic posts, this ambassadorship put its occupant close to the top of the social world of two continents. For Joseph Patrick Kennedy it meant that after years of striving he had got about as far as he could hope to go. His position would also mean social preferment for his children. His older daughters, now in their teens and all of them tall, dark, lovely girls, were soon meeting and winning the attentions of young British gentry. Kathleen met the Marquess of Hartington, heir of the Duke and Duchess of Devonshire, and the two fell in love. They were married later, during the war.

Moreover, Joseph Kennedy had reached a high station in his church. Father of a model Catholic family, husband of a deeply pious woman, he had contributed heavily to Catholic charities, hospitals, and other undertakings. He was on his way to being appointed a Knight of Malta and a Grand Knight of the Order of Pius IX. Yet there existed a dichotomy in his attitude toward the church. He had sent his daughters to Catholic schools, but not his sons. His daughters, he seemed to feel, should be trained in the values and shaped by the character of the church. But his sons should have secular education to prepare them for the competitive struggle.

The family was increasingly dispersed geographically, but not psychologically. Some of the older children at their own request were godfather and godmother to the younger. The clan still gathered when it could on the Cape or in Palm Beach, playing parlor games and sports as fiercely as ever, and when the parents moved to London, Joe and Jack visited the embassy at Grosvenor Square as often as possible. About this time the father settled separate trust funds on each of his children amounting to well over a million dollars each. "I fixed it," he later told a reporter with a grin, "so that any of my children, financially speaking, could look me in the eye and tell me to go to hell." But he was mainly anxious, as a speculator, to give them security against the vicissitudes of the future.

So, by the late 1930's, the Kennedys seemed to have everything—money, looks, education, brains, high standing in society, in their church, and in the nation. They were something new in America—the immigrants' final surpassing of the blue bloods. Yet, something seemed missing. Perhaps it was that the family lacked roots. They seemed to live everywhere and nowhere. When the new Ambassador went to London, he simply added one more mansion to his homes in Florida and Massachusetts and his apartments and hotel suites in Boston and New York and Chicago and other way stations. The family had left Boston and the tenements far behind without identifying with any new locale or group. They were part of the New Deal upsurge but no longer emotionally kin to it, part of the highest income group but politically separated from it, moving in high social circles but not wholly accepted in them, worshipers in the Catholic Church but not willing, at least on the part of the men, to submerge themselves in her.

It was this detachment, perhaps, that explains one of the most curious of Joseph Kennedy's actions—sending his beloved eldest boys to study in London under Harold Laski, who, as a Jew, a Socialist, an agnostic, a dogmatist, was at polar opposites from him. Only a man with absolute confidence that his sons would not fall for "political nostrums" would take such a chance. The father knew what he was doing. By the late '30's his son Joe held views that were almost a carbon copy of his father's—Democratic, but not New Deal, conservative socially, tending toward isolationism.

But Jack? He was even less committed than his father or Joe. He seemed even more detached than the rest of the family. Alert, inquisitive, receptive, but somewhat remote, he looked at the world with quizzical gray eyes.

3 ★ WAR AND PEACE

Jack Kennedy's last two years at Harvard fell in the shadow of tumultuous world affairs. About the time he began his junior year, in September 1938, Neville Chamberlain yielded Czechoslovakia to Adolf Hitler at Munich. While Jack studied international relations during the fall months, the Führer planned the military and economic isolation and domination of the Danube and the Balkans. While Americans concentrated on their internal problem, Europeans prepared to make the final commitments to war. Thousands of young men of his age were leaving school and work; millions more would soon follow.

The coming war years would try the detachment and neutrality with which Jack had viewed the passionate causes of the New Deal era. Those years would be fateful ones for other members of the family. The father, opposed both to Nazism and to an absolute American commitment against it, would eventually end up on the sidelines during the great conflict. Kathleen would be drawn by marriage into the tumult and tragedy of Britain's battle for survival. And Joe, Jr. would make the ultimate commitment—life itself.

In London, Ambassador Kennedy watched the growing crisis with open alarm. He told Britain's Navy League a few weeks after Munich that the democracies and dictatorships, instead of emphasizing their differences, should solve their common problems by trying to re-establish good relations on a world basis. "After all, we have to live together in the same

51

world, whether we like it or not." From Cambridge, Jack wrote that this speech, "while it seemed to be unpopular with the Jews etc. was considered to be very good by everyone who wasn't bitterly anti-fascist, although it is true that everyone is deadly set against collective security and don't seem to have a very accurate conception of England's position, due to the type of articles that have been written."

In the same letter, Jack squeezed in some news about the Kennedy family. He had just seen Victor Moore and Sophie Tucker in "Leave It to Me." In the play, Sophie, wife of the Ambassador to Russia and mother of five daughters, claimed that with four more she "would have had London." She was making plans, she said, and after five years, at the rate of one child a year, she wouldn't give *that* for the Kennedys. "It's pretty funny and the jokes about us got by far the biggest laughs whatever that signifies," Jack wrote. He noted also, "Tonight is a big night in Boston politics as the Honorable John F. Fitzgerald is making a speech for his good friend James Michael [Curley]. Politics makes strange bedfellows. . . ."

But Boston politics and political satire seemed pretty small potatoes in the winter of 1938-39. Jack watched restlessly while Europe girded for war. Eager to see the tension points at first hand, he won permission from Harvard to spend the second semester in Europe, and crossed the Atlantic late in the winter of 1939 just before the Nazis swallowed the rest of Czechoslovakia. After spring in Paris, he went to Poland, stayed two or three weeks, then went on to Riga, Russia, Turkey, Palestine, and back to the Balkans, Berlin, and Paris. During his grand tour of Europe on the eve of the war, he used the American embassies as stopping-off places and observation posts. He stayed with Ambassador William Bullitt in Paris—the embassy was so large it was like living in an apartment house, Jack thought—with Ambassador Anthony Biddle in Warsaw, with Charles ("Chip") Bohlen, then Second Secretary, in Moscow.

His father, whose position made these contacts possible, asked of his son only one thing—that he send him detailed reports from each capital. After each stop, young Kennedy mailed to London his summation of the situation. The literary quality of his reports was not the highest, and the spelling was still atrocious, but they showed a cool detachment. He deliberately talked with representatives of all parties to get a balanced point of view. In Warsaw, for example, he saw newspapermen, embassy people, "plenty of Poles, rich and poor"; in Danzig he saw a leading Danzig senator and the German, British, Norwegian, and American consuls. In a

2,500-word letter, he carefully summarized the German and Polish arguments about Danzig.

"Probably the strongest impression I have goten is that rightly or wrongly the Poles *will fight over* the Question of Danzig," he concluded.

Russia struck Jack as a "crude, backward, hopelessly bureaucratic country," he later remembered. His Russian plane had a broken window, which seemed to bother no one, and he had to sit on the floor. The wide streets in the big grim cities were swept by dusty winds. He saw Leningrad, Moscow, and the Crimea before taking a ship for Istanbul. Upon leaving Jerusalem, he sent his father another long report, part of it a historical survey of British-Arab-Jewish relations, and concluded that British policy sounded just and fair but that what was needed was not a just and fair solution "but a solution that will work." He admitted, though, that he had become "more pro-British down there than I have been in my other visits to England. . . ."

The long-gathering storm burst over Europe soon after Jack had concluded his tour and had reached his father's embassy. Rejecting any compromise over Danzig, the Nazis on September 1 suddenly overran the Polish border and lunged toward Warsaw. Britain and France honored their commitments to Poland and declared war. Russia stayed neutral; the "backward" nations had outwitted the Western democracies in the game of power politics—at least for a time.

Jack was shortly pulled into a tiny backwash of the storm. Early in September, the British liner *Athenia* was torpedoed by the Germans and the American survivors taken to Glasgow. Dispatched by his father to a Glasgow hotel to help the Americans, Jack got a noisy reception. As he assured them that an American ship would take them home, they shouted, "We want a convoy—you can't trust the God-damned German Navy!" Jack could do nothing but return to London and advise his father that a convoy should be sent.

It was a brief moment of action, but he was still a college student and classes were beginning at Harvard. Later in the month Jack sailed for home.

"Why England Slept"

"Am getting along fine here," Kennedy wrote his father from Harvard late in the fall of 1939. His term in Europe had boosted his prestige; "I am quite a seer around here." He was taking an interesting course from a political-science professor. "I am still incognito," he added playfully, "but expect to go up and shake his palm and start discussing what a big impression he made on you when those papers start getting marked." He was not neglecting his social life. He was "doing better with the gals," and was taking a friend of Kick's to the Princeton game, "which will be my first taste of a Catholic [school?] girl so will be interested to see how it goes."

Now a lordly senior, Kennedy cut a bigger figure on the Harvard campus. He took an active part in the social life of Winthrop House, on one occasion leading the "Big Apple" at a house dance. He had not risen very far on the *Crimson,* but wrote a few editorials for the undergraduate daily. He was devoting some time to the stock market and earned a couple of hundred dollars after some cautious speculation in aviation stocks. He was drawn at the same time more to intellectual activity than he had ever been. To make up for the semester in Europe, he took extra courses his senior year, all either in government or economics, and he won B grades in all of them. He was now a candidate for a degree with honors in political science.

To gain such honors he needed to submit an undergraduate thesis, and this was Kennedy's main intellectual effort during his senior year. His subject was "Appeasement at Munich." He had been struck by the criticism of Chamberlain he had encountered during his travels abroad. In America, also, the Prime Minister was viewed with contempt. Was Chamberlain, Kennedy wondered, simply a scapegoat for deeper, more impersonal forces of defeat? Under the supervision of Bruce Hopper and Payson Wild, political-science professors, Kennedy toiled in Harvard's Widener Library during the winter months of 1939-40, studying parliamentary debates, Foreign Office minutes, issues of the *Times* of London and the *Economist.*

On the face of it, the thesis that Kennedy submitted in the spring was a typical undergraduate effort—solemn and pedantic in tone, bristling with statistics and footnotes, a little weak in spelling and sentence structure. Starting out with London's disarmament policies of 1933-35, the dissertation treated of the reasons for Britain's slow response to Hitler's rearmament, with particular stress on the influence of the pacifists, the economizers, the all-out League of Nations supporters, business and labor concern with immediate self-interest, and petty party politics. The second half of the thesis dealt with the slowness and inadequacy of Britain's rearmament of the late '30's.

The thesis had two arresting qualities. One was Kennedy's emotional detachment from the crisis he described. The urgency in his paragraphs was purely intellectual. He criticized people for being too emotional over Munich. He was no alarmist, he insisted, as though being an alarmist in the spring of 1940 were a sin. The other arresting aspect was closely related to this—his emphasis on the point that men like Chamberlain and Stanley Baldwin were not mainly responsible for Munich, but, rather, that Munich was caused by deeper forces inherent in democracy and capitalism, by general apathy, concern with profits and security, pacifism, fear of regimentation, and so on. In this sense the thesis was mature and judicious in tone.

". . . Most of the critics have been firing at the wrong target," he concluded. "The Munich Pact itself should not be the object of criticism but rather the underlying factors, such as the state of British opinion and the condition of Britain's armaments which made 'surrender' inevitable.

"To blame one man, such as Baldwin, for the unpreparedness of British armaments is illogical and unfair, given the conditions of Democratic government."

But perhaps the most significant aspect of his work lay in its agreement with his father's position on the European war. During late 1939 and early 1940, while the son was working out his conclusions in Widener Library, the father, in his reports from London to President Roosevelt and Secretary of State Cordell Hull, "was sympathetic," says an authoritative study, "to the Chamberlain Government and its policies and tended to project his isolationism to the European problem. For the United States he prescribed complete abstention from the conflict brewing in Europe and urged that every effort be made to arm in self-defense against all eventualities."

Kennedy, Sr. did not conceal his pessimism about the future of Britain and France. Poland was gone for good, and even if Hitler fell, chaos and communism would follow in Germany, he wrote Roosevelt at the end of September 1939. England didn't have a "Chinaman's chance" against Germany and Russia but would go down fighting. Then much later he returned home and told a group of Army and Navy officers that another year of war would leave all Europe ready for communism. The collapse of France in the spring of 1940 deepened his fears and sharpened his isolationism. "It seems to me," he wired home, "that if we had to protect our lives, we would do better fighting in our own backyard."

Like his father, Kennedy showed, in his thesis, that he was worried that a democracy could not long bear a huge defensive force without becoming totalitarian. "She is forced to pay for everything out of her budget, and she is limited by the laws of capitalism—supply and demand." Like his father,

Kennedy excused Munich as inevitable because of Britain's delay in rearming and even as desirable, as a way of buying time. Like his father, Kennedy wanted America to build up its own armaments as quickly as possible, even if it meant jettisoning some democratic luxuries. But while events forced the father eventually to take a position on aid to the Allies —chiefly against it—the son in his Harvard paper could avoid this burning question of 1940. "I of course don't want to take sides too much," he wrote his father.

As Kennedy handed his dissertation in to Professor Hopper in the spring of 1940, events in Europe dramatized his thesis of democracy's weakness. Germany smashed through Dutch and Belgian defenses, cut to pieces French infantry corps, and pinned British troops against the sea at Dunkirk. France was gone; Britain was in grave danger. To Kennedy, the great consolation was that Churchill, whose efforts to arouse Britain he had often cited in his thesis, was now leading the British. But would America wake in time?

In June, Kennedy was graduated from Harvard amid the traditional pomp and pageantry—the parade in the Stadium, the ivy oration, the final singing of "Fair Harvard" as an undergraduate, the concert at the House triangle, the baseball game with Yale, dancing in Winthrop House, the confetti battle, and next day the solemn Commencement in Harvard Yard. But all the bands and songs could not drown out the roar from abroad. The class poet told of lying lazily on the banks of the Charles during the past four years, but—

> And now the war, and—rolling over on our bellies
> —we say,
> "We must fight."
> "We must not fight."

Kennedy's mother and sisters came up for Commencement, but the Ambassador had to stay in London. When he told his father that he was graduating *cum laude* in political science and had got *magna cum laude* on his thesis, a cable of congratulations flashed back, ending: TWO THINGS I ALWAYS KNEW ABOUT YOU ONE THAT YOU ARE SMART TWO THAT YOU ARE A SWELL GUY LOVE DAD.

His thesis had been so well received at Harvard that Kennedy decided to try to get it published. He showed a detached attitude toward his work in a letter to his father: "I thought I could work on rewriting it and making it somewhat more complete and maybe more interesting for the average reader—as it stands now—it is not anywhere polished

enough although the ideas etc. are O.K." His father heartily
concurred and sent him from London a stream of advice on
rewriting, editing, and publishing contacts. In a long letter
of May 20, 1940, he contended that his son had gone too far
in absolving Baldwin and Chamberlain from responsibility
for Britain's weakness at the time of Munich. The Ambassador granted that ultimately the blame must be placed on the
people as a whole, but a politician should do more than keep
his ear to the ground, "he is also supposed to look after the
national welfare, and to attempt to educate the people. . . ."
He suggested that Jack blame *both* the people and their
leaders. His son agreed. "Will stop white washing Baldwin,"
he replied.

The facts and views in the book were little changed from
the thesis, except for a surprisingly rhetorical ending: "To
say that democracy has been awakened by the events of the
last few weeks is not enough. Any person will awaken when
the house is burning down. What we need is an armed guard
that will wake up when the fire first starts or, better yet, one
that will not permit a fire to start at all.

"We should profit by the lesson of England and make our
democracy work. We must make it work right now. Any system of government will work when everything is going well.
It is the system that functions in the pinches that survives."
Actually, these and a few other sentences of exhortation he
had taken almost verbatim from a letter from his father.

At the Ambassador's request, his good friend Arthur
Krock, of the New York *Times,* recommended an agent and
a title, *Why England Slept,* intended as a follow-up of the
earlier Churchill title *While England Slept.* Jack told his father he hoped Churchill, then prime minister, would not
mind. Another friend of the Ambassador, Henry Luce, of
Time, Inc., agreed to do a foreword. Kennedy scrubbed up
the spelling, took out the footnotes, vastly improved the
style, and added chapters that brought the book up to date
and made it more relevant to America. After being turned
down by Harper & Brothers on the grounds that it had been
outdated by the fall of France, the manuscript was accepted
by Wilfred Funk, Inc., which got the book out under forced
draft during July.

Why England Slept was a surprising success. It appeared
on the eve of the Nazi blitz of Britain, sold 40,000 copies in
the United States and a like number in Britain, and won a
gratifying reception from the critics. Reviewers were intrigued that this twenty-three-year-old could marshal his material so skillfully, make his judgments so temperately, and
relate his conclusions so tellingly to America's situation.

Some felt, however, that he was still too easy on Baldwin and Chamberlain, that he distributed the blame for Munich so widely among so many impersonal forces, economic and political, that he left the reader unsure as to what exactly was the lesson for Americans. Kennedy had raised grave questions about the capacity of Western capitalist democracies to cope with totalitarianism, but he offered little advice as to what democrats could do about this except to produce strong leaders—more easily said than done.

But while the reviewers studied the book's ideas, Ambassador Kennedy looked at it through a proud father's eyes. "You would be surprised how a book that really makes the grade with high-class people stands you in good stead for years to come," he wrote to his son in August. "I remember that in the report you are asked to make after twenty-five years to the Committee at Harvard, one of the questions is 'What books have you written?' and there is no doubt you will have done yourself a great deal of good." He sent copies of the book to Laski, to Churchill, and to the Queen.

By the time *Why England Slept* reached the best-seller lists, Roosevelt was grappling with problems of leadership far more complex than those described in it. All at the same time, the President had to begin his campaign for re-election, send aid to the desperately pressed Churchill, rearm his own country, and soft-pedal the possibility of war. And he had to cope with members of his party who disapproved of a third term or of his decision to help Britain.

The Kennedys had a curious relationship to these great events. Joe, Jr., still in Harvard Law School, shared his father's opposition to intervention in behalf of Britain. In the spring of 1940, when Roosevelt was evading the third-term issue, Joe made his debut in Massachusetts politics by running for delegate to the Democratic national convention on a pledge to vote for Farley for president. Even when Roosevelt was nominated at Chicago on the first ballot, Joe stuck with Farley. A Roosevelt leader phoned the Ambassador and asked him to talk with his son, but he refused: "I wouldn't think of telling him what to do." After the convention, Farley quit his post as chairman of the Democratic National Committee, and Joe went on to become a fiery critic of Roosevelt's interventionist foreign policies, even to stating in January 1941 that the United States would be better off for economic reasons under a barter system with a Nazi-conquered Europe than engaging in a total war on the side of Great Britain.

Kennedy, Sr. was a much more serious problem for the President. While the Nazis stepped up their massive bombing attacks during September 1940, the Ambassador dispatched telegram after telegram paying tribute to the British "stiff upper lip" but doubting that the country had either the leadership or the resources to withstand the Nazis for long. In Washington, campaign rumors were circulating that Kennedy might come home and stump for Wendell Willkie, the Republican candidate. He did come home, but Roosevelt quickly and shrewdly brought him into camp. He invited him to the White House, heard out his complaints about his treatment by the State Department, emphatically agreed that Joe had been badly abused, promised a real house cleaning after the election, and immediately won the Ambassador's agreement to make a radio speech for him.

In the last week of the campaign, Kennedy came through for the President with a speech, sponsored by him and his family and broadcast over 114 stations of the Columbia network. He announced his support of FDR and defended his own role as ambassador. He had been subjected, he said, "to deliberate smear campaigns." "If by that word [appeaser], now possessed of hateful implications, it is charged that I advocate a deal with the dictators contrary to the British desire . . . the charge is false and malicious. . . ." But he went on to proclaim his opposition to war intervention: "Unless we are attacked, the American people do not have to go to war."

The next night, in Joe's old home town, Roosevelt told a big crowd in the Boston Garden that he had been happy to "welcome back to the shores of America that Boston boy, beloved by all of Boston and a lot of other places, my Ambassador to the Court of St. James, Joe Kennedy." And in this same speech, the President said: "And while I am talking to you mothers and fathers, I give you one more assurance. . . . Your boys are not going to be sent into any foreign wars." Some were to label Roosevelt a hypocrite for that last statement; others were to point out that he could not lead too far ahead of the people and that by December 7, 1941, the war would be no longer a "foreign" war, but a war brought home to America.

In Boston, after the election, Kennedy indiscreetly poured out his feelings to a newspaper reporter, saying that democracy was finished in Britain, that if the United States got into the war with Britain "we'll be left holding the bag," that he was going to see Hearst about a campaign to keep America out of the war, and much else. When the story was published and the storm of protest broke at home and abroad, he knew that his ambassadorship was finished.

And where was Jack Kennedy during his father's diplomatic crisis? He favored Roosevelt's re-election, too, but he was not active in the campaign. His main role, it seems, was to bring Grandfather Fitz around to see the President when he was campaigning in Boston. As usual, Roosevelt showed his masterly touch, greeting Fitzgerald warmly: "Everywhere I went on my South American trip they were asking after you. They all remember your singing 'Sweet Adeline' when you were down there. Yes," said the President, while Fitzgerald beamed, "all the Latin Americans are singing 'Adelina Dulce' down there now!"

For a year following the summer of 1940, Jack Kennedy marked time. He first planned on Yale Law School, but changed his mind, attended business school at Stanford for six months, but his heart was not in that either. Once again he got wanderlust and left to take a long trip through South America. During 1941, war spread to the Balkans and to Russia; it looked more and more likely that the United States would become involved, though the isolationists stepped up their pleas for "America First."

Kennedy, Sr. had returned to his embassy for a few weeks after the 1940 election, but to the British he had become a symbol of appeasement and defeatism, and at the end of the year he resigned as ambassador. He never succeeded afterward in clearing the image of his position on foreign policy. He seemed so isolationist that the America First Committee considered him for its national chairman. ". . . I do not want to see this country go to war under any conditions whatsoever unless we are attacked," he had said. And another time, "England is not fighting our battle. This is not our war." On the other hand, he saw the Nazis as hostile to the rule of conscience and reason, "to law, to family life, even to religion itself," refused the label of isolationist or appeaser, and vastly preferred the British, though they "snub us or sneer at us", to the world of "Nazi brutality." He simply refused to make a final commitment at a time when the world was choosing up sides—We or They.

While his father retired to the sidelines, Jack moved near to direct involvement in the war. In the spring, he tried to enlist in the Army but was rejected because of his old back condition. He went through five months of strengthening exercises, however, and managed to pass a Navy fitness test in September. For a time he worked in Intelligence on a news digest for the Navy Chief of Staff in Washington. When Pearl Harbor came he applied for sea duty, but it was a long time coming. He was assigned for several months to a project in the South for protecting defense factories against bombing—a job he found dull and distasteful. Part of his spare time was devoted to Navy correspondence courses in Foreign Intelligence and Navy Regulations and Customs. Fearing that he might be given a desk job, he asked his father to use his influence with the Navy Department to insure that he would get sea duty. His father successfully pulled some strings for his son. This episode had an ironic side, for Kennedy, Sr. had tried to get back into action the day of Pearl Harbor with a wire to the President: NAME THE BATTLEFRONT. I'M YOURS TO COMMAND. Somehow this telegram never reached the President; indeed, his fellow Bostonian, House Majority Leader John W. McCormack, told Kennedy that Roosevelt was surprised that Kennedy had not volunteered. He wrote then to FDR that he *had;* a friendly exchange of letters followed, but somehow Kennedy never did receive a wartime assignment.

Late in 1942, Jack realized his hope of training for the kind of sea duty that seemed fitting for a man who had almost grown up in small boats—assignment to a Motor Torpedo Boat squadron. For six months he learned how to handle the speedy, brittle PT boats, most of the time at Portsmouth and Newport. His instructors graded him near perfect in ship handling, good in technical matters like engineering, and "very willing and conscientious."

Early in 1943, he shipped out from San Francisco for the South Pacific, where Allied forces were beginning slowly to turn back the long Japanese advance. By March, Lt. (j.g.) Kennedy was commanding his own PT boat in the Solomons, off Tulagi and the Russell Islands. By August, he was part of a vast air-sea-ground counterattack against the Japanese around New Georgia.

"Jesus Loves Me"

Shortly after midnight on August 2, 1943, the Japanese destroyer *Amagiri* cut through the dark waters of Blackett Strait west of New Georgia. On the bridge, Kohei Hanami, commander of the destroyer, peered through the cloudy, squally night; bedeviled by American planes during the day and by PT boats at night, he had ordered his men to maintain attack positions. Suddenly he saw a PT boat moving about a half-mile off.

"Starboard ten degrees!" Hanami called to the helmsman. "PT boat—steady." At thirty knots, he bore down on the boat, smashed into her amidships, cut her clean in two, and slid on without a jar. The PT boat was crunched apart with an unearthly noise, and the two halves flamed up in the water.

On the PT boat, Lt. John F. Kennedy, skipper, and his

twelve officers and men had watched helplessly as the destroyer bore down on them. The PT was leaden, for it was running on one engine to keep down noise. Two men were killed outright or were sucked down to die in the churning vortex of the destroyer's wake; others struggled to keep afloat and away from the gasoline fire burning on the water. Kennedy was thrown hard in the cockpit and fell on his back across the deck. He thought: "This is how it feels to be killed." But his half of the PT boat stayed afloat, and he and four others clung to it. He shouted for survivors in the water, and six more responded. One man, McMahon, was badly burned; another, Harris, had hurt his leg. Kennedy swam to them and half-tugged, half-guided them back to the PT boat.

"I can't go any farther," Harris protested.

"For a guy from Boston, you're certainly putting up a great exhibition out here," Kennedy retorted. Harris and the others, buoyed up by their life preservers and the skipper, made it to the drifting hulk after three hours.

As day came, the eleven men waited for other PT boats to come to the rescue. Unaccountably, no one arrived. To the northeast, west, and south were islands swarming with Japanese. The boat was now listing badly and settling.

"What do you want to do if the Japs come out?" Kennedy asked. "Fight or surrender?"

"Fight with what?" someone asked. They had one Tommy gun, six 45-caliber automatics, and one .38.

"Well, what do you want to do?"

"Anything you say, Mr. Kennedy," someone said. "You're the boss."

"There's nothing in the book about a situation like this," Kennedy said. "Seems to me we're not a military organization any more. Let's just talk this over." But talking led to arguing, and Kennedy finally realized he would have to take command. He ordered all but the three injured men into the water to give the wounded room. But soon the hulk turned turtle. Kennedy decided that the only hope lay in their swimming for a small island three miles to the southeast. He towed McMahon, holding in his teeth one end of a long strap on the burned man's Mae West. Although he swallowed a lot of salt water through his clenched teeth, Kennedy made it to the island in five hours. He had been in the sea for almost fifteen hours.

The men sprawled exhausted on the little island. Kennedy decided to strike out on his own to a further island and try to intercept a PT boat along the regular route through Ferguson Passage. In the twilight he swam to the reef, hugging

the ship's lantern. Once he saw a huge fish in the water; he remembered one of his men saying, "These barracuda will
come up under a swimming man and eat his testicles." Like a
drunken man, he made his way slowly along the reef, the
sharp coral cutting his shins and ankles, swam out into Ferguson Passage; and there, treading water, chilled to the
bone, he waited for a PT boat. Nothing came. He started
back, but the current was faster now, he was tired, and he
drifted right by the little island where his men waited. At
last he stopped trying to swim; he seemed to stop caring, as
if in a trance; but he held the heavy lantern as if it were a link
with his men. At times he drifted off into sleep or uncon-
sciousness. He thought he might be dying. But the current,
slowly carrying him in a huge circle, took him back into Ferguson Passage to the spot where he had been. Once again
he started home, picking his agonizing way along the rough
coral reef, in bare feet. Finally he made the island,
crawled up the beach, and vomited on the sand. His men
moved up to him. Kennedy looked at his third officer. "Ross,
you try it tonight," he said. Then he passed out.

Back at the squadron's base, hope had been given up for
the thirteen survivors. Services were held in their memory.
One of the officers wrote to Ross's mother that her son had
died for a cause he believed in "stronger than any one of
us." Jack Kennedy, the Ambassador's son, the letter went on,
was on the same boat and also lost his life. "The man that
said the cream of a nation is lost in war can never be accused of making an overstatement of a very cruel fact. . . ."

Ross swam out into Ferguson Passage that evening but met
no better luck than had his chief. Kennedy, cold and sick,
was awake most of that night. The men were terribly thirsty.
In the morning Kennedy insisted that they keep moving;
he swam out with them toward an island nearer Ferguson
Passage. Three hours later, they landed and found coconuts.
The thirsty men broke them open and greedily drained their
milk, only to turn sick and spew it out. Rain fell during the
night, and the men crawled through the brush licking water
off the leaves. In the morning they saw that the leaves were
covered with bird droppings. Sourly they named the place
Bird Island.

This was now the fourth day. One sailor pointed to a
rosary another wore. "McGuire, give that necklace a working over." McGuire said quietly, "Yes, I'll take care of all
you fellows." But to Kennedy the only hope was to keep
moving, so he and Ross swam to Nauru Island, even nearer
the passage, and here their luck turned. They found two na-

tives, some Japanese provisions, and a canoe. The natives fled, but later, when the canoe was swamped, other natives appeared. Kennedy found a coconut with a smooth shell and cut a message on it with his knife: ELEVEN ALIVE NATIVE KNOWS POSIT AND REEFS NAURU ISLAND KENNEDY. "Rendova, Rendova," he said to the natives. One seemed to understand; taking the coconut, they paddled off.

Kennedy lay sick and dazed on Nauru all day and then determined that he and Ross must go out into Ferguson Passage in the dugout and watch for PT boats. The wind was high and the choppy waves soon overturned their canoe. The two men struggled for two hours against a tidal current headed for the open sea.

"Sorry I got you out here, Barney!" Kennedy shouted.

"This would be a great time to say I told you so," Ross shouted back, "but I won't!"

They forced their way out of the current and toward the island. Ahead was the heavy roar of the waves smashing on the dangerous reef. A wave tore Kennedy from the canoe and spun him around and down, but miraculously he landed not on coral but in an eddy. Ross was badly cut on the arm and shoulder, and his feet were now so lacerated that Kennedy had to lay the paddles down, step by step on the beach, so that Ross could walk on them. They fell on the beach at Nauru and slept.

Their ordeal was almost over. In the morning four natives awakened them. One said in excellent English, "I have a letter for you, sir." It was from the commander of a New Zealand infantry patrol on New Georgia urging them to follow the natives back to his camp. The rescue could not have come much later. McMahon's burns had begun to rot; Ross's arm had swelled to the size of his thigh. The natives placed Kennedy in the bottom of their canoe, concealed him from Japanese planes with palm fronds, and paddled him to the New Zealand patrol. A few hours later, a PT boat arrived. "Hey, Jack!" someone called.

"Where the hell you been?" Kennedy called back.

"We got some food for you."

"No thanks," Kennedy said. "I just had a coconut." A moment later, he jumped into the boat, and hugged the men aboard—they were his friends from the base.

The native guided them back to Bird Island for the rest of the men; and in the middle of the night the PT boat sped back to the base with its joyful passengers. On the way, one of the survivors tippled rather heavily of the brandy that the squadron surgeon had sent to revive them. Then he sat topside, his arms around a couple of plump, missionary-trained natives. Together they sang a hymn all three happened to know:

"Jesus loves me, this I know,
     For the Bible tells me so;
     Little ones to him belong,
     They are weak, but He is strong.
     Yes, Jesus loves me; yes, Jesus loves me. . . ."

War's End

Kennedy's mates welcomed him noisily at the base. Both officers and enlisted men liked him; they thought he lacked the airs a millionaire ambassador's son might have been expected to have. The survivors' stories of their experiences and of Kennedy's tenacity spread through the base. The Navy bestowed official recognition when it awarded to him, in addition to the Purple Heart, the Navy and Marine Corps Medal. Admiral William F. Halsey signed the citation, which read in part: "His courage, endurance and excellent leadership contributed to the saving of several lives and was [in] keeping with the highest traditions of the United States Naval Service."

The rest of the war for Kennedy was anticlimactic and studded with frustration and tragedy. He contracted malaria and dropped down to 125 pounds. His flip-flop on his back after the PT boat explosion had aggravated his old back injury, and this caused him a good deal of pain. In December 1943, he left his MTB squadron and was rotated back to the States. For a time he was an instructor in a PT training program at Miami; a pleasant life, with plenty of time on the sea and plenty of recreation, too. One day Kennedy visited James Cox, the Democratic presidential candidate of 1920, who lived nearby, and discussed war and politics. His Navy superiors found Kennedy pleasant, quiet, conscientious, and intelligent; they gave him a low rating only in "military bearing and neatness."

Kennedy hoped for more overseas duty, preferably in the Mediterranean. But he was not well, and, in the late spring of 1944, entered Chelsea Naval Hospital, near Boston. It was not far to Hyannisport, and he could spend weekends with his family. It was there one weekend—the date was August 2, the anniversary of the PT-boat crash—that word came in to the family that two priests had asked to see Mr. Joseph Kennedy. He left the room and came back a few moments later, his face gray. Joe, Jr. had been reported missing. The family held out hope for a time—perhaps the miracle of the previous year would be repeated—but Joe had never really been missing. He had been killed instantly during a desperate mission, for which he had volunteered, to destroy the seemingly invulnerable submarine pens on the Belgian coast. Under the plan, Joe's plane, heavily packed with explosives, was to fly close to the pens; at the last minute, the crew would bail out and other planes, by remote control, would crash the ammuniton plane into the pens. But before reaching the bail-out point, the plane, for unknown reasons, suddenly blew up.

Jack could not believe that Joe was dead. Only when, back at the hospital, he saw the headlines and Joe's picture on the front page did the terrible finality come home to him.

A month later, came news that Kathleen's husband, the Marquess of Hartington, then a captain in the Coldstream Guards, had been killed in action in France. The couple had been married only four months, and their decision to marry had been difficult, for Hartington was a Protestant. The first Duke of Devonshire, indeed, had withdrawn from the Privy Council of King Charles II in the seventeenth century in protest against Roman Catholic influence. But Joe, Jr., then in England, had characteristically backed up his sister, and she and the Marquess had been married in a civil ceremony in the Chelsea Registry Office. They had had only a few days together—and now he, too, was gone.

Jack's heart ached for his beloved Kick—but not nearly so much as it would several years later when Kathleen herself was killed in a plane crash on a vacation trip to the Riviera.

"The thing about Kathleen and Joe was their tremendous vitality," Kennedy said many years later. "Everything was moving in their direction—that's what made it so unfortunate. If something happens to you or somebody in your family who is miserable anyway, whose health is bad, or who has a chronic disease or something, that's one thing. But, for someone who is living at their peak, then to get cut off—that's the shock."

After a long stay at Chelsea, where a disc operation was performed on his back, Kennedy, still thin and ailing, appeared before a Navy board in Washington and retired from service. He returned to civilian life at the beginning of 1945. The outcome of the war was no longer seriously in doubt. Men's thoughts turned toward plans for keeping the peace. In February, Kennedy produced a short paper, "Let's Try an Experiment in Peace," arguing that an arms race would mean heavy taxes and hence the stifling of private enterprise and full employment, and proposing an agreement among the postwar Big Three—Britain, Russia, and the United States—

for limiting postwar rearmament plans. It was a curious position for the author of *Why England Slept*, but he contended that Germany and Japan could and should be rendered impotent after World War II. But how could unity among the Big Three be maintained? Here Kennedy was lamentably vague and unconvincing. He called for "workable, practical machinery for settling disputes" and better understanding between Russia and America, but how all this was to be achieved he did not say.

Just how elusive unity would be, Kennedy was to see at first-hand a few weeks later. As Allied troops speared into Germany and American forces seized Okinawa, emissaries from the united nations gathered in San Francisco to lay plans for a permanent world organization. Kennedy was there covering the conference "from a GI viewpoint" for the New York *Journal American* and other Hearst newspapers.

From the start, he took a sympathetic but realistic view of the proceedings. His first dispatch complained that the conference had been given too much of a build-up, that the best to be hoped for was the strengthening of the voting procedure in the new security council and the yielding of the Russians' "stiff-necked attitude" toward the Polish question. In subsequent dispatches, he reported at length on the "belligerent Russian attitude." After a week at the conference he had concluded that the Russians could not forget their years of being treated as a second-class nation and it would be a long time before Russia would entrust her safety to any organization other than the Red Army. Hence, "any organization drawn up here will be merely a skeleton. Its powers will be limited. It will reflect the fact that there are deep disagreements among its members."

Kennedy's pessimism deepened as the conference proceeded. "The world organization that will come out of San Francisco will be the product of the same passions and selfishness that produced the Treaty of Versailles." The only ray of light he could see was realization that humanity could not afford another war. But soon he was reporting "talk of fighting the Russians in the next ten or fifteen years." At the parley's end, Kennedy approved the new United Nations Organization, provided that it did not interfere with the Monroe Doctrine, but thought the only hope was unity among the Big Three and in this he believed no progress had been made.

He tried his hand at journalism once again by reporting the British election from London in the summer, also for the Hearst papers. After that, he had had enough of reporting. The war was coming to an end in the Pacific, too. Tens of thousands of demobilized soldiers and sailors were streaming back home. Most of them had formed definite plans for civilian life—plans lovingly shaped and solidified in long months of waiting. But not Jack Kennedy. By the age of twenty-eight he had earned a B.A. degree, learned how to swim and to sail and to golf; he had written a successful book, traveled extensively and learned courage and endurance in the years of war. But the man and the political leader of a dozen years later was unformed; his political views and his personality were still in the making.

4 ★ THE POOR LITTLE RICH KID

According to a Boston legend, Kennedy's decision to enter politics took place on a particular evening a few weeks after Joe, Jr.'s death. Jack, still recovering from his Navy injury, was summoned to his father's presence. In a dramatic scene, the Ambassador was supposed to have said that with Joe gone Jack must now carry on the family tradition of public service. He must be the champion of the Kennedy clan in politics. The whole family would unite to help him. And Kennedy, then and there, answered the family call.

Unhappily, things are always tidier and more dramatic in legend than in fact. To be sure, the Ambassador wanted his son to enter political life and made his views known on many occasions. But Jack was undecided. He still toyed with the notion of making a career of journalism; and he was attracted also to academic life and intellectual pursuits. On the other hand, newspaper work was an undependable trade for a beginner, and he had no graduate degree for teaching. Business lured him not at all.

He had mixed feelings about a political career. He liked the idea of being part of the top circles of government—making decisions, working on legislation, handling the affairs of state. But he was not at all sure that he would like politics at the level where he would have to start. He was still shy with people outside his social circle, a bit withdrawn and unassertive. He disliked the blarney, the exuberant backslapping and handshaking, the exaggerated claims and denunciations that went with politics, especially Boston politics. Nor was he convinced of his own talents as a speaker, or as a "mixer."

Then, too, for what office would be run—and where? If he had lived in England, Kennedy could have made a national name for himself and then asked his party for a good seat where he could run for Parliament. But this was not England, nor even America, but provincial Massachusetts. And here lay the cream of the irony. Kennedy had no roots in Massachusetts, no place that he could call home. He had lived briefly as a child in several parts of Boston, then in New York, then in Connecticut as a schoolboy, then at Harvard (which was never considered a Massachusetts voting precinct), then in England and in the Navy. A politician must have a home base. Kennedy had none.

Finally, Boston politics had changed since his grandfathers Fitzgerald and Kennedy had entered politics. This change was important, for it would deeply influence Kennedy's future.

In his grandfather's day, the Irish had won control of Democratic politics and seized power from the Yankees. For a time that power was undisputed; the Yankees were increasingly outnumbered, and the newer immigrants were politically helpless and docile. But after the turn of the century, Italians, Slavs, and Poles began to rise from the ditch and the dock to semiskilled jobs, just as the Irish had done; some went to college, entered law, medicine, and other professions, and in turn became the respected "prominenti" of their ethnic group. Following closest on the heels of the Irish were the immigrants from Italy, and soon the Italian counterparts of the Kennedys and Fitzgeralds were welding their groups into political organizations that rivaled the Irish.

For a while the newer immigrants worked with the Irish as junior partners, but as their numbers and their competence grew they demanded higher status. Some Irish leaders, including Fitzgerald, shared a few political plums with the Italians, but many Irish reacted to the newcomers as the Yankees had to them. Of course, the newer immigrants were Catholics, too, but they had brought from Europe a different strain of Catholicism, and the Italian Catholic, French Catholic, and Polish Catholic churches often chafed under the dominance in Boston of the Irish Catholic hierarchy led by Cardinal O'Connell.

Partly for this reason, partly because Woodrow Wilson's foreign policies alienated immigrant groups, partly because Republican Yankees began to cater to the Italians and Jews, the loose Democratic coalition of Irish, Italians, and other immigrants fell to pieces in 1920. Chastened by their loss of office, the Irish during the following decade grudgingly shared power with other ethnic leaders and even with Yankees, such as Joseph B. Ely, as the only way of winning elections during a Republican era. Al Smith's nomination in 1928, however, and the Great Depression brought such a powerful Democratic tide in Massachusetts that the Irish could go it alone. The Democratic leaders during the '30's were all Irish and virtually all from the Boston area: Jim Curley, Maurice Tobin, John McCormack, the rising Paul A. Dever, and others.

The Democratic party had become, more than ever before, less a unified organization than a holding company for personal organizations that often warred with one another more fiercely than with the Republicans. Italians and other groups, denied recognition by the Democrats, turned to the Yankee Republicans, who often made room for them. These and other forces also cut the Massachusetts Democratic party off from the national party; the Bay State Democrats were mainly concerned with patronage and bread-and-butter liberalism, while the national party, under Roosevelt, had taken over the broader liberal, internationalist, and "good government" traditions personified by Cleveland, Theodore Roosevelt, and Woodrow Wilson.

Such matters, if he recognized them at all, might have seemed highly academic to Jack Kennedy in 1945. But they were not. He was Irish and hence a member of the dominant force in the Democratic party, but Boston politics was mightily affected by the feuds between the Irish and the Italians. Then, too, the provincial and separatist ways of the Bay State Democracy would have important implications for a man hoping to build a base in Massachusetts for a national political career. And the chaotic condition of the Democratic party meant that he would have to build a personal machine to win office.

Still, these were problems of the future. During the summer of 1945, as the war drew to an end in Japan, Kennedy restlessly pondered his prospects.

Political Baptism

The issue was decided by, of all people, Jim Curley. In recent years the "Purple Shamrock" had been down on his luck. Vigorous young men had beaten him for the United States Senate, for governor, and even for mayor of Boston. Old and broke, under court orders to pay back to the city $42,000 as a result of a judgment of fraud, Curley had partly recouped his political fortunes in 1942 by winning a seat in Congress. But Washington was not his political forte. He hungered for one more crack at being mayor of Boston, one more chance to pay off political friends, to pay back political foes, and to refurbish the fading Curley legend. In the spring of 1945, he announced his candidacy for mayor in the fall election. If he won—and his chances looked good—the Eleventh Massachusetts Congressional District would be open. Kennedy eyed it with interest.

The Eleventh District was not an attractive one to a genteel political fledgling. Sprawling across East Boston, the North End and West End, and then over the Charles River into Charlestown, Cambridge, and part of Somerville, it enclosed a patchwork of some of the ugliest blighted areas in America. Irish, Italians, and a score of other immigrant groups were packed into grimy red-brick tenements sandwiched between smoking factories, oil tanks, elevated railways, dumps, and freight yards. In these tenements lived the thousands of longshoremen, teamsters, warehousemen, crane operators, and others who worked in or out of the docks and grain elevators of Boston Harbor that bounded the district on the east. Landmarks in the district were Bunker Hill monument and the grisly old State Prison, Boston's cesspool, some called the worst part of the area. The crime rate in sections of the district was among the highest in the country.

Tacked together by gerrymanders, the Eleventh had no resemblance to the "compact and contiguous" districts that the law enjoins. Quite the contrary, it fell into several distinct parts. East Boston—Pat Kennedy's old bailiwick—was now mainly Italian and dominated by street-corner politicians who promised to deliver their blocks for a consideration. Charlestown was peopled by varied groups, but all Catholic, who fought among themselves but united against outsiders, including those from across the Charles River. Cambridge and Somerville were more pleasant, lower-middle-class areas; the highest aspiration of many in East Boston or the North End was to move out of their slums into one of the huge frame "three-deckers" in these parts of the district.

Tucked into a corner of this district was a very different area—Harvard University and nearby precincts peopled by academics, old Yankee families, and executives commuting to the city. For many years, the "Harvard" part of Cambridge had been part of another congressional district, the Ninth, represented in Washington by Republican Robert Luce, a dignified Harvard alumnus and authority on Congress. Luce had been beaten in 1940 by another Harvard man, Thomas H. Eliot, grandson of a Harvard president and son of a prominent Unitarian minister, and a New Dealer who had helped write the Social Security Act. Two years later, after elaborate tinkering with district boundaries by the state legislature, the "Harvard" area—and along with it Eliot's own residence—was torn out of the suburban, middle-class Ninth District and stuck into the immigrant, proletarian Eleventh. Eliot found himself on Curley's own home grounds, and Curley had easily beaten him in the next Democratic primary.

Surely this was not a very inviting constituency for young Kennedy. But what else could he do? Some of his friends, knowing that he was looking around, urged him to run for statewide office—lieutenant governor, for example. Kennedy was cool to the idea. A host of politicians had their eye on the statehouse, men who had built up what Kennedy so painfully lacked—a political base of operations. Moreover, he far preferred office in Washington to Boston. So when Curley won the mayoralty early in November 1945, Kennedy decided to make the run for the Democratic nomination for Congress. In this district the Democratic nomination was equivalent to election.

He still, however, had not sunk political roots. After the war he had taken a suite at the Bellevue, a hotel that teemed with politicians from the statehouse nearby. Grandfather Fitz still lived there, grumpily offering advice to political neophytes, and Jack's rooms were usually filled with a motley group of former Navy officers, self-appointed political advisers, veterans still in uniform, old school chums, and family friends. To get away from the hubbub, Kennedy would hold political discussions in the corridor or the lobby downstairs. He lived in the Bellevue throughout the campaign; many a business has been run from a hotel room but Kennedy's was perhaps the first congressional campaign so conducted. The parochial politicians of the Eleventh were not happy about it. When a friend took Kennedy around to pay his respects to party leaders, one of them looked at him scornfully.

"I can't support you."

"Why not?"

"You're a god-damned carpetbagger!"

Boston thought it had seen everything in politics, but here was something new. Kennedy was only twenty-eight years old. Still yellow from the Atabrine he had taken to fight malaria, reserved, gaunt, almost emaciated-looking, he was a polar opposite to the familiar image of the derby-hatted, loud-talking, paunchy Boston politician. Many of the latter did not take the young candidate very seriously. He would get a bad case of burned fingers, they told one another;

Boston politics was for big boys. Wait till the pros got into the race. But he had the Kennedy name, money, and a determination to make good that became almost fanatical as the months passed.

Knowing he had to establish his claim to office in his own right, Kennedy got into the race early. In 1946, the Massachusetts primary elections took place in June. Kennedy campaigned for several months before the other candidates jumped off from the starting line. And in the process he began to build a big personal organization. It was this group that was most responsible for Kennedy's victory.

Its nucleus was a number of old friends from Choate, Harvard, and the Navy. Republicans or Democrats, liberals or conservatives, they converged on Bowdoin Street to "help out Jack." One Navy friend flew in all the way from San Francisco. Brother Bob, just out of the Navy, came in to take over some wards in East Cambridge. Les Billings, in from Pennsylvania, plunged into the campaign and even surprised himself with his zeal—a Republican working for a Democrat, an Episcopalian working in a Catholic district, a Pittsburgh native working in Boston, he later noted wryly.

Kennedy was shrewd enough, however, to know that he could not win with a bunch of non-Bostonians. It was bad enough that he himself was an outsider. Early in the operation, he began to hunt out people who had grown up in the different parts of his district. The men he found were much like himself—young, vigorous, politically inexperienced, not active in party politcs, vaguely Democratic but uncommitted ideologically. His "junior brain trust," Kennedy called them.

There was Francis X. Morrissey, a jaunty, voluble young Bostonian who helped run the Community Fund. There was sunny, likeable Timothy J. (Ted) Reardon from Somerville, who had been a close friend of Joe, Jr. at Harvard and was now just out of the service. There were Mark Dalton of Boston, Tom Broderick of Brighton, Dave Powers, who took over the tough Charlestown district, Billy Kelly of East Boston, John Droney of Cambridge—all veterans, all weary of Boston's noisy and corrupt politicos, all hardheaded and businesslike, all looking for new faces in politics. And they in turn recruited scores of volunteer helpers from outside the usual political channels. Despite the polyglot nature of the district, almost all Kennedy's leaders were Irish.

At times they looked at their own candidate a bit anxiously. Could this slight, reserved, charming young man fight a Boston primary battle? One day Frank Morrissey found out. He drove Kennedy to Maverick Square, a gathering place for swarthy Sicilians, who stood about, coat collars turned up, hands in their pockets, broad-brimmed hats pushed low over their eyes, staring coldly at the throng. Morrissey watched while Kennedy went up to each of these characters, stuck out his hand, extracted a handshake, and soon had them talking and even smiling. Kennedy, Morrissey decided, would make out fine.

Free-for-All

Primary elections are rather special affairs. Almost anyone who has a mind to can run for the party nomination, which means that a dozen or more politicians may join the race. Some jump in planning to be bought off to get out. Since all the contestants belong to the same party, the battle is one of personalities and name-calling rather than issues and program. Confused and bored, most of the voters do not show up at the polls on primary day. All this is doubly true of Boston primaries. In this most political of cities, primaries are a hurly-burly of neighborhood vendettas, ethnic-group rivalries, and obscure clashes of street-corner politicians, occasionally enlivened by stunts and mudslinging.

Kennedy's primary was no exception. To make things worse, the decision to hold primary election day in June meant that the nomination of candidates came five months before Election Day in November and hence at a time when the voters were even more apathetic than usual. It was also apparent by early 1946, as candidate after candidate filed for the Democratic nomination for Congress in the Eleventh District, that this race would be a typically wide-open affair.

Kennedy's rivals were a rather mixed lot. Best known was Mike Neville, of Cambridge, an old-timer who had climbed the political ladder to state legislator and mayor. Another favorite was John F. Cotter, of Charlestown, who, as secretary to former Congressman Jim Curley, had built close contacts in the district. Of wholly different cast was Joseph Lee, of Boston, a patrician Yankee who valiantly ran for office year after year in this Catholic area and occasionally won. Catherine Falvey, of Somverville, who had served as a WAC major, lent color to the contest, for she liked to show up at rallies in her gleaming white dress uniform. Also in the race were a Somerville schoolteacher—an idealist who wanted to show that he could campaign without accepting contributions—and four Bostonians of Italian origin, *two* of whom were named Joseph Russo.

At first the rest of the candidates laughed Kennedy off—at least tactically. "The poor little rich kid," Catherine Falvey dubbed him. Mike Neville offered him a job as a secretary

if Kennedy would drop out. It became increasingly evident
that Kennedy was working hard and running strong, and the
taunts changed to indignation. Who was this kid who had
invaded the Eleventh District? Nothing but an outsider
trying to slide in on the Kennedy name and money. Kennedy's father, it was charged, was buying the election; according to one story, the old man claimed that with the
money he was spending he could elect his chauffeur to Congress. And if the boy was a carpetbagger, he came by it
naturally, for hadn't old Fitzgerald run for office while he
was living in Concord?

Actually, the "kid" was taking no chances on the power of
his name and money; he was relying on sheer hard work. Day
after day, he made whirlwind tours of his district's endless
sidewalks, darting into barbershops, saloons, grocery stores,
factories, wharves, fire stations for quick handshakes. He
turned more hollow-eyed and anemic-looking than ever, his
war injury bothered him, and sometimes his harried workers
wondered if he could get through the day. But he always did
—though living on nervous energy.

Kennedy learned campaigning as he campaigned. At first
his speaking was nervous and hesitant; he showed little poise
and certainly no magnetism. But he slowly developed a
style of direct, informal, simple speaking, without high-blown
rhetoric or bombastic exaggeration, that to some of his lis-
teners was in happy contrast to the oratory of the old-fashioned politicians. Kennedy's way of speaking was appropriate for what he talked about. Shunning personal attacks,
ignoring his opponents altogether except toward the end, he
talked factually about problems closest to the needs of the
Eleventh District—jobs, housing, low rents and prices, medical care, veterans' benefits, social security, and other bread-
and-butter matters. While on all these issues he took a New
Deal–Fair Deal position, he spoke not in generalities but in
terms of concrete help that he could supply from Washington. The only foreign-policy issue of importance in the campaign was the British loan, which Kennedy supported and
several other candidates opposed.

The young candidate learned, too, the power of suggestion
and the quirks of voters. At one rally he was speaking
vehemently for veterans' housing when an old character
named Jackie Toomey suddenly stood up in the front row.

"What about the *non*-veteran?" Toomey hollered.

"Yes, sir, the *non*-veteran too," Kennedy shot back, and
Toomey was seen going around to his pals afterward with
the happy report, "You see—he's for the non-veteran too."

With that cold realism that has marked his whole career,

however, Kennedy saw early that orthodox campaigning was not good enough. People who turned out for rallies had already made up their minds. Sidewalk handshaking helped, but most voters quickly forgot his name, or at least what he was running for—hardly surprising, since there were nine other candidates in his own race, and several score other contestants for a dozen other state and local nominations. Radio time and newspaper advertising were useful, but much of this was wasted because these media covered all of Greater Boston.

How could he reach the thousands of apathetic voters who looked on politics as an odious business monopolized by crooks and windbags? If they would not come to him, he would go to them in their homes. So Kennedy, through his hundred or more volunteers, arranged for house parties in every corner of his district. There was nothing new in this—house parties were an old campaign technique—but what was different was the sheer number of parties, the care with which they were planned, and the scheduling that enabled Kennedy to cover at least half a dozen in one evening. In poorer neighborhoods, Kennedy workers supplied coffee and cookies, cups and saucers, silver and flowers. Names were carefully noted and added to mailing lists. Kennedy was at his best at these affairs—coming in a bit timidly but with his flashing, picture-magazine smile, charming the mothers and titillating their daughters, answering questions with a leg draped over an arm of his chair, wandering into the kitchen for a word with proud grandparents about news from the "old country," a final round of handshaking before leaving for the next affair. This social type of politicking was climaxed by a huge affair at a Cambridge hotel that featured, not the candidate, but his mother and sisters.

Kennedy reached the voters wherever he could—even on their way to and from work. It was said that his streetcar and subway advertising beat anything ever seen before in a congressional fight in Massachusetts. A single streetcar would have as many as four Kennedy placards, on which four different people—for example, a housewife, a dockworker, an executive, and a veteran—would explain "why I am for Jack Kennedy." A condensation of the *New Yorker* account of the PT-boat episode was widely distributed.

By now the slush and ice had long since gone from Boston's streets, spring was turning to summer, and the long campaign was nearing the end. The lesser candidates knew they were licked; one of them—the idealistic Somerville schoolteacher—obligingly played the piano to hold the crowd when Kennedy was late. But the tempers of the front runners grew short. When Miss Falvey, after peppering Kennedy with accusations at an outdoor rally, then whispered in his ear, "Don't pay any attention—it's just politics," Kennedy was not to be disarmed. He got up and delivered a biting counter-attack on the lady. When one of Lee's supporters wrote humorous vitriolic pieces for an East Boston newspaper playing up the "rich kid" theme and, far worse, charging (falsely) that Kennedy's sister had married a descendant of Oliver Cromwell, despised by all good Irishmen, Kennedy begged Lee to have his friend lay off, and Lee reluctantly complied. By primary day, the race was rapidly developing into one of those zany, bellicose, and feverish battles so well described by Edwin O'Connor in *The Last Hurrah*.

On primary election day Kennedy went to the polls with Grandmother and Grandfather Fitzgerald, and squeezed in a movie—"*A Night in Casablanca*"—before the returns came in. The results showed how well Kennedy had done his work. By amassing a total of 22,183 votes, he almost doubled the vote of Neville, who came in second, and beat Cotter by better than three to one. Major Falvey came in fifth. Kennedy ran ahead of all his opponents in Boston and Charlestown, and was beaten only by Neville in Cambridge. His share of the vote—about 42 per cent—was impressive for a ten-man race.

Jack took his victory with his usual self-possession. But Grandpa Fitz danced an Irish jig on a table and sang "Sweet Adeline."

Safe Seat

In winning the nomination, Kennedy soon began paying the penalty of success. Stung by their defeat at the hands of this youth now just turned twenty-nine, some die-hard supporters of his opponents charged that Kennedy's father had masterminded the election, had put a small fortune into radio and newspaper advertising, and had induced politicians with Italian names to enter the primary (to split the "Italian vote") or had tried to keep others with Yankee or Irish names out of the race.

Without question, Kennedy, Sr. was as active as he could be behind the scenes. He supplied money, pulled strings, and worked on publicity and public relations. Doubtless his agents were active in obscure maneuverings. But his activities probably had only a small effect on the outcome. There is no way to buy or rig a wide-open, ten-man primary race, for there is no way of telling just what effect the entrance of one candidate or the departure of another will have on the final vote. Any manipulation on behalf of one candidate is counterbalanced or canceled out by manipulation for other candidates.

The greatest contribution of father to son was the name Kennedy. This was the magic word that opened doors and gave the candidate a chance to put over his charm. The other main ingredients of success were Kennedy's tireless stumping over a long period, the intensive use of house parties, the availability of money when needed, and, above all, the enthusiasm of his aides and volunteers.

Kennedy won his first big race mainly on his own. The result hardened not only his self-confidence but his belief that he could make realistic political decisions, sometimes against the advice of the pros. He had heard much conflicting advice during the campaign—from his father, from Grandpa Fitz, from old Boston pals, from New Deal liberals, from conservative friends—and his victory vindicated the political judgments that he had reached.

The results also left him with a disdain for routine politics and "party hacks" that he would not lose for many years, if ever. He had found that the Democratic party hardly existed as an organization in the Eleventh District; after he won office and consolidated his position, he could say, "*I* am the Democratic party in my district." Thus he learned early that the key to winning politics—at least in Boston—was a personal organization, not the party committees. And he was careful to keep his organization intact as a nucleus for a bigger group.

Kennedy's primary victory was, of course, a final victory, since the Eleventh District had not gone Republican for decades. A Somerville Republican valiantly entered the regular election in the fall of 1946, and Kennedy, without campaigning very much, swamped him by more than two to one. He had that prize of American politics, a safe seat. How safe it was, was shown two years later, in 1948, when Kennedy had no opposition in the Democratic primary, nor Republican opposition in the fall. Two years after that, he easily bested five primary opponents—four of them Italians—in winning with five times their combined vote, and in the fall of 1950, he defeated the Republican nominee, a young Boston lawyer named Vincent J. Celeste, by almost five to one. Kennedy had the firm base of operations he wanted so badly.

But all this was in the future. During the summer and fall of 1946, while other candidates across the nation toiled on the hustings, he could swim, sail, and relax on the Cape. While he did so, the pendulum was swinging in American politics. Capitalizing on postwar shortages, frustrations, and letdown, the Republicans, under the leadership of Senator Robert A. Taft and the slogan of "Had Enough?," won their first majorities in Congress in almost two decades. Even this outcome was helpful to Kennedy, for with few new Democrats elected to the House, he gained a better choice of committee assignments. Without trying very hard or thinking much about it, and without knowing much about the subject, he became a member of the House Committee on Education and Labor, a step that would be of considerable significance in his later career.

5 ★ THE GENTLEMAN FROM BOSTON

Kennedy was only twenty-nine years old when he took his seat in Congress in January 1947. He looked years younger, with his shy, boyish smile, big shock of hair, and gangly frame. Kennedy denies that he was mistaken for a page boy, but some of the old hands around Congress thought he was a college boy who had picked up a patronage job. And those who knew him paid him little notice at first. The Kennedy name might mean a lot in Boston, but scions of famous political families were a dime a dozen in the nation's capital. Kennedy was amused by some of his experiences.

"Well, how do you like that?" he demanded with mock indignation as he burst into his office one morning. "Some people got into the elevator and asked me for the fourth floor!" The young Congressman at first did little to correct this impression. He might appear on the House floor in his old khaki pants, perhaps with a rumpled seersucker coat. Sometimes his tie was spotted and his shirt-tail hung out. This was not affectation, but a habit of grabbing the nearest piece of clothing handy in the morning, or even a suit that his valet had put aside to be cleaned.

It was, in short, hard for older congressmen to take him seriously. When crusty Ed O'Neal, veteran farm lobbyist, kept addressing him as "laddie" in testifying before the House Labor Committee, he spoke not out of contempt; it was just the natural way to talk to someone who seemed more like a college freshman than a member of Congress. Nor was it easy for Kennedy to step into the statesman's routine. Still fond of sports, he sometimes left his office early, donned an old sweatshirt and sneakers, and hurried over to a Georgetown playground with a football or a softball and mitt. Soon he would be the center of a gang of boys, white and colored, who had no idea that they were catching passes from a congressman. Sometimes he sailed in the Tidal Basin with Ted Reardon. Evenings he went to the movies, read at home, or had dates with girls around town, sometimes jointly with other bachelor members of Congress, especially his close friend George Smathers, of Florida, who had entered Congress the same year as Kennedy.

He lived in a Georgetown house, attended by a doting housekeeper, Margaret Ambrose, and his Negro valet, George Thomas, formerly employed by Arthur Krock. George brought Kennedy's luncheons to his office in a big heated container. Part of the time Kennedy stayed with his sister Eunice, before her marriage to Sargent Shriver, of Chicago. Occasionally his mother came to town to take an anxious look at his domestic arrangements, just as she had come to school to check on his progress years before; brothers and sisters often stopped in on their way through Washington. His father rarely came to the office but often called him long-distance.

At first, business in the office was light, until people in the district—and outside of it—found that they could get quick service on favors and problems. Routine affairs were handled by Reardon and by a secretary, Mary Davis, who had had experience on the Hill. Sometimes the young Congressman read in his inner office, feet up on the desk; occasionally a secretary found him staring out his office window into space. Kennedy enjoyed legislative work more than the political glad-handing. Sometimes he returned from the House to find a waiting delegation; he would greet them pleasantly, retire to his inner office, buzz for Ted or Mary, find out the names, and return to the delegation with cheery, first-name greetings. He maintained an office in Boston, too, and an apartment at 122 Bowdoin Street. When he came to the office, politicians, job-seekers, and hangers-on would begin to crowd the outer room, until Kennedy, feeling overwhelmed by the endless demands, might escape by a side door.

One day, after watching a high-school football practice, he borrowed a uniform from the coach and joined the workout. He was just a new boy to halfback Freddy Greenleaf, who shouted: "Hey, kid, come on over here and snag some passes." Kennedy snagged, then passed and punted.

"How's the Congressman doing?" the coach asked.

"Is that what they call him?" Freddy asked. "He needs a lot of work, coach. What year's he in?"

Bread-and-Butter Liberal

Kennedy did not arrive in Washington with a full and rounded set of principles. On some issues he was ill-informed; on others he was unsure of his position and would allow events to rule. But on one type of issue he had definite notions—the economic problems of wages, working conditions, social security, housing, prices, rents, and aid to veterans and the aged. By every test—the needs of his urban constituents, the promises he had made in the campaign, the social-welfare tradition in the Kennedy-Fitzgerald family, and his own Democratic views on economic matters—he had reason to fight for social-welfare programs.

The problem was not what but how. The 80th Congress was not a hopeful arena for any kind of liberalism. The small band of liberals were hard put even to salvage New Deal welfare programs from Republican and Southern Democratic attacks, much less to extend them. But in many fields the need for broader programs had grown more acute, especially because of the postponement of action during the war. In no field of welfare was the need greater than in public, low-cost housing. And nothing was closer to Kennedy's heart. Believing in the home as the citadel of the family, he had seen at first hand during his campaign for Congress the drab and noisome tenements in Charlestown and East Boston, places that drove men into the bars and children into delinquency.

Kennedy's fight for housing legislation propelled him into one of the high-pressure areas of American politics, and the pressure was never higher than in the postwar period. Building had almost stopped during the war, returning veterans were getting married, and married veterans were fathering babies. The political support for housing legislation was so strong that even conservative Senator Taft had cosponsored a comprehensive, long-range housing bill with Democratic Senators Robert F. Wagner and Allen Ellender.

Fiercely opposed to the "TEW" bill was an array of conservative interests, headed by realtors' groups, with powerful support in Congress. The TEW backers reasoned that they could broaden their appeal by working through veterans' groups. In the summer of 1946, following his nomination for

Congress, members of the Veterans of Foreign Wars asked Kennedy to serve as chairman of their forty-seventh national encampment in Boston in September. Kennedy not only chaired the convention, but offered from the floor a resolution endorsing TEW, which passed. But the anti-TEW forces also had friends in the VFW leadership. One of these was the new national commander, who told the press in Washington that the VFW had taken this action in a moment of confusion, because the acoustics were bad. Kennedy, now in office, tartly replied that in that event the commander had not been legally elected, since the acoustics must have been poor during the balloting, too.

Working from the inside, Kennedy and his cohorts managed to neutralize the VFW in the housing struggle, only to face a more formidable foe in the American Legion, which boycotted a Massachusetts Veterans' Housing Rally in Boston designed to set up a united veterans front for the housing bill. The freshman Congressman publicly attacked the Legion, of which he was also a member, for opposing TEW, and quoted the Jesuit weekly *America*'s description of the Legion's housing committee as a "legislative drummer boy for the real estate lobby." When the Legion dismissed him as an "embryo" congressman, Kennedy called for an "avalanche of mail" on Capitol Hill from TEW supporters. He spoke vehemently for the bill on the House floor. But the housing measure simply did not have the votes, and Congress adjourned without acting on it.

With veterans still living in garages and basements, the housing issue flared up again in the 1948 session of Congress. At a huge veterans' housing conference in Washington, Kennedy spoke for the VFW, now converted to his side, Franklin D. Roosevelt, Jr., for the American Veterans Committee, Robert F. Wagner, Jr., for the Catholic War Veterans, and Jacob K. Javits for the Jewish War Veterans. Kennedy urged the delegates to turn the heat on Congress and, above all, not to weaken their impact by becoming sidetracked away from TEW to any other issue. In Congress he denounced the "sell-out to the real estate and building lobbies that have swarmed over the Hill for the past two years." He heatedly debated the issue over a coast-to-coast radio hook-up with a young, unknown senator from Wisconsin named Joseph McCarthy. But once again, despite all the oratory, the housing measure was stopped by Republicans and Southern Democrats in the House.

A year later, Kennedy introduced a housing bill to provide federal funds for slum clearance and for low-rent public-housing projects initiated by local agencies. Once again high Legion officials opposed him. Kennedy was incensed, as he said later, "at the way Legion leaders were wrapping the flag around the poor old veteran" on the wrong issues, such as a veterans' bonus. One day during debate on a bonus bill, Kennedy's indignation boiled over.

"I am a member of the American Legion," Kennedy told the House. "I was never consulted about this plan. Who in the American Legion was consulted?" A congressman said that the national convention of the Legion had endorsed it. Only a handful of World War II veterans had been present at the American Legion convention, Kennedy replied. Then he blurted out: "The leadership of the American Legion has not had a constructive thought for the benefit of this country since 1918!"

Members looked up, startled. No congressman had ever made such statements in the House—certainly no stripling like this. Member after member rose to dissociate himself from such lese majesty. The Legion was one of the greatest American organizations the country had ever had, said John Rankin, of Mississippi. Congresswoman Edith Nourse Rogers, of Massachusetts, after carefully paying homage to the Legion, asked members to remember that Kennedy and his family had made great sacrifices in the war. Friendly congressmen rushed over to Kennedy and urged him to retract. Do it right away, they said, to correct the record. Kennedy asked for the floor—not to retract, but again to denounce the Legion leaders for opposing a "good housing bill."

"Well, Ted, we're gone!" Kennedy told Reardon laughingly back in the office. Reardon asked him whether he had attacked just the leadership of the Legion or the Legion in general; Kennedy could not remember, so Reardon checked the record and felt better when he found that his boss was not attacking the whole three-million membership. But Kennedy was never really worried. The mail was in favor of his action, and the next state Legion convention was friendly. Late in the session, Congress, now under Democratic leadership, finally passed an effective housing bill. The short-run effects of defying the Legion were negligible; in the long run, Kennedy's action showed that political daring might have more advantages than disadvantages. Kennedy looks at such affairs dispassionately. "The rockets go up and last for three or four weeks, then people forget because they have so many problems of their own," he says.

The sharpest issue in Congress during Kennedy's first year there was labor policy. The Wagner Act—probably the New Deal's most radical measure—had bolstered organized labor's economic and political power. For years, Republicans and Southern Democrats had sought to change the act and shift the balance of power back toward business. Now at last they had the votes. They had a skilled parliamentary leader, too, in Senator Taft.

Here was another political high-pressure area—but it seemed unlikely that Kennedy would be affected by it. Although a member of the House Labor Committee, he had little experience in the labor field. Labor reform had not been an issue in his campaign. During hearings on a labor measure the month after he entered Congress, he rarely spoke up, appropriately for a freshman member, and when he did speak up his questions were none too impressive. Hence it was all the more surprising that he took such an active part in House consideration of the key labor-reform measure, the Hartley Bill.

Kennedy plunged into the fray not only by signing the Labor Committee minority report opposing the Hartley Bill, but by filing a one-man report of his own. He was clearly unhappy over the extreme positions of both sides, over the charges by Taft's supporters that the Wagner Act had made unions into a "despotic tyranny" and over the charges by laborites that labor reform would mean the destruction of free unionism. His remarks, which were the opening gun in what turned out to be a thirteen-year, and, ultimately, successful, effort to gain moderate labor reform, reflected Kennedy's middle-of-the-road approach to the problem.

"Management has been selfish. Labor has been selfish," he stated in his report. He accused the Labor Committee majority of succumbing to old and deeply rooted antilabor prejudices. He warned the conservatives that repressive and vindictive labor legislation would set off "a tide of left-wing reaction" that might well destroy our existing business system. "Equally fundamental," on the other hand, was "the right of each individual union member to a square deal from his union." Kennedy favored democratizing union elections by use of the secret ballot for electing union officers and calling strikes; free speech for union members; no arbitrary or excessive initiation fees and dues; due process for members threatened with expulsion from their unions. Then, almost as if he had tilted the balance too far against labor, he attacked the Hartley Bill for its blanket approach in condemning all forms of jurisdictional and sympathy strikes and secondary boycotts and for failing to see that some such strikes and boycotts were wholly proper.

Kennedy's one-man report was but a firefly's flicker in the supercharged atmosphere of Washington. The Hartley Bill came to the House floor in mid-April 1947, at a time when the nation was swept by strikes. The young legislator took the floor to admit the irresponsibilities of some unions, but also to plead that the House reject a bill that would "strike down in one devastating blow the union shop, industry-wide bargaining, and so strangle collective bargaining with restraints and limitations as to make it ineffectual." Passage of the bill, he warned, would bring labor war, bitter and dangerous, and would play into the hands of union radicals who preached the doctrine of the class struggle. Few were listening; the opposition's mind had long been made up. The House passed the Hartley Bill by a top-heavy majority.

From a labor standpoint, Kennedy went down the line against the labor bill. He was one of a small band of forty-seven representatives to vote against consideration of the bill in the first place; he tried to soften the bill's restrictive union-shop provisions through an amendment, which failed; he voted to recommit the Hartley Bill, and then voted against its passage. Although the Taft-Hartley Bill, as it emerged from conference committee, was a much more moderate bill from labor's standpoint, the Congressman maintained his opposition. He was one of seventy-nine to vote against the Taft-Hartley Bill, and one of eighty-three to uphold President Truman's unsuccessful veto of the measure.

When the new labor policy was securely on the books, however, Kennedy changed his tactics. Most labor leaders were cool to efforts to modify the legislation; dubbing it a "slave-labor act," they preferred to keep it intact as a hateful device against which to rally their battalions of union voters. When the Democrats, with labor's help, re-elected Truman and regained congressional majorities in 1948, union leaders demanded repeal of the act. But Kennedy would not go along. While still opposed to Taft-Hartley as a whole, he did not consider it a slave-labor act, and he did not think it could be repealed. Nor did he simply want a symbol against which labor leaders and liberals could rally their forces in subsequent elections. He supported a bill to soften several antiunion features of the legislation; when it became clear that the Republican-Southern Democratic coalition could defeat this amendment, Kennedy reluctantly fell back to the next line of defense, a more modest effort to moderate Taft-Hartley. But this effort failed, too. In the end, Kennedy's differences with organized labor over the legislation chiefly concerned methods rather than goals, but some union leaders interpreted his tactical flexibility as an effort to compromise on the legislation itself.

On other labor and social-welfare measures Kennedy followed a straight labor-liberal line during his six years in the House. He opposed reduction in the appropriation for school lunches, a tax relief bill because it favored the rich rather than the poor, a sales tax in the District of Columbia, weakening of rent control, and tax relief for the oil industry. He favored broadened social security, higher minimum wage provisions, more immigration, and, always, expanded housing programs.

On all such bread-and-butter matters, the young Congressman hewed close to the Truman Fair Deal policies. But on other matters he failed to follow the White House lead.

Defying the White House

During his first two years in Congress, Kennedy seldom spoke up on foreign policy. To be sure, he strongly backed the Truman Doctrine for aid to Greece and Turkey, in a speech at the University of North Carolina, and he also supported the Marshall Plan bill authorizing aid to Western Europe. And, of course, he showed special interest in nations whose sons and daughters had emigrated to Massachusetts, calling for interim aid to Italy and for admission of former Polish soldiers to the United States as atonement for the "betrayal" of Poland at Yalta. Still, he seemed mainly concerned with domestic matters.

During his first term of office, however, violent shifts took place in the world situation. Czechoslovakia fell to the Communists, America began large-scale foreign aid, the airlift saved Berlin, and Congress authorized a peacetime draft. By the end of 1948, the situation in Europe seemed stabilized. In China, however, the situation was anything but stable. By late 1948, the Communist armies of former library assistant at Peking University, Mao Tse-tung, were overwhelming Nationalist forces in a long sweep southward. Chiang Kai-shek's American-trained divisions were melting away. Affairs came to a climax in January 1949, when Chiang gave up the fight and prepared his retreat to Formosa.

In the House of Representatives on January 25, the invocation had hardly ended when Kennedy was on his feet, requesting unanimous consent to address the chamber for one minute. Nobody objected; nobody knew what was to come. The Congressman did not exhibit his usual calm, detached manner.

"Mr. Speaker, over this weekend we have learned the extent of the disaster that has befallen China and the United States. The responsibility for the failure of our foreign policy in the Far East rests squarely with the White House and the Department of State.

"The continued insistence that aid would not be forth-coming, unless a coalition government with the Communists were formed, was a crippling blow to the National Government.

"So concerned were our diplomats and their advisers, the Lattimores and the Fairbanks, with the imperfection of the democratic system in China after 20 years of war and the tales of corruption in high places that they lost sight of our tremendous stake in a non-Communist China. . . .

"This House must now assume the responsibility of pre-venting the onrushing tide of communism from engulfing all of Asia."

By now, Speaker Rayburn was pounding his gavel to signify that time was up, somewhat more heavily than usual, thought Reardon, watching from the gallery.

The House, its mind on more immediate affairs, went on to routine business without comment. A few days later, Kennedy repeated his remarks in a speech at Salem, Massachusetts, and elaborated on them. Those responsible for the tragedy, he proclaimed, must be searched out and spotlighted. Once—during the war—America had fought for China's freedom. But at Yalta a "sick" Roosevelt, with the advice of General Marshall and other chiefs of staff, "gave" the Kurils and other strategic points to the Soviet Union. The administra-tion had tried to force Chiang to bring the Communists into a coalition. President Truman had even treated Madame Chi-ang with "indifference" if not "contempt." "This is the tragic story of China," Kennedy concluded, "whose freedom we once fought to preserve. What our young men had saved, our diplomats and our President had frittered away."

Strong words for this boyish, tousled Congressman hardly past his freshman days on the Hill. Far stronger, in-deed, than the words he had used about Chamberlain and Daladier in *Why England Slept*, ten years before. His friends speculated about his motives in challenging his President and party leader and so august a figure as Marshall.

Kennedy's sudden show of revolt against the White House and the Democratic-party foreign-policy makers was no flash in the pan. The following month—February 1949—he voted to recommit the Trade Agreements Extension Act. (When re-committal failed, 151-241, Kennedy, along with several score other representatives, reversed himself and voted for final passage.) His opposition to a three-year extension of the Trade Agreements Act was an attack on one of the programs most sacred to the Democratic party—the reciprocal-trade policies sired by the revered Cordell Hull and backed by both Roosevelt and Truman. He complained publicly about inadequacies in civil defense, and just in case the White House failed to hear him, he sent his complaints direct to Mr. Truman by mail. During 1948 and 1949, Kennedy also attacked the administration for its economy program in the defense establishment; for example, he favored a seventy-group air force rather than the fifty-five groups requested by Defense Secretary Louis Johnson. In February 1950, he inserted an article by Joseph and Stewart Alsop into the *Congressional Record* as a warning of the "effect that economies are having in our defense structure."

Communist aggression in Korea four months later seemed to Kennedy to vindicate his attack on defense policies. Curiously though (in the light of his China stand), he showed no enthusiasm for Truman's vigorous stand on Korea. But while all eyes were turned toward the desperate holding operations in Korea, he warned on the floor of the House and in speeches back home against denuding of troops other areas that had more strategic importance. "I think that we are heading for a major disaster in Western Europe," he told the House in August 1950.

Late in 1950, as the cold war deepened in Europe and hot war flared and flickered in Korea, Washington came hard up against a pressing question: Should American ground troops be sent to Western Europe to man the defenses against Soviet attack? As a backer of greater military power, Kennedy had little doubt that American divisions must take up their posts in Europe. To him the big question was whether Western Europe would do its part.

To answer this question, he took a six-week trip to Europe early in 1951. He visited the chief countries of the North Atlantic Treaty Organization in Europe—Britain, France, and Italy—and three other nations—Spain, Yugoslavia, and West Germany—whose policies closely touched the defense of the West. Although Kennedy paid his own way, it was no vacation trip (nor should it have been, since Congress was in session the whole time he was away). He kept notes of his interviews and impressions, sometimes scribbled on the back of hotel bills or envelopes during plane rides. Aside from an interview with Tito and an audience with the Pope, he gained his most useful information from off-the-record talks with second-level officials such as deputy ministers. On returning home, he carefully converted these notes into a long statement of his views.

Early in 1951, the Senate committees on Foreign Relations

and on Armed Services were jointly considering the question that preoccupied Kennedy—the assignment of United States troops to duty in the European area. A closely related issue had been raised by Republican Senator Kenneth Wherry, who had brought in a resolution barring the assignment of troops to Europe without congressional approval. After hearing General Eisenhower, Dean Acheson, the newly appointed Secretary of State, General Marshall, now Secretary of Defense, and a host of generals, admirals, and other famous men, the committee invited Kennedy to testify as an on-the-spot observer.

Kennedy was not slow to accept. Before a dozen eminent Senators, including the formidable Tom Connally and Richard Russell, he spoke in emphatic terms of the strategic importance of Western Europe, the likely collapse of its defenses without more American troops, and especially of the need to compel the Europeans to intensify their own military efforts. On this last point he urged—in sharp contrast to the administration's position—the adoption of a ratio system under which the Europeans must supply six divisions for every division sent from America. On the Wherry Resolution itself, Kennedy took no stand, but he urged congressional supervision of the proposed ratio system, arguing that the administration would not favor it and hence would not enforce it. This suggestion ran directly contrary to the advice of administration spokesmen, who saw immense complications in a ratio system, especially in one supervised by Congress.

If the Congressman seemed to be lining up with the antiadministration forces in Congress, he was not doing so as an isolationist. Under sharp questioning from committee members, he insisted that he wanted to force the Europeans to do more, not to allow America to do less. "It is not a backhanded way of trying to pull out of Western Europe," he said. Later in the year, Kennedy criticized the White House for not demanding more stringent economic controls for the defense effort, and especially for what he considered Truman's failure to request the necessary power to head off inflation. He also proposed a rigid embargo on the shipment of materials useful for war to Red China, which he dubbed "trade in blood."

By his third term in Congress, in short, Kennedy was staging a personal revolt against crucial parts of the Truman defense policies (though he defended Truman's position on the MacArthur firing episode). On economic aid to Europe, Kennedy sometimes took a compromising stand. He publicly differed with McCormack on the floor of the House in 1950 when the latter put heavy emphasis on the need for the mutual-aid program. A year later, Kennedy offered an amendment cutting economic aid to Africa and the Near East from $175 million to $140 million, and he voted for an amendment cutting economic aid to Europe by $350 million.

But he had not lost the capacity to learn. In the fall of 1951, accompanied by his sister Pat and his brother Bob, Kennedy took a trip around the world, with "study stops" in the Middle East, Pakistan, India, Indochina, Malaya, and Korea. Though disturbed by the caliber of some American officials in these areas, Kennedy was impressed with the enormous difficulties and potentialities of this "two-thirds of the world." The next year he reversed himself and supported Point Four aid to the Middle East. "Many of us feel," he told the House, "that the United States has concentrated its attention too much on Western Europe."

Just after Kennedy had finished testifying in February 1951 before the Senate committee on the issue of sending troops to Europe, courtly old Senator Walter George looked over his spectacles at the witness and said:

"The question I am going to ask you I want to assure you in advance is an impersonal one, although you might at first blush think it is a personal one. I mean it not as personal.

"You come from a very distinguished American family that exercises a great influence on American public opinion. I want to ask you very impersonally, whether you remember the able speech of your father in December 1950?" In case he didn't, the Senator quoted from Joseph P. Kennedy's address to the University of Virginia Law School Forum two months before, in which he condemned American commitments overseas. He had advised the United States to "get out" of Korea, and he had said, "It is idle to talk of being able to hold the line at the Elbe or the line at the Rhine. Is it not best to get out now? The truth is that our only real hope is to keep Russia, if she chooses to march, on the other side of the Atlantic. It may be that Europe for a decade or a generation or more, will turn communistic."

Did the son differ with his father? Senator George asked. Kennedy's answer was diplomatic. To lose Europe and its productive facilities would threaten American survival. But he knew from his trip the difficulty of building a strong-enough Western European army soon enough, and he could understand his father's despair: "To him and to a lot of other Americans it looks like an almost hopeless job and that we are committing troops to be lost." But, adding up all the factors and "considering them as coldbloodedly as I can," he felt personally that the risk should be taken.

"That is my position," he concluded. "I think you should ask my father directly as to his position."

A Subject of the Pope?

Then there was the touchy issue of schools. By the time Kennedy took office in 1947, federal aid to education had become one of the pressing issues before Congress. The problem was immensely complicated by the question of whether federal aid should extend to Catholic and other private schools.

Kennedy had no illusions about the plight of public education in Massachusetts or in other states. A few months after taking office, he spoke on a radio forum about the educational crisis and came out flatly in favor of federal aid. He avoided for the moment the burning question of federal aid to parochial and private schools. But during the hearings in the spring of 1947 on federal-aid bills before an Education and Labor Committee subcommittee, of which Kennedy was a member, he made no effort to hide his view that federal aid should include funds to parochial schools for such services as school-bus transportation and health examinations.

It took Elmer E. Rogers, Assistant to the Sovereign Grand Commander, Supreme Thirty-third Degree, Ancient and Accepted Scottish Rite of Freemasonry, Southern Jurisdiction, United States of America, to break through Kennedy's customary reserve on religious matters. In a long statement to the committee, Rogers declared that the Roman Catholic Church was out "to destroy our liberties and further expand their theocracy as a world government." Catholics had a dual allegiance, he said, to their country and to the Vatican.

Did Mr. Rogers believe, asked Kennedy, that any Catholic parent who did not send his child to a parochial school would be excommunicated?

Rogers referred to a statement appearing in a Jesuit magazine twenty-four years before.

"I never went to a parochial school," Kennedy said. (Canterbury was run by Catholic laymen.) "I am a Catholic and yet my parents were never debarred from the sacrament, so the statement is wrong."

"You are pretty prominent people up there in Massachusetts," Rogers answered. "I know something of the prominence of your father, and the bishops are pretty diplomatic and have good judgment about such things."

"But the statement is wrong because you have a living example," Kennedy said. "I do not want to get in an argument about Catholic theology, but you do not want to make statements that are inaccurate. . . . Now you don't mean the

Catholics in America are legal subjects of the Pope? I am not a legal subject of the Pope."

Every devout Catholic bore a dual allegiance, Rogers maintained. Under prodding from Kennedy, he cited canon law enunciated by Benedict XV, overriding "all contrary regulations, constitutions" and the like. Kennedy was clearly uninterested.

"There is an old saying in Boston," he observed, "that we get our religion from Rome and our politics at home, and that is the way that most Catholics feel about it. . . ."

It was one thing to tangle with Freemasons, but what stand would Kennedy take on legislation? So delicate was the issue that the House of Representatives avoided a stand on the question during 1948, although the postwar crop of babies was nearing school age. In 1949, the whole question flared up in what was perhaps the country's most acrimonious religious quarrel since 1928.

Late in July 1949, Cardinal Spellman suddenly struck out publicly at Mrs. Eleanor Roosevelt for her newspaper columns opposing federal aid to church schools and backing complete separation of church and state. Dubbing her columns "documents of discrimination unworthy of an American mother," the Cardinal ended, ". . . your record of anti-Catholicism stands for all to see. . . ." A public uproar followed, with political leaders and spokesmen for Protestant and Jewish groups springing to Mrs. Roosevelt's defense.

In a temperate answer to the Cardinal, Mrs. Roosevelt insisted that "spiritual leadership should be spiritual leadership" and that temporal power should not become too important in any church. "The final judgment, my dear Cardinal Spellman, of the worthiness of all human beings is in the hands of God." Shortly before, she mentioned her work for Al Smith in 1928 as evidence that religious prejudice did not influence her political decisions. Although the prelate backtracked two weeks later in a moderate statement of his own, the clash hardened further the conflicting attitudes among the public. When Cardinal Spellman stated early in August that the parochial schools wanted funds only for buses, health services, and nonreligious textbooks, Methodist Bishop G. Bromley Oxnam answered a day later that what the Cardinal really wanted was not milk and medicine, books and buses, but "the support of parochial schools by taxes levied on all the people." In such a stormy atmosphere no education bill had much chance.

During the controversy following Cardinal Spellman's letter to Mrs. Roosevelt, Kennedy introduced in the House a general federal-aid bill authorizing funds for buses, health services, and textbooks for private and parochial schools, but this proposal was turned down in the Education and Labor Committee, whose chairman, Graham Barden of North Carolina, a strong opponent of aid for parochial schools, had been tongue-lashed by Cardinal Spellman in even harsher terms than the Cardinal had used for Mrs. Roosevelt.

A year later, 1950, Kennedy proposed a new, somewhat milder, amendment. Concerned solely with the issue of school-bus transportation, it provided that in states where state and local funds could be legally spent for such purposes, such states would be permitted to use part of the federal money to augment their own expenditures for school-bus rides for pupils in all kinds of schools. It also provided that in those states where such use of public funds was prohibited, the federal government would pay directly to the school up to half the cost of pupils' transportation.

The atmosphere was still too tempestuous for agreement. Catholic spokesmen were insisting on funds at least for buses, while some Protestant and Jewish groups refused to settle for anything less than an outright ban, on the grounds that to yield on the bus issue would mean opening the door to more and more appeals for aid to parochial schools. The New York *Times* editorially supported Kennedy's essential position, but at a New York meeting of the Committee on Federal Aid to Public Education, Representative Barden called Cardinal Spellman "a cruel authoritarian," and Mrs. Roosevelt stated that she was "certainly opposed" to Kennedy's amendment. In Washington the next day, Kennedy's amendment was defeated in the committee by a strong margin.

The 1950 federal-aid bill died in committee at the hands of members, including Kennedy, who felt it did not go far enough to help parochial school children, members who felt it went too far, and conservatives who opposed any bill and were delighted to see proponents of federal aid split apart by the parochial-school issue.

"A white Knight," Kennedy was dubbed by the *Pilot*, Boston archdiocesan newspaper, after his fight for bus aid. "This gentleman of youthful appearance but extremely mature intelligence fought valiantly in the interests of large groups of citizens who are merely asking for their just share. . . ."

If there was a "Catholic" side to Kennedy, there was also a conservative side. His conservatism, reflected in votes for government economy, fiscal orthodoxy, congressional restrictions on presidential power, and governmental reorganization, showed itself sporadically during his first three years in the House and seemed to increase toward the end.

In one of Kennedy's first votes on an appropriation bill in the House, he favored cutting in half an item in President Truman's budget of $295 million for the Interior Department. In 1949, he opposed a big veterans' pension bill, and a year later he joined Republican budget-slasher John Taber in the economy bloc's effort to reduce total appropriations by $600 million. "How long can we continue deficit financing on such a large scale with a national debt of over $258 billions?" Kennedy demanded of the House. During his last three years in the lower chamber, he voted often to cut Agriculture and Interior Department appropriations. He voted against a Public Library Services Demonstration bill, which authorized federal aid to states for promoting library services, and in 1952 he voted for a cut of $14 million in funds for the Tennessee Valley Authority.

He took one of the strongest positions in the House for a balanced budget during the Korean war, coming out even for higher excise taxes and increased taxes on personal and corporate income. He generally supported the recommendations for government reorganization of the Hoover Commission, of which his father was a member. He was "agin inflation" and had some ideas of what to do about it. He consistently opposed the dismantling of wage and price controls following World War II and backed Truman's request for control legislation after the Korean war broke out. Reflecting opinion in his district, Kennedy was particularly sensitive to increases in food prices and rents.

As for the balance of legislative and executive power, Kennedy's support of congressional supervision of sending troops to Europe was a policy that many authorities would consider an infringement on the President's constitutional power. But perhaps his most surprising vote, at least from the vantage point of later years, was that in favor of the Twenty-second Amendment, limiting the President to two terms. "When I voted for this amendment," Kennedy says today, "I had very much on my mind a talk I had had in February 1945 with Dr. Lahey of the Lahey Clinic, who had been one of a three-man committee to look over the President before the 1944 campaign. He felt that the President should not have run again and the doctors should have told him not to. Two months later Roosevelt was dead." A two-term limit, however, is scanty protection against presidential illness, as the Eisenhower case later showed; doubtless Kennedy had other motives for this vote, too. The Twenty-second Amendment was something of an anti-Roosevelt gesture, and there was strong feeling among Kennedy's constituents that Roosevelt had been ill and incompetent at Yalta. More important, Kennedy shared the conservatives' belief in maintaining the traditional balance between congressional and presidential power, and he was, in effect, voting into the Constitution the anti-third-term tradition that had lasted as an unwritten law for a century and a half until Roosevelt ended it in 1940.

Kennedy as a Congressman

It was clear—at least to those few who were following Kennedy's career at the time—that this man could not be neatly defined and put into a pigeonhole marked "Fair Dealer," "Conservative," "Isolationist," or with some other handy tag. What was he, then? Could his mixed voting record be explained by any single set of motives?

Was he, for example, under his father's influence? Friends of the Kennedys talked often about the old man's powerful personality, his strongly held views on public policy, his tendency to meddle in his children's lives. During his son's years as a congressman, moreover, the former Ambassador was speaking out on foreign policy with his old-time vigor, with most of the old-time attitudes, and even with some of the old-time phrases. "Our policy today is politically and morally a bankrupt policy," he said in December 1950. And, "What have we gained by staying in Berlin? Everyone knows we can be pushed out the moment the Russians choose to push us out. Isn't it better to get out now?" He criticized the British loan, aid to Greece and Turkey, reliance on the United Nations, American participation in Korea, and, by implication at least, the Marshall Plan—all on the grounds that American money had not won friends, after all. A Republican congressman, terming him neither "an isolationist nor an ostrich," credited him with helping to bring Herbert Hoover back into active public life and with opening the "great debate" of 1951 on foreign policy.

The son's views on foreign policy coincided with his father's at certain points and then went off at a tangent. They both opposed heavy spending abroad as utopian. Representative Kennedy told the Boston Chamber of Commerce in November 1951: "We cannot reform the world. . . . Uncle Sugar is as dangerous a role for us to play as Uncle Shylock." Certainly he showed some of his father's misgivings about Asiatic policy and some of his father's pessimism about the chances of holding Europe in the face of Russian power. They both wanted a strong defense at home.

Otherwise, however, their views diverged sharply. The

young Kennedy favored bill after bill—from the British loan to, in the end, Point Four—that his father would have flatly opposed. They were operating from wholly different premises: the father from the premise that the United States should not commit itself abroad but should withdraw into strong continental defenses; the son from the premise that it should make commitments abroad provided that its allies bore their share of the burden. On domestic matters they differed considerably; the Congressman was far more willing than his father to achieve reform and welfare through governmental action. There is little evidence of direct paternal influence on the son's views; his files contain a number of letters from his father, but almost all relate to family and financial matters. His father states flatly today that he never asked his son to vote for or against any bill in Congress.

Did the Congressman follow the Democratic party line? Decidedly not. Although he usually voted with administration Democrats on economic and social-welfare matters, he often refused to go along with the White House. He opposed bluntly some of its foreign policies, especially after Truman's "miracle victory" of 1948, when the doughty President was at the height of his popularity and prestige. He departed from Democratic party policy in voting for cuts in Interior and Agriculture spending programs. He was not a "party man"; he did not think in terms of party loyalty. It is doubtful that Representative Kennedy ever delivered one of those fervent, extravagant addresses of the type rendered by keynote speakers at party conventions; temperamentally and intellectually, he was incapable of it. In his talks he preferred to discuss specific issues, and often he did so heedless of the official party position. He strongly supported most Democratic party doctrine but he was not an "organization" Democrat.

Nor was he much influenced by the Democratic leaders back in Boston. The party as an organization hardly existed in his district. Like most candidates for the House, he had built his own personal organization, staffing it with young independent-minded supporters. With Democratic leaders in Boston he had pleasant but cautious and reserved relations. Especially was he reserved in his attitude toward House Democratic Leader McCormack, who was a potent figure both in Boston and on the floor of the House. McCormack ruled over federal patronage for Massachusetts, and Kennedy, like his fellow Democratic representatives in the House, complained that the Majority Leader kept too much for himself. And often he did not go along with McCormack in his voting.

For his part, McCormack liked Kennedy but found him something of a trial. One time, he sat down with a group of congressmen considering housing legislation, looked around elaborately for the absent Kennedy, held aloft a Boston newspaper headlining a Kennedy demand for more housing, and asked: "Where's Johnny? Where's Johnny?"

It was Jim Curley who put Kennedy's independence from the Boston party and his courage to the acid test. In 1947, Jim was in trouble again. Convicted for using the mails to defraud in war contracts, he had just been sentenced to jail despite his plea to the judge that he was suffering from nine separate ailments, including an impending cerebral hemorrhage. Now, still mayor of Boston, he was in Danbury penitentiary and pulling all wires to get out. Party chieftains in Boston and Washington urged President Truman to pardon him. McCormack drew up a petition to the President and got the prompt signatures of Massachusetts representatives, Republican and Democratic alike. Spotting Kennedy on the floor of the House, McCormack handed him the petition. Would he sign? The two men eyed each other tensely.

"Has anyone talked with the President or anything?" Kennedy asked.

"No," said McCormack. "If you don't want to sign, don't sign it."

"Well, I'm not going to sign it," Kennedy said. And he did not. His decision was taken against the advice of close friends. McCormack was annoyed, and Curley was to seek political retribution the first chance he had. Kennedy's rebuff of Curley, long a foe of the family, took considerable political courage, for the Mayor had a fanatically devoted following in Boston, especially in his old congressional district. It also reflected Kennedy's distaste for the Curley element in the party.

On other matters, however, Kennedy spoke and acted for his district. His votes against appropriations for Western projects reflected not only opposition to the "pork-barrel" aspects of this spending, but a Bostonian's lack of interest in such matters. His vote against federal aid for rural libraries suggested that his perspective was still from Boston and not even from that of the whole state, for rural central and western Massachusetts would have certainly benefited from the bill. His sponsorship of federal aid to parochial schools from 1947 to 1950 also was popular in his heavily Catholic district.

"All you have talked about since you have been here is New England," a Midwestern representative remarked during debate on an appropriations bill.

"Do you object to that?" Kennedy asked.

It was not surprising that Kennedy could ignore the weak party leadership in his district. But how could he dare defy national party leaders like McCormack and Truman, who had the power to help or hurt a young man's national career? "For one thing," Kennedy says, "we were just worms over in the House—nobody pays much attention to us nationally. And I had come back from the Service not as a Democratic wheelhorse who came up through the ranks—I came in sort of sideways. It was never drilled into me that I was responsible to some political boss in the Eleventh District. I can go it the hard way against the politically active people. I never had the feeling I needed Truman."

What about the economic pressure groups congressmen are often pictured as submissive to, the potent organized interests of the nation? Kennedy not only defied them, but did so outspokenly and perhaps judged them overseverely. He battled the leadership of the Legion and the VFW in the housing fights and on a veterans' bonus for World War II veterans and other special veterans' measures. His strong position on economic austerity after Korea put him at odds with a host of groups seeking exemptions from the anti-inflation program. At one time or another, he took on real-estate interests, oil interests, processors of farm commodities, airlines (in a hard fight for separation of airlines' subsidies from airmail payments), and various agricultural and other producer interests.

Was Kennedy a liberal? Not by any current definitions of the word. Certainly he had no hankering for the label and perhaps went out of his way to avoid it. In November 1950, when Kennedy addressed professors and students at a Harvard seminar on the legislative process, he specified that he was no follower of a "liberal line."

On voting tests of liberalism established by such publications as the *New Republic* and such organizations as Americans for Democratic Action, Kennedy usually scored 80 to 90 per cent. The main reason for this, however, was his solid support of market-basket liberalism. On noneconomic matters, like civil liberties, his record was highly ambivalent, many liberals decided. Most distressing to liberals was his refusal to become aroused against men like McCarran, whose record was clearly right wing, and McCarthy, who had aroused the country with his unsubstantiated charges of communism in government since February of 1950.

But certainly Kennedy was no straight-out conservative, either, despite many conservative votes. He repudiated the central conservative idea (in America) that government is inherently incompetent, wasteful, and evil; on the contrary, he saw the enormous potential of an ably staffed public service. He consistently supported social-welfare programs, progressive taxation, business regulation; he strongly opposed stringent labor reform. Some issues, such as economy and efficiency in government, he discussed so persuasively and supported so strongly that he attracted many conservative businessmen, but they had to ignore other pages of his voting record.

Was there, then, no pattern to the man? Was he completely outside the ordinary definitions of American politics? Certainly if Kennedy had had his choice, the answer would have been "yes." He got quiet satisfaction apparently from shocking his liberal auditors at Harvard by what had seemed his conservative opinions, from telling an anticommunist audience in Boston that America had been negatively anticommunist and "pro-nothing," from telling off the Truman administration on foreign policy, from steering clear of party leaders in Massachusetts.

But no man is an island, entire of itself. The only pattern that fits Kennedy is, on the face of it, quite simple: he was very much a representative of his Boston constituency. But underneath, this was not simple at all, for his constituency was deeply divided. It was divided not only in the manner in which most districts are divided—between rich and poor, liberals and conservatives, businessmen and workers. It was deeply divided ideologically and culturally, and, most important of all, that division was deeply imprinted on Kennedy's family background and his own development despite his family's long sojourn outside Massachusetts during his boyhood.

The political differences long ago between the immigrant Irish and non-Irish in Boston, Handlin says, testified to the barrier of diametrically opposed ideas. "Resting on basically different premises, developed in entirely different environments, two distinct cultures flourished in Boston with no more contact than if 3,000 miles of ocean rather than a wall of ideas stood between them." A century after Pat Kennedy came from Ireland to this divided world, its differences were still deep in Boston and deep in Kennedy's own personality. On one side was the great majority of his constitutents—immigrant Catholic, liberal on economic and social matters, conservative on issues of public education and civil liberties, rigidly anticommunist, somewhat isolationist. On the other hand was a small minority of Yankees, Jews, some Catholics —internationalists, libertarian, vehemently pro-public education. Some politicians might have settled the issue by counting heads, but Kennedy could not. Representing sheer numbers would have been distasteful to him temperamentally; politically it was unnecessary, for he had a tight grip on the district. His difficulty was that as a Choate and Harvard alumnus he had a vast respect for the Arthur Holcombes and Bruce Hoppers, the Conants and, in former days, the A. Lawrence Lowells and Eliots who had presided over the intellectual, reformist, and cosmopolitan life of Cambridge.

Some politicians might have broken away from the immigrant world and embraced the more edifying, more sophisticated, and more exciting world of the liberal intellectuals. But for Kennedy this would have meant breaking away not just from a remote background but from a dominant family whose powerful way of life was still strong within him. And symbolizing that family—standing guard, as it were, over the links between him and the Fitzgeralds and the Kennedys —was his father. The most potent forces on a legislator, a keen student of Congress has said, are not the pressures *on* him but the pressures *in* him; and this was the role of his father. Whatever influence Joseph Kennedy, Sr., exerted on his son to keep him responsive to the Boston Catholic conservative ways was by example—the example of a self-confident man of affairs who had succeeded as a Catholic and an immigrant's grandson. A man has as many different social selves, William James said, as there are distinct groups of persons about whose opinions he cares.

Some friends of Kennedy have felt that his early independence stemmed from his detached attitude toward most burning issues; because he was neutral and dispassionate, they said, he rejected the ideologies and stereotypes of both conservatives and liberals, both isolationists and interventionists. But where did the detachment come from in the first place? It was both a product of and a cloak to cover the divisions within him. Committed to neither world, though related to both, he could sit back and regard each with a cool and judicial eye. Kennedy was committed only to noncommitment.

Still, he was a politician. While the divergent forces operated within him, they also operated upon him, from the outside. One social scientist has pointed out that it was somewhat similar to the problem of the "inner-directed" versus the "outer-directed" man which David Riesman has described. The real test of the durability of Kennedy's detachment and independence would come as he shifted his electoral base. The story of his next decade is of the expansion of that base to encompass a far greater range of interests and loyalties than the twofold division of the Eleventh Congressional District. The puzzle of that decade concerns the extent to which the pressures *in* Kennedy remained the same while the pressures *on* him changed so strikingly.

Six years as a congressman did not seem to age Kennedy very much. Looking closely one could see faint lines in his face, but people noticed not these, but the picture-magazine profile and the quick, radiant smile. The Congressman often wore a deep tan, acquired in Florida or on Cape Cod or the Potomac, and this took a few more years off his appearance.

Nor did legislative responsibilities give him a dignified mien. He had still not "settled down"; he liked long, energetic weekends, quick trips to Florida or Europe, madcap drives to get to an airplane or dinner on time. He read a great deal on these trips or at home sprawled in a chair; a reporter noted that Kennedy "never sits in a chair; he bivouacs in it." Another described him as tall, frail, genteelly rumpled, with an air of boyish, well-bred emaciation that attracted mothers and daughters alike.

By 1952, Kennedy had an assured future in the House. His district was safe indefinitely (unless a Republican legislature should regerrymander it), for the migration of families outward to the Boston suburbs was making it more, rather than less, Democratic. He now ranked fifth out of the fourteen Democrats on the Labor Committee. Although he had few close political friends, he was well liked by his colleagues in the House; and not only his fellow Democrats from New England, but many Southerners and Republicans as well felt that, despite his economic liberalism, he had special sympathy for them and their problems. It was

104

quite likely that his youth, his safe seat, and his appeal to all Democratic factions would have made him a safe bet to be Democratic leader and perhaps speaker within two decades.

But the Congressman did not want a House career. It is doubtful that he spent ten minutes considering the possibility of the speakership. In fact, the life of the House did not excite him. He was one of 435 members—and a not very important member. It was hard to win the spotlight to dramatize his position on an issue. House rules and customs were frustrating; to strike out on one's own meant running up against barrier after barrier, while working with the leadership meant the watering down of a bill until it could satisfy a host of Democratic factions and perhaps some Republicans.

Where to go next? Since his early days in Washington, Kennedy had been weighing the possibility of a statewide run. In 1948, his second year in the House, he eyed the senatorial seat of Republican Leverett Saltonstall with longing. But Saltonstall had always been a strong campaigner. And 1948—the closer he got to it—did not look to Kennedy like a good year to run. Wallace Progressives were veering off on the left and the 1946 undertow against the Democrats still seemed to be running strong. Truman looked so unpopular that important Democrats were thinking of ditching him and nominating someone else, perhaps General Dwight D. Eisenhower himself.

So Kennedy let 1948 go by. But he did not waste time. Clearly he must win a statewide name before he could win statewide office. So during his second term in Washington he began to campaign across the state. He still did not know what office he was seeking. Paul A. Dever had won the governorship in 1948 and could be expected to seek a second term in 1950. No Senate seat would open up until 1952.

Surely this was a remarkable thing—a thirty-two-year-old congressman, still hardly more than a freshman, launching an intensive statewide campaign at a time when he did not know the office he was seeking, the year he would seek it, or the man he would run against. But Kennedy was in dead earnest. In 1946 he had snared a prize congressional seat by starting early, months before the regular campaign season had opened. Now he would use this proven weapon against bigger game.

Kennedy's lieutenants still talk of this period with amazement and exasperation. The Congressman would fly up to Boston late on Thursday for a long weekend on the hustings. On hand were Frank Morrissey, who now ran the Boston office, and Bob Morey, a talkative former prize fighter who, as chauffeur, could meet tough speaking schedules. Since invitations were sought and accepted in every corner of the state, the little party might crisscross the state several times in one weekend. Factories, schools, fishing boats, communion breakfasts, women's clubs, veterans' conclaves—Kennedy appeared anywhere he could wangle an invitation. Trying not to look like a candidate, he rarely talked politics or took a stand on an issue. He usually discussed local matters, economy in government, social-welfare legislation, or some other relatively safe subject. He was campaigning for one purpose—to put across the Kennedy name and the Kennedy record.

"I'll bet he talked to at least a million people and shook hands with seven hundred and fifty thousand," Morrissey said later, without much exaggeration.

The pace was hard—and so was the candidate. Kennedy drove himself and his aides almost ruthlessly. Rising before dawn, driving for hours in the fog or rain or snow, racing to be on time, sleeping in motels or dingy hotels or in the car, wading through muck to greet hip-booted tannery workers, autographing the books of pushing, chirruping schoolgirls—this was the endlessly repeated cycle, growing in intensity as 1952 neared. Unenchanted by food, Kennedy allowed the party ten minutes to eat. Meal after meal might consist of cheeseburgers or hamburgers and milk shakes. The Congressman was often late, and he hated to be late. A stop for a train, an unnecessary delay, a buttonholing admirer would tauten Kennedy's face and send him into short tirades back in the car. Other times, the threesome, returning home early in the morning, would remember some funny incident and burst into tired, ironic laughter.

No man could stay healthy under such a schedule for so long a time, and Kennedy did not. Soon his back was throbbing painfully. He eased it by tearing his clothes off and settling into a brimming tub of hot water at every hotel stop, and by putting a stiff board under his mattress or sleeping on the mattress on the floor, but he grew worse. He could climb upstairs only by dragging his leg, when he thought people were looking the other way. By 1952, he was on crutches again.

The Battle Joined

By early 1952, Kennedy had stumped in almost all the 351 cities and towns of Massachusetts. But what was he running for?

It was certain that Senator Henry Cabot Lodge's term expired in 1952. It was almost as certain that Lodge would run again. What would the Democrats do? Everything turned on the plans of Governor Dever, a sure-footed graduate of the political school of hard knocks, now midway through his second term in the statehouse. Dever had a problem of his own. Like most American governors, submerged in executive detail and local politics, he looked forward to a gracious senatorial career and a chance to parade on the national stage. But could he beat Lodge? For months, Dever hesitated while his aides sniffed the political wind.

Meanwhile, Kennedy fidgeted. He had to wait for the Governor to decide. Many of his friends hoped that Dever would choose the Senate race so that Kennedy could run for governor. In the statehouse he could make a name for himself as an executive, and after one term he could go after Saltonstall's senatorial chair. But Kennedy felt differently. The Massachusetts governorship had been hard on political fortunes, especially those of Democrats. The 280 senators and representatives were notoriously independent, the governor's powers limited, and the legislature tended to stay stubbornly Republican even when the state as a whole went Democratic. Besides, Kennedy had become more and more excited by national affairs.

The national political scene was equally murky. Since Truman would not run again, the race in each party seemed wide open. A sharp struggle between Eisenhower and Taft was splitting the Republican forces; a dozen Democrats were behaving like possible candidates for their party's presidential nomination.

Finally, Dever took one last look at the redoubtable Lodge and decided that he was too tough to beat. On an early April night in 1952, he called Kennedy in and told him that the Senate race was open. Kennedy did not hesitate. He announced publicly: ". . . There is not only a crisis abroad, but there is a crisis here at home in Massachusetts. . . . For entirely too long the representatives of Massachusetts in the United States Senate have stood by helplessly while our industries and jobs disappear. . . ." He concluded by drawing a bead squarely on his target.

"I, therefore, am opposing Henry Cabot Lodge, Jr., for the office of United States Senator from Massachusetts."

Some friends of Kennedy were aghast at his decision. Lodge had a mighty record as a campaigner. He had first gained his Senate seat by beating Jim Curley by 142,000 votes in 1936, the year of the high-water mark of New Deal voting power. He won re-election six years later, resigned from the Senate in 1944 for combat service, and returned after the war to defeat the "unbeatable" isolationist David I. Walsh. He was a hard campaigner who for years had been shaking hands throughout the Commonwealth of Massachusetts, from the Berkshire hills to his estate in Beverly on the North Shore. If Kennedy was a household name in Boston, Lodge was a potent political trade-mark throughout the state.

Rarely in American politics have hunter and quarry so resembled each other. Not only were they both tall, young, handsome, and winning, each a Brahmin in his own way, but their careers were remarkably parallel. Like Kennedy, Lodge was a Harvard man who had had a fling at newspaper work before entering politics at an early age. Both possessed noted isolationist forebears; Lodge's grandfather, of the same name, had led the effort to spike Woodrow Wilson's efforts to bring America into the League of Nations. Both Kennedy and Lodge could boast of their war records. Both had a reputation for appealing to the "women's vote." Of the two, Lodge was more suave, polished, and mature, Kennedy more tense, detached, and boyish, but each could be cool and stiff under pressure.

The astute Paul Dever summed up the situation in six words: "Jack is the first Irish Brahmin."

Ironically, the two men differed little over public issues. Lodge had a mixed record on issues of bread-and-butter liberalism; he had, for example, voted for the Taft-Hartley Act. But on other matters the records of the two men crisscrossed. Forsaking his grandfather's isolationism, Lodge had supported the Truman Doctrine, the Marshall Plan, the North Atlantic Treaty, and the sending of troops to Europe. A member of the Senate Foreign Relations Committee, he had carried on the Vandenberg policy of nonpartisanship in foreign policy, and he had, in fact, been less critical of Truman's foreign policy than Kennedy had been. Like Kennedy, too, he had been silent on McCarthyism.

Events in early 1952, moreover, dramatized Lodge's right to the liberal Republican tag. While Eisenhower stayed in Europe stating that "under no circumstances" would he ask for relief from his NATO command to seek political office, Lodge led the pro-Eisenhower forces back home. This put the Massachusetts Senator directly at odds with Taft and his conservative and isolationist followers. By 1952, indeed, Lodge was becoming something of a liberal hero; at a convention of a CIO union in Boston, for example, he was given an ovation.

Lodge's politicking for Eisenhower made him miss some key votes in the Senate and opened him up to the charge of absenteeism. But by a final ironic twist, Kennedy was even more vulnerable on this score, as a result of illness, trips abroad, and campaigning for the Senate. It seemed that fate had conspired in every way to balance the political scales between the two young politicians.

How could David conquer David? The more Kennedy's advisers studied Lodge and his record, the more they despaired of finding the vulnerable point. He was an internationalist with an isolationist heritage, a "liberal conservative" who had veered back and forth on domestic issues.

Faced with this dilemma, Kennedy's advisers began to split into two camps. On the left were some labor leaders and Fair Deal Democrats who urged him to go down the line for more welfare programs, civil liberties, civil rights, and continued economic and military commitments abroad. It was a presidential year, they argued; he would have to campaign on national issues. His record was essentially a Democratic record; how could he campaign as anything but a Fair Deal Democrat?

The other camp held far different views. Kennedy, they argued, was in a perfect position to conduct an elaborate flank attack on Lodge from the right. The Congressman's own record would lend itself to this tactic; he had sounded off against some of Truman's foreign policies, favored cuts in certain foreign-appropriations bills, spoken and voted for governmental economy, scolded Europe for not carrying its share of the load. Indeed, these advisers went on, Kennedy's position was not too far from that of the Republican nationalists, who believed that Europe was worn out, that the Democrats had "lost" China, that Korea was "Truman's war." Elaborate studies were prepared to prove that on foreign policy Kennedy stood closer to Taft's position than did Lodge.

"Kennedy has been an outspoken critic of many elements of the Administration's Foreign Policy," one such study began. "In this respect, he has been much closer to the position of Taft than has Lodge. Indeed, the latter has been riding at the head of the so-called bi-partisan foreign policy parade since 1947. . . ."

The strategy, then, was apparent to this group: attack Lodge as a Republican who had deserted his party, a political adventurer clinging to Eisenhower's coattails, an internationalist who had repudiated his own grandfather. Leader of the "Keep Right" group was the Congressman's own father. During 1952, Joseph P. Kennedy was in and out of Boston, seeing publishers and politicians, conferring with speech writers and researchers, discussing public-relations programs with advertising agencies. As spry, vocal, and aggressive as ever, the old man had no formal position in the campaign setup, nor did he need any. Of course, as a friend of Taft and other Republican nationalists, he had good reason to dislike Lodge. But politics was the least of it. Here at last was the supreme opportunity for his son. Joseph P. enlisted for the duration.

Young Kennedy listened dutifully to both camps. He was not yet ready to decide between the two strategies, if, indeed, a decision ever would be necessary at all. He had his own plans.

By the Left—or Right?

The national spotlight shone on Chicago in July 1952. Early in the month, Eisenhower and Taft forces locked in mighty battle at the Amphitheatre. Charging Taft's men with attempts to "steal" delegates, the Eisenhower forces outvoted the Ohioan's delegates in the early contests and then beat them in the first roll call. Despite Ike's quick visit to the Senator at his headquarters to present a united front, Taft's diehard supporters went home from the convention sore and vengeful.

Two weeks later, the Democrats convened in the same arena. Governor Adlai E. Stevenson, of Illinois, captivated the convention within an hour of its start in his welcoming speech as governor of Illinois. "For almost a week," Stevenson said of the Republicans, "pompous phrases marched over this landscape in search of an idea, and the only idea they found was that the two great decades of progress in peace, victory in war, and bold leadership in this anxious hour, were the misbegotten spawn of bungling, corruption, socialism, mismanagement, waste and worse. They captured, tied and dragged that idea in here and furiously beat it to death." The delegates roared. "But we Democrats were not the only victims here. First they slaughtered each other, and then they went after us. . . ."

Kennedy was active for Stevenson, contributing money to help maintain his volunteer headquarters and organizing a group of Democratic candidates for the Senate to endorse Stevenson at the beginning of the convention. He was not conspicuous in the Massachusetts delegation, however, for Dever headed it, and old Jim Curley attracted the most attention as he strode down the center aisle to his seat in the delegation. Kennedy was pleased with Stevenson's quick nomination. Stevenson was the type of Democrat he liked—moderately liberal, polished, articulate, a foe of banal phrases and stereotyped thinking.

After the delegates enthusiastically nominated Stevenson on the third ballot, Kennedy immediately flew home to tune up his own campaign organization. In his months of campaigning, he had quietly looked over in each area of the state men and women who might organize his local campaigns. By now he had a network of 286 "secretaries," backed by several thousand workers. It was an odd mixture of local civic leaders, professional people, housewives, heads of fraternal groups, mayors, businessmen. Many of these secretaries were independents or independent Democrats; some even had Republican leanings. This was not accidental. Kennedy was trying to win votes from the hosts of independents who usually hold the balance of power in Massachusetts elections, and, in any event, most of the Democratic committeemen were interested mainly in Dever or in local candidates.

The first test of this amateurish-looking organization made the professionals sit up and take notice. Kennedy had no opposition in the primary, partly because of his head start, partly because no other Democrat wanted to take on Lodge. This was a help—and also a problem. Without a primary fight it would be hard to give his organization a workout. It was necessary, however, to get 2,500 signatures on his nomination papers. Why not get ten times, a hundred times, as many? The 262,324 signatures finally amassed were a record total. And all the names were filed also in headquarters to be approached again in the fall.

Kennedy wanted to avoid the usual campaign situation of too many generals and too few privates. He needed people who would go out and ring doorbells instead of gossiping at headquarters. Who better to start with than the energetic Kennedy sisters? Soon the clan was gathering: from Chicago came Jean, who had been assisting her father at the Merchandise Mart, and Eunice, a social-service worker for the House of the Good Shepherd; from New York came Patricia, who was working in television. Perhaps on the theory that only a Kennedy could slave-drive Kennedys, the candidate also summoned young Bobby and made him campaign director. This was a shock to the old pros, who could not imagine this twenty-seven-year-old managing a statewide campaign. It was even more of a shock to the girls, who would return to their Boston apartment footsore after a long day, only to be called back to headquarters by the imperious Robert for some new emergency task.

The family also put a good deal of money into the campaign. Seven Kennedys gave $1,000 each to each of the five committees set up to help finance the campaign—committees for "Improvement of Massachusetts Fish Industry," for "Improvement of the Shoe Industry," for "Improvement of the Textile Industry," along with the "Build Massachusetts Committee" and "Citizens for Kennedy and a More Prosperous Massachusetts." Such multiple giving was necessary, since $1,000 was the maximum under state law that one person could give one committee. Through additional donations, the family gave a total of $70.000. Kennedy received over two hundred other $1,000 contributions.

Headquarters in Boston was now a ceaseless bustle of activity. Girls at typewriters spent hours making up lists of special groups to be circularized: Albanian-Americans, insurance men, Independent Greek-Americans, college professors, railway mail clerks, taxi drivers. A stream of instructions and exhortations, including even fund-raising requests, went out to area secretaries. Area workers carted off thousands of copies of the *Reader's Digest* reprint of "Survival" on Kennedy's P-T boat experience to be left, as nonpolitical reading matter, in barbershops and hairdressers' salons. Advertising men planned an intensive television campaign. Reardon prepared a huge campaign book detailing Kennedy's votes, excerpts from his speeches, and Lodge's record. Publicity men worked up several press releases a day; the more important were hand-carried to the newspaper offices. Hardly a detail was overlooked. A Kennedy message concerning the Jewish New Year was prepared weeks ahead for Jewish newspapers.

The tactics were fine—but what about strategy? Campaign advisers, including the self-appointed, still argued whether their candidate should attack Lodge from the left or the right, as an isolationist or internationalist.

The issue was sharpened when the Taft delegates from Massachusetts returned home after their rout at Chicago. Still bruised over the tactics of Ike's men, they turned their aim toward the convenient target of Lodge. Kennedy, after all, was not so bad, they told one another; he might be a Fair Dealer on domestic matters, but hadn't he been more critical of the Truman foreign policy than Lodge? And Kennedy's father was a close friend and admirer of Taft. Many of these unreconstructed Taft men worked quietly for Kennedy. A few spoke out publicly. Basil Brewer, publisher of a New Bedford paper and a Taft die-hard, scored Lodge in his editorials and kept in close touch with men in the Kennedy campaign. A retired wholesaler and former Taft lieutenant set up the "Independents for Kennedy" at the request, he told friends privately, of Ambassador Kennedy himself.

Then there was the thorny problem of Joe McCarthy. The Wisconsin Senator created a dilemma for both Lodge and Kennedy. Lodge disliked McCarthy and opposed his tactics. But coming from Massachusetts, where McCarthy sentiment, especially among the Irish Catholics, was strong, Lodge had steered a cautious course. His main hope was that McCarthy would stay away from Massachusetts. But what if he came anyway? Kennedy asked the same question. Lodge was being attacked in Boston for his coolness toward McCarthy. What if McCarthy came and endorsed Lodge? What if he endorsed Kennedy? There was no way of knowing what the wild man from Wisconsin would do. Both candidates pretended he did not exist.

But events made evasion difficult. Any group—a Legion Post or "Americanism" committee—might get the notion of inviting McCarthy to town. Indeed, McCarthy had sent word to Kennedy, Sr. that if Lodge asked him to come to Massachusetts, he would do so. Was this a warning to his son? The father preferred to wait and let Lodge jump first—"if you have to make a tough choice," he argued, "let the other man make it." But Kennedy's anti-McCarthy advisers urged him to take a bold position—to denounce, if not McCarthy, at least McCarthyism. One night, Gardner ("Pat") Jackson, a down-the-line liberal, veteran of the Sacco-Vanzetti case and of the New Deal wars, and then on loan to the Kennedy campaign from the CIO, prepared a ringing statement against McCarthyism for Kennedy to endorse and publicize. The next morning he took it around to the Bowdoin Street apartment.

When Jackson entered the apartment he was surprised to find the living room filled with people. Usually the place was deserted at this early hour. He soon saw why—sitting on the sofa was Joseph Kennedy. The father, who usually operated from his own rooms, was making one of his rare visits to the apartment. The candidate was evidently still in bed. The others were mainly advertising and public-relations people. While the group watched nervously, Jackson pulled out his document and started to read it.

He had got through three sentences when Joseph Kennedy sprang to his feet with such force that he upset a small table in front of him. He stormed over to Jackson almost as if he would attack him.

"You and your friends are trying to ruin my son's career!" He was not opposed to McCarthy, he shouted; he had contributed to his campaign. Again and again he returned to the charge that liberals and union people were hurting his son. The Jews were against him, too. In the midst of the hubbub, young Kennedy appeared. He took neither side—indeed, he hardly spoke to Jackson or to his father—and soon he and Reardon slipped out for the day's campaigning. Jackson left soon afterward, the great challenge back in his pocket.

A few days later, Jackson was sitting in the same living room at the same hour, while the candidate dressed in the bedroom.

"They gave you a bad time, Pat?" Kennedy called casually through the half-open door.

"How do you explain your father, Jack?" Jackson asked.

Kennedy was silent for a few moments. "Just love of family." He paused and then corrected himself: "No. Pride of family."

Kennedy kept mum on the McCarthy issue. Lodge's eventual endorsement of McCarthy for re-election in Wisconsin was not enough to mollify conservative Republicans in Massachusetts. Basil Brewer continued to busy himself in Kennedy's behalf. He visited John Fox, publisher of the Boston *Post*, and urged him to oppose Lodge and support Kennedy on the grounds that Lodge had no firm convictions, and perhaps, too, on the grounds that he had been soft on communism. When Lodge later refused to "explain himself" to Fox, the publisher wrote a front-page editorial endorsing Kennedy. Fox said long afterward that he then had tried to reach Kennedy without success; at one of the telephone numbers, however, he found Joseph Kennedy, who came over for a drink and a talk. Shortly after the election, Fox obtained a loan of half a million dollars for the money-losing *Post* from Joseph Kennedy. This loan, the senior Kennedy later said, was a regular commercial transaction and was repaid in sixty days at full interest.

Battle of the Teacups

Dogged by discord in his own ranks, and still faced with an elusive opponent, Kennedy did what successful politicians often do under such circumstances—he let the two sides follow their own strategy separately while he pursued his. While his cohorts peppered away at Lodge from both right and left, Kennedy attacked him for taking contradictory positions on a host of issues, including trade with communist countries, civil rights, price control, China, troops to Europe, rent control. However, he evaded a clean confrontation on national issues—to the extent this was ever possible between two such like-minded men—by basing his campaign on local and state problems.

"Kennedy will do MORE for Massachusetts," billboards and posters proclaimed.

Lodge was not to be outdone.

"Lodge has done—and Will Do—the MOST for Massachusetts," his placards proclaimed back.

Kennedy's billboards outnumbered Lodge's, but the Congressman learned early that billboards could not do the job alone. One night, returning to Boston from Worcester, he and a friend stopped off at a roadside restaurant. As they got out of the car, Kennedy observed happily a huge Kennedy billboard of the most expensive kind looming over the restaurant, and blazoning forth in enormous letters, "JOHN F. KENNEDY FOR SENATOR." After gulping down a chocolate milk shake, Kennedy paid his check to the manager. He stuck out his hand.

"Hello, I'm John Kennedy."

The man looked at him vaguely. "Who?"

"John F. Kennedy, running for United States Senator."

"Oh—John Kennedy. Running for what?"

Kennedy walked out, took another look up at the sign, and drove on in eloquent silence.

Lodge's whole offensive was now in full swing, but for a Massachusetts campaign the contest was remarkably mild and gentlemanly. Cautiously, the men shadowboxed with each other; it seemed hard for the blue blood and the green blood to join battle. Lodge backed Eisenhower's program in the hope that the General would sweep the state, but otherwise he, too, was forced back on local issues. He made something of Kennedy's absenteeism, only to have his opponent charge him with absenteeism on more important issues. The two men met face to face on one or two occasions. Once, 1,200 people crowded into a junior-high-school hall in Waltham to watch the expected fireworks, but the two men argued affably and even said nice things about each other. On debating points, the result was a standoff, although Kennedy proved that in force and in presence he compared well with his more experienced rival. Kennedy disarmed his opponent at the start by admitting that the Truman administration had made some serious mistakes, although it had done a good job as a whole. Two of the most serious issues on the national election front—Korea and McCarthyism— seemed out of bounds in Massachusetts' campaign.

Still, by late September, Kennedy's campaign showed signs of faltering, mainly because he had been stumping so long and Lodge was just getting under way. The Senator was especially effective in speaking to French-American groups in fluent, idiomatic French, in appearing before Italian audiences in the company of a noted Italo-American artist, Francesca Braggiotti (the wife of his brother, Governor John Lodge, of Connecticut), and in talking to isolationist Irish-Americans who remembered his grandfather's battle against the League. Jim Curley, hoping to get revenge for Kennedy's refusal to sign his pardon petition, was giving aid and comfort to the Lodge forces. And Lodge finally met the McCarthy problem by saying bluntly that he was supporting all Republican candidates, specifically including Joseph McCarthy.

There were signs, too, that an Eisenhower sweep was in the making even in Massachusetts, which had not voted for a Republican candidate for President since Coolidge. Stevenson's independence and his divorce disturbed many Democrats who regularly voted for their party. Kennedy asked his workers to help Stevenson, too, and he appeared with him when the Governor toured Massachusetts. But Kennedy was running his campaign separately from all other candidates —an old custom in Massachusetts—and it was clear that many of his supporters liked the combination of "Ike and Jack." For his part, Stevenson strongly endorsed Kennedy, calling him "my type of guy."

With betting odds now even between the two candidates, Kennedy unsheathed a secret weapon unusual even in Massachusetts, where the politicos felt they had seen everything. For weeks, thousands of Massachusetts women had been finding in their mail formal invitations to a series of receptions throughout the state. The invitation for one such affair read:

Reception in honor of
Mrs. Joseph P. Kennedy
and her son
Congressman John F. Kennedy
Wednesday evening, October 1, 1952
at 8 o'clock
at the
Commander Hotel, Cambridge, Mass.
Guests Invited   [union label]

Printed on sleek white cards, encased in hand-addressed vellum envelopes, the invitations seemed to have no relation to politics, except perhaps for the union label. The star of the affair was Rose Kennedy. Still youthful-looking and stylish in a dignified way, she gave a simple, motherly tribute to her son that made the real campaign seem far off and somehow unimportant. At first, Kennedy's aides tried to write her speeches for her ("Of all places on earth, Boston is, and always has been, dearest to me . . .). But ghostwriting was unnecessary; Rose's own stories about bringing up her children were better even than tributes to local pride. Sisters Eunice, Jean, and Pat managed the affairs with their usual charm and gusto. The candidate gave a short talk, barely touching on issues and ending with a request that each of the ladies come up on the stage so that he and his mother and sisters could meet them and later have a cup of tea with them.

"For approximately two hours," a newsman reported of one such affair, "an unbroken line of women filed slowly across the stage, shaking hands with each of the Kennedys, mumbling confused introductions and pleasantries, and pushed on through a side door into the lobby still packed with those waiting their turn to go through the receiving line. Along one side of the spacious room were long tables with harassed waitresses—pouring tea and coffee and serving cookies. (Total consumption was reported later at 8,600 cups.) . . . An air of pleasant, chattering amiability prevailed in spite of a few splattered dresses and two faintings. When the handshaking in the ballroom was finally completed around 10:30, the Kennedys, looking wilted but determined, came in for tea themselves."

The Kennedy receptions were a smashing success. In this television age, when it is almost impossible to induce people to leave their TV sets to see candidates in the flesh, 50,000 women, by a conservative estimate, turned out to meet the Kennedys. Most important, the women went home talking about it—gossiping over the back fence, telling their in-laws, and planting the Kennedy name firmly in the minds of women who would not dream of following an election campaign. And the guests were carefully selected from a racial, religious, national, and political cross section, so that Kennedy talk would go back to every part of their communities.

As election day neared, the activity of the Kennedy family reached its peak tempo. The sisters held house parties; their mother toured Boston wards; Kennedy shook hands on city sidewalks. To blanket the state in one fell swoop, the family twice put on a homey "Coffee with the Kennedys" television program, showing mother and children chattering happily on a sofa, for the viewing of which campaign workers were asked to arrange little parties in their homes. The campaign almost ran out of Kennedys; on one occasion, Bob had to leave headquarters to give one of the shortest political speeches on record:

"My brother Jack couldn't be here, my mother couldn't be

here, my sister Eunice couldn't be here, my sister Pat couldn't be here, my sister Jean couldn't be here, but if my brother Jack were here, he'd tell you Lodge has a very bad voting record. Thank you."

On election eve, Kennedy toured the Gloucester water front in the fog and drizzle of a November afternoon. The sisters buttonholed astonished riders of the Boston subways. Nearby, at the Boston Garden, Eisenhower was the center of a glittering all-star political extravaganza that the Kennedy forces suspected had been put on in Boston to rescue Lodge. On election night, Kennedy sat, tense but cool, with a large group of friends at campaign headquarters. Down the street, they could see the lighted windows of the opposition camp. The returns swayed back and forth, but Kennedy was serene throughout. Early in the morning, when Eisenhower's sweep was clear and Lodge was ahead, Kennedy and Torby Macdonald left the feverish campaign headquarters and went for a walk in the Boston Public Garden. "I wonder what job Eisenhower's going to give Lodge," Kennedy speculated. He had no doubt of his own victory. At six in the morning, Lodge conceded and left his office. Only then did the Kennedy forces relax, too tired to celebrate.

Kennedy beat Lodge by 1,211,984 to 1,141,247, a margin of over 70,000 votes. Eisenhower overcame Stevenson in Massachusetts by 208,800 votes. Dever lost to the Republican candidate for governor, Christian Herter, by a close margin. Like a sapling, left standing amid uprooted oaks, Kennedy was suddenly the dominant political figure in the state, eclipsing even McCormack.

How had he done it? Political pundits in Boston had a multitude of theories—Kennedy's money, his father's influence and mobilization of public-relations people, the tea parties, the Kennedy family, Lodge's inability to campaign during most of the year, the defection of the Taft men. Certainly all these were factors. Undeniably, Kennedy outspent Lodge by a substantial margin; he had more television and radio time, more billboards, and probably more newspaper space. The various Kennedy committees, which operated independently of the Democratic-party committees, officially reported expenses of $349,646; the whole cost of the Kennedy campaign was probably more than half a million dollars. The Lodge campaign cost, officially, $58,266; but he was also one of the chief beneficiaries of the one million dollars spent by the Republicans for their state ticket.

Lodge's desertion by the Taft forces hurt him some but

probably not decisively. The Taft leaders were disgruntled, yet the bulk of the Ohioan's supporters in Massachusetts were too strongly Republican to vote for Kennedy. Brewer and other Taft backers simply could not deliver. Nor is it likely that Joseph, Sr.'s tactics had a vital part in the outcome. Whatever votes he picked up for his son on the isolationist right were probably balanced by losses on the internationalist left.

Seen in retrospect, the contest was essentially a battle between Yankee Republicans and Catholic immigrant Democrats. Kennedy held the Democratic vote, which usually is slightly in the majority in Massachusetts, and added to it some of the Taft Republicans. His major achievement was in pulling up even with Lodge by his lengthy "pre-campaign" campaigning and his tea parties. The main effect of the teas was to hold for the Democrats the "lace-curtain" Catholic vote that had gone earlier to Yankee Brahmins like Lodge and Saltonstall. In two or three years, he had made himself as well known as Lodge had done in sixteen. The TV, radio, and billboards simply channeled the Kennedy sentiment into the act of voting. Essentially, Kennedy outstumped Lodge by old-fashioned campaign methods, and by the tea parties.

The campaign was not won on issues; the differences between the two men were too obscure. Like most congressional and many senatorial campaigns, the outcome turned on personality rather than national policies. To be sure, Kennedy's consistent support of bread-and-butter legislation in Congress and in the campaign helped tie down the labor vote. But on foreign policy, civil liberties and civil rights, military policy, and absenteeism, the voters could not see clear alternatives. Kennedy had taken what seemed to be a major strength of Lodge—his ambiguous record—and at the very least had managed to neutralize it.

Never a sentimentalist, Kennedy would not think of his victory as vengeance for his grandfather's defeat by the earlier Henry Cabot Lodge thirty-six years before. But the day after the election, some old Irishmen sitting on a park bench in East Boston were sure that they heard—from the place where Boston politicians go for their reward—the faint but happy rendering of "Sweet Adeline."

7 ★ THE SENATOR FROM NEW ENGLAND

The story goes that when, early in January 1953, Senator-elect Kennedy first tried to board the quaint little subway car that runs between the Capitol and the Senate Office Building, a guard told him to "stand back—let the Senators go first." If this happened, the guard must have been even newer to the place than Kennedy, for the young man did not arrive unheralded. Anyone who had knocked Lodge out of his Senate seat had come sharply to the notice of the observant politicians of the upper chamber.

Kennedy, indeed, moved into the Senate, and into its inner life, with ease. He liked the spaciousness of the Senate, its decorum, gentility, sense of tradition. The upper chamber, as William S. White has said, is an odd, mixed place—both hard and efficient and soft and dawdling, harsh and kind, dignified and disorderly, democratic and "majestically undemocratic." And because these qualities of the Senate mirrored the contradictions and ambivalence of American life, the place was all the more congenial to the young Bostonian, who himself still held an ambivalent and undeveloped set of political views.

The Senate was a storeroom of history. Here had strode the colossi whom Kennedy had been reading about for years—Webster and Clay and Calhoun, Norris and La Follette and all the others. Here had been hammered out great decisions of state, especially in the days when the initiative in policy lay more with Congress than with the President. Here, too, "willful men" had thwarted presidential projects through the filibuster and other engines of delay and destruction.

The upper chamber was still the habitat of famous men. Robert A. Taft, beaten by Eisenhower at the convention but imperishably "Mr. Republican" on Capitol Hill, was majority leader of his party. Lyndon Johnson, of Texas, led the Democratic minority. Patriarchal Walter George and apple-cheeked Harry Byrd, who had both defied Franklin D. Roosevelt and got away with it, symbolized the durable strength of the old South. Veteran New Dealers like Herbert Lehman, of New York, and Lister Hill, of Alabama, still carried on the liberal tradition. The radical right was fully represented by a score of Republicans; one of its spokesmen was a man named McCarthy, who, under the inverted logic of senatorial politics, held the seat once held by Bob La Follette, of Wisconsin.

Entering the Senate meant associating with such men; it meant, also, access to the wider, more sophisticated world to which the Senate was a direct route. This was the world of Cabinet members and Supreme Court justices, of foreign envoys and high State Department officials, of potentates of business and labor, of noted journalists like the Alsop brothers, Marquis Childs, and James Reston. Kennedy had known such men through his father's connections; now he was to rub shoulders with them almost daily, not as an ambassador's son, but in his own right. Much has been made of the Senate as a poky, parochial place, but for some men it can also be a broadening and liberating institution.

On January 3, 1953, Kennedy marched down to the well of the Senate on the arm of his senior colleague from Massachusetts, Leverett Saltonstall, and took the oath of office. Then he took his seat in the rear row behind the Democratic phalanx. On his right sat the eloquent, mettlesome young Senator from Minnesota, Hubert Humphrey, now beginning his fifth year in the Senate; just in front was the liberal statesman Paul H. Douglas, of Illinois. Over the heads of the rows of Democratic senators, Kennedy could see the dark, heavy jowls of the new President of the Senate, Richard M. Nixon. Seventeen days later, Dwight D. Eisenhower was inaugurated President of the United States.

The Open Door

Duly sworn a United States senator, Kennedy returned to the suite of four rooms that had been assigned to him on the third floor of the Senate Office Building. This office, which would be his official home for at least eight years and from which he would launch his presidential campaign, was already beginning to reflect the Kennedy personality. The middle room, where visitors entered, was jam-packed with desks, filing cabinets, and three chairs for visitors. The room led on the left to two small offices, one occupied by Ted Reardon, now the Senator's administrative assistant; on the right was the Senator's own roomy office.

From the beginning, Kennedy ordered that the door to the middle room always be kept open. The open door was symbolic. The young Senator knew well that American legislators are tested more on the basis of their diligence in doing a host of little favors than for the part they play in actual lawmaking. In any case, the role of a freshman senator in legislating for the whole nation is sharply limited. Kennedy drew one good committee assignment—Labor and Public Welfare—but, despite his six years on the House Labor Committee, he now had to start all over again at the bottom of the ladder behind five other Democrats and seven Republicans. His other committee assignment—Government Operations—for a time would have little to do with legislation, since its chairman was Joseph R. McCarthy, of Wisconsin, the Senate's investigator in chief.

So Kennedy concentrated at first on making his office a businesslike service agency for the folks back home. He had ample help. By law, a senator from a state the size of Massachusetts was allowed a maximum of $36,900 for secretaries, and Kennedy could supplement this with extra hire out of his own pocket. In time, his office staff overflowed into a basement room in the Senate Office Building. Supplementing the Washington office under Reardon was an enlarged office in Boston, under Frank Morrissey, which supplied many services on the spot.

The Senator's office soon gained a reputation for prompt action on constituents' requests. And as the reputation grew, so did the volume of favors sought. Some were routine: requests for copies of government documents, for help on application for veterans' benefits, for information on passports, and the like. Some were more troublesome: a professor's request for study space in the Library of Congress, a small businessman needing guidance through Washington's bureaucratic maze, a disappointed father anxious to know why his son was turned down at Harvard or Georgetown. Could the Senator do anything about it? In an amazing number of cases, the Senator—usually meaning Reardon or Morrissey—did.

Legislatively, the new Senator devoted himself in the first two years mainly to the special needs of Massachusetts. He had no real choice, since the question "Who could do more for Massachusetts?" had come to be the main issue between Lodge and himself. With imagination and skill, Kennedy and his aides applied themselves to the needs of every organized interest in Massachusetts; and sometimes, when the interest groups exerted no pressure, the office alerted them to their opportunities.

At the end of his first two years in the Senate, Kennedy could boast in a memorandum to his constitutents of the results of his labors. His efforts are worth listing in part (with Kennedy's own evaluation of his success in parentheses), because they show the range and variety of special-interest activity of a resourceful representative:

For the Massachusetts Fishing Industry: Kennedy Fishing Research and Market Development Bill (passed); Kennedy Fish Sticks Tariff Bill (passed); Kennedy *et al* Fishing Boat Protection Bill (passed); requested import relief from Tariff Commission and President (denied); urged federal purchases of surplus fish (pending); testified in 1953 for increase in Fish and Wildlife Budget (passed).

For the Massachusetts Textile Industry: Kennedy Bill to prevent excessive speculation in raw wool (passed); urged bill in 1953 permitting price of wool to fall to normal market level, lowering cost to mills (adopted in Administration Farm Bill, passed); requested Senate Committee, Tariff Commission, and President to adopt policy of low tariffs on raw wool imports (adopted); testified at Labor Department hearing favoring new Walsh-Healey woolen minimum wage to prevent substandard competition (adopted); requested Treasury in 1953 to adopt countervailing duties on subsidized wool top imports (adopted); urged passage of amendment to Flammable Fabrics Act to save several New England mills (passed); requested Bureau of Labor Statistics to continue at least sample wage studies of Southern textiles (agreed to); Kennedy Bill to prevent move of Army Quartermaster's Texile Office (defeated).

For the Massachusetts Shipbuilding Industry: Kennedy-Butler *et al.* Bill for modernization of reserve-fleet merchant vessels in private yards (passed); urged award of *Forrestal* carriers and other contracts to Quincy Fore River Shipyard (no carriers; some awards).

For the Massachusetts Watch Industry: Urged President and Senate Committee to adopt appropriate watch tariff protection (adopted).

For the Port of Boston and Massachusetts Transportation

Industry: Kennedy-Saltonstall-McCormack Bill for federal $10-million rehabilitation of Boston Army Base Pier (passed); Kennedy Longshoremen Safety Bill (pending); urged I.C.C. to reopen case denying Port of Boston and New England Railroads opportunity to receive iron-ore shipments (agreed to); joined other New England senators in urging C.A.B. to grant early hearings on extension of Northeast Airlines routes (granted).

"Parliament," Edmund Burke declared in 1774, "is not a congress of ambassadors from different interests; which interests each must maintain, as an agent, and advocate . . . but Parliament is a deliberative assembly of one nation, with one interest, that of the whole; where, not local purposes, not local prejudices, ought to guide, but the general good, resulting from the general reason of the whole. . . ." Kennedy did not subscribe to Burke's thesis for America; as a member of the Senate, representing areas, he would fight for local advantage against the agents of other states. Besides, Edmund Burke had lost his seat in the next election.

What's the Matter with New England?

Late in the afternoon of May 18, 1953, Kennedy gained the floor of the Senate by previous arrangement. Looking up at the presiding officer from a thick manuscript, he started out:

"Mr. President, I wish to address the Senate today in the first of a series of speeches concerning the economic problems of New England and the role of the Federal Government in the solution of such problems. . . ."

He stood in the well of the Senate, lean and erect, with his heavy brown hair dropping down over one eye, and somehow managing to look serious and informal, grave and youthful, all at the same time. For well over two hours he spoke, almost without interruption. He was no prophet of gloom, he said. New Englanders had every reason to be optimistic and little reason to complain. They had, indeed, one of the more prosperous areas of the country. "But, Mr. President, I believe we must speak frankly with respect to the very real problems which threaten that prosperity."

This was, in fact, Kennedy's maiden speech in the Senate. He had spoken briefly on the educational crisis and several other matters, but this represented his first major effort. He had good reason to take the New England approach. Economically, the problems of Massachusetts were inseparable from those of the rest of the region. Politically, this approach enabled the young politician to widen his political base.

Kennedy had prepared his program with the utmost care. As his main researcher and writing assistant, he had hired a young lawyer, Theodore Sorensen. Son of a pro-Roosevelt, insurgent Republican attorney general in Nebraska, Sorensen had joined Kennedy only after deciding that the Senator was a durable liberal. Astute, solid, and resourceful, he soon made himself an expert on a region he had hardly seen. He and Kennedy in turn picked the brains of regional experts, most notably a hardheaded professor of economics at Harvard, Seymour Harris, who had recently written an analysis of the New England economy. Kennedy himself had become something of an expert on key New England problems as a result of the complaints and problems that flowed into his congressional offices, talks with labor, business, and civic leaders during campaign tours, and legislative matters he had worked on in the House.

In his first speech, Kennedy gently chided those who thought nothing could be done, or should be done, about New England's problems, or who denied that such problems existed. He argued that he was really dealing with a national situation, since so many of his region's difficulties were to be found in other depressed areas. He denied that federal help was a panacea. Then he got down to business. Industrial expansion and diversification, tax amortization, incentives, job retraining, aids to small business, resource development, power, flood control, water-pollution control, subsidies for the fishing industry—one by one he carefully dissected the problems and proposed federal action.

Loaded with facts and specific proposals, the speech sounded very much like an economics lecture at Harvard Business School. Kennedy spurned rhetoric and oratorical eloquence. He carefully set the regional problem in the wider and more complex national context. He did not bother with any stories, jokes, or even illustrative references for "human interest." He simply drove straight along his course. His second speech, two days later—equally analytical and again well over two hours in the delivering—dealt with national legislation, such as Taft-Hartley and minimum-wage laws, that should be strengthened for New England's advantage. In his third talk, he discussed general federal policies, such as fair competition and economy in government, that related to New England, and concluded with a thirty-six-point program for the diversification and expansion of commercial and industrial activity, the prevention of further decline and dislocation of business, elimination of tax privileges, the reduction of hardships caused by recession or dislocation.

It was an impressive performance. The Senators who con-

gratulated Kennedy on the floor—mainly liberals like
Humphrey and Lehman—could do so with more than the
usual enthusiasm for a freshman's first major effort. There
was a scattering of applause in New England's newspapers;
Kennedy's conservative friend Basil Brewer, for example,
commended him for his "remarkably keen penetration."

Still, the speech failed as a springboard to national attention. The New York *Times* did not mention it; leaders of
national opinion dismissed it as just another push in the
endless scuffle for local or regional advantage. This anticli-
max was unfortunate for several reasons. For one thing, by
almost any test except eloquence, the speech was a cut far
above even the better senatorial performances. For another,
Kennedy showed a good deal of follow-through. One of his
proposals was that New England senators organize themselves more thoroughly to fight for their goals as a solid
bloc, regardless of party ties. By no means a new idea, such
a project turned mainly on getting an able person to do the
job of co-ordinating the senators' efforts. Sorensen took over
this task, and by working with the other legislative aides he
was able to turn the New England bloc into one of the
strongest regional groupings on the Hill. Kennedy and Sorensen also publicized the program through articles by the
Senator in the New York *Times Magazine*, the *Atlantic*, and
the *New Republic*. Within the next few years, Kennedy could
claim substantial progress on the New England program, especially his proposals involving specific regional needs.

The heart of his program, and probably the most realistic
part of it, called for liberalization of New Deal–Fair Deal
measures such as minimum wages, social security, public
housing, natural-resource development, and the like, for the
excellent reason that such action would be bound to help
New England if only by raising standards in the South and
thus reducing its "unfair" competition. More than this, Kennedy made a brilliant case for regional-development corpora-
tions, he attacked discrimination against Negroes and other
minority groups in government employment, and he even
gave a distinctly favorable nod toward the controversial
Brannan farm plan. Still, the dressing up of all these positions in the garments of regional advantage left Kennedy
more in the posture of a delegate from New England than of
a spokesman for American liberalism.

Within a year of his "New England program," there was
to reach the Senate floor an issue that would subject that
commitment to a harsh test. This was the St. Lawrence Seaway.

It was symptomatic of American political processes that the Seaway was still an issue in 1953. Advocated by President after President, strongly pushed by Canada, endorsed by engineering and transport experts, the project had been thwarted repeatedly by an alliance of domestic interests that felt imperiled by the low rates that the Seaway would permit. No section had opposed the scheme more vigorously than had Massachusetts. As Kennedy himself pointed out, on six different occasions over a period of twenty years not one Massachusetts senator or representative had ever voted for the Seaway.

Other forces put Kennedy under heavy pressure on this issue. The loudest of all the Seaway's foes was the Port of Boston, and thousands of dock workers lived in the Senator's old congressional district. His own grandfather John F. Fitzgerald had stumped American and European cities giving speeches on the port's advantages. His senior colleague, Leverett Saltonstall, was outspoken in opposition to the Seaway and would vote against it. And Kennedy could never forget that he himself had lined up against it in the 1952 campaign as part of his pledge to do MORE for Massachusetts. Reardon had never seen his boss so torn over a decision.

There was more than ordinary interest in the Senate when Kennedy arose to speak on the Seaway bill early in the 1954 session. He admitted that few issues had troubled him as much as this. But he came out emphatically for the bill. Briskly running through a dozen arguments for the Seaway, he based his position mainly on the point that Canada would go ahead with the project anyway—a point he had denied a year and a half earlier in the campaign. He also went to some pains to show that the Port of Boston would be only slightly hurt by the Seaway and indeed would gain ultimately from its benefits to the whole economy.

A "fine and very thoughtful speech," Senator Lehman said. Yet once again Kennedy seemed almost deliberately to drain any element of drama out of his action. His speech was one of his typically dry and logical efforts. He avoided the temptation to say that the Seaway would be of direct and immediate benefit to his state; he coolly admitted that it would not. He openly admitted that one reason he supported the bill was that he wanted the Midwestern senators to help him on New England's needs.

The Seaway was not the only occasion when the young spokesman for New England took a national stand. In the 1954 session he also voted for an amendment to clarify and extend the President's power under the reciprocal-trade program. He was the only New England senator to support the measure. This was Kennedy's general position, however; when it came to specific tariff problems, few senators surpassed him in his zeal for guarding local interests. During the Eighty-third Congress, for example, he asked the administration for higher duties for the watch, fishing, and textile industries against foreign competition. On the other hand, he opposed the old system of legislating tariffs on behalf of particular interests in Congress or its committees; instead, he believed that the interests should present their case to the Tariff Commission under the reciprocal-trade-agreements program.

But his first year as senator was not all work.

The Girl from Newport

At thirty-six, Kennedy was still a bachelor—to the delight of society columnists, who made glittering forecasts out of even his more casual dates. "Many women have hopefully concluded that Kennedy needs looking after," according to an article in the *Saturday Evening Post*. "In their opinion, he is, as a young millionaire senator, just about the most eligible bachelor in the United States—and the least justifiable one."

But the "gay young bachelor," as the *Post* called him, was already courting his future wife. In 1951, while still a congressman, he had met at a dinner party a lovely young student from George Washington University. Jacqueline Lee Bouvier was then twenty-one years old. She was the daughter of Mr. and Mrs. John V. Bouvier, III; her parents had been divorced, and her mother had married Hugh D. Auchincloss. She grew up in New York and Washington, and attended Vassar and the Sorbonne before returning to the Capital. A Catholic of wealthy background, widely traveled, she came from somewhat the same social environment as her future husband.

Jacqueline's exquisite features and lovely hair, her soft, shy charm and beautifully modulated voice almost instantly attracted the Senator. "I leaned across the asparagus," he later remembered, "and asked for a date." Kennedy grew increasingly attached to her, but he was in no hurry. The fight against Lodge was coming up, and a serious decision must wait. At least one good friend doubts that Kennedy would be married today if he had lost his Senate battle.

"It was a very spasmodic courtship," Jacqueline said later. "We didn't see each other for six months, because I went to Europe again and Jack began his summer and fall campaigning in Massachusetts. Then came six months when we were both back. Jack was in Congress and I was in my last year

Eight of the nine Kennedy children, about 1927: *(left to right)* Joseph Jr., John, Rosemary, Kathleen, Eunice, Patricia, Robert and Jean

The Kennedy family at Antibes, France, 1939: *(back row, left to right)* Kathleen, Joseph, Jr., Rosemary, Mrs. Kennedy, Edward; *(middle row, left to right)* John, Eunice, Joseph Kennedy, Sr., Patricia; *(front row)* Robert and Jean

John Kennedy on his graduation from Choate, 1935

Ambassador Joseph P. Kennedy with three of his sons, Joseph, Jr., Robert and John, in Boston in 1939 *(Wide World Photos)*

Lt. John Kennedy *(far right)* with his PT-boat crew off Guadalcanal, July 1943, a few days before their boat was sunk

Congressman John Kennedy with his grandfather John F. Fitzgerald and his father Joseph P. Kennedy, in 1946

John Kennedy campaigning in Boston for the Senate in 1952, with Governor Adlai E. Stevenson and the late Governor Paul A. Dever

John Kennedy and his fiancée Jacqueline Bouvier, sailing in 1953 at Hyannis, Mass. *(Photo by Hy Peskin, Courtesy LIFE Magazine, © 1953, Time Inc.)*

Senator and Mrs. John Kennedy with their baby Caroline, after her christening in December 1957 at St. Patrick's Cathedral in New York, with Archbishop Richard J. Cushing of Boston, who performed the ceremony *(W i d e W o r l d Photos)*

Senator Kennedy with members of his family on the Senate
subway, April 1953: *(left to right)* sisters Jean, Eunice and
Patricia, John Kennedy, Mrs. Robert Kennedy and Robert
(Photo by Ollie Atkins, reproduced by courtesy of the
Saturday Evening Post, *Curtis Publishing Company)*

John Kennedy stepping out for football practice with his
brother Robert and his two assistants, Ted Reardon *(far
left)* and Ted Sorenson *(far right)* *(Photo by Ollie Atkins, reproduced by courtesy of the* Saturday Evening
Post, *Curtis Publishing Company)*

Former President Harry S. Truman *(left)* greets John Kennedy as the Democratic candidate for President, in St. Louis, October 1960. Also present at the speaking engagement was *(right)* Senator Stuart Symington of Missouri *(Wide World)*

Mrs. Eleanor Roosevelt with John Kennedy, outside her New York residence, after a breakfast meeting, October 1960. The Democratic Presidential candidate has a record album of speeches of President Franklin D. Roosevelt, which was presented to him at the meeting *(Wide World)*

Vice-President Richard Nixon and Senator John Kennedy, during a nationally televised debate, broadcast from a New York studio in October 1960 *(Wide World)*

A shower of confetti and paper strips greets John Kennedy in Los Angeles, one week before the Presidential election in November 1960 *(Wide World)*

Inauguration

John Kennedy takes the oath of office as President of the United
States, January 20, 1961, from Chief Justice of the Supreme Court
Earl Warren *(U.P.I.)*

of George Washington University. But it was still spasmodic because he spent half of each week in Massachusetts.

"He'd call me from some oyster bar up there, with a great clinking of coins, to ask me out to the movies the following Wednesday in Washington." Jack, she found, loved Westerns and Civil War pictures.

Kennedy campaigned so hard for the Senate that Jacqueline did not hear from him for six months. But when he came back to Washington as a senator, he resumed his courtship more seriously. Jacqueline was now inquiring photographer for the Washington *Times-Herald*. Developing her pictures she found a dismaying experience, but fellow photographers helped her out, and nobody approached for an interview on the streets of Washington could resist this charming young lady. She found Kennedy disconcertingly intellectual in his approach. Instead of candy and flowers, he presented her with history books such as *The Raven*, Marquis James's biography of Sam Houston, and one of his favorites, John Buchan's autobiographical *Pilgrim's Way*. But Jacqueline was not to be outdone; adept at drawing and sketching, she gave him two books she had illustrated herself.

After two years of a rather helter-skelter relationship, Jack finally proposed and Jacqueline accepted. They were married in St. Mary's Roman Catholic Church in Newport on September 12, 1953, a few weeks after Congress adjourned. A close friend of the Kennedy family, the Most Reverend Richard J. Cushing, then Archbishop of the Archdiocese of Boston, performed the ceremony, celebrating the nuptial mass and reading a special blessing from the Pope. Bob Kennedy was best man. More than 1,200 persons attended a reception at the three-hundred acre estate of the bride's mother and stepfather overlooking Narragansett Bay. Despite the glamorous couple and guests, the affair had political undertones. All senators and many political leaders had been invited; Kennedy's campaign aides were there in force; and the groom's good congressional friend George Smathers, of Florida, was an usher. A crowd of 3,000 broke through police lines and nearly crushed the bride when she arrived for the wedding. They pressed forward again as the newlyweds left the church and posed for photographers. Jack, used to crowds, kept his big smile; Jacqueline, startled, recoiled a bit.

Jacqueline was now officially part of the Kennedy family. It was a formidable experience. When working, the family seemed to infiltrate the whole country. Joe, Sr. still kept his hand in a variety of business and banking affairs. In Chicago, Eunice, former executive secretary of the Justice Department's juvenile-delinquency section, supervised the re-habilitation work of the House of the Good Shepherd. In New York, Jean was an aide to Father James G. Keller, founder of the Christophers, an organization attempting to combat corruption and communism "by urging Christians to enter professions where Communists most often operate—in the fields of government, education, labor relations, litera-ture and entertainment." At St. Coletta, a Catholic school near Milwaukee, Rosemary helped care for mentally retarded children. In California, Patricia, wife of actor Peter Law-ford, assisted in the Family Rosary Crusade, which urged families to pray together once a day. Bob was an attorney in Washington for Senator McCarthy's Government Operations' subcommittee; and Teddy, the youngest, and considered by many the handsomest and friendliest of the three boys, was headed for the University of Virginia Law School.

Although Kennedy and the older of his sisters were now in their thirties, they still behaved like children out of school when they congregated together at Hyannisport. All in-laws, Jacqueline included, had to conform to the hard physical and mental pace. She was introduced to the family's com-petitiveness and watched in amazement a five-year-old Ken-nedy push a four-year-old Kennedy, who promptly went over and pushed a three-year-old. She plunged into family sports —and soon broke an ankle playing touch football. She was forced back on genteel forms of sabotage. Once in a while, she confessed to a reporter, when the Kennedys were all play-ing Monopoly after a strenuous day of outdoor sports, she got so sleepy that she deliberately made a mistake to end the game.

"Does Jack mind?" she was asked.

A gleam crept into her dark eyes. "Not if I'm on the other side." Like her husband's mother, she may have felt that a little independence was the price of survival in the clamorous Kennedy family. Once when Jack saw her pensive and quiet and offered her a penny for her thoughts, she answered gravely, "But they're *my* thoughts and they wouldn't be my thoughts any more if I told them!"

Guests were also subjected to the gruelling schedule. One of them later tabulated a terrifying set of "Rules for Visit-ing the Kennedys," which read in part:

"Prepare yourself by reading the Congressional Record, US News & World Report, Time, Newsweek, Fortune, The Nation, How to Play Sneaky Tennis and The Democratic Digest. Memorize at least three good jokes. Anticipate that each Kennedy will ask you what you think of another Ken-nedy's a) dress, b) hairdo, c) backhand, d) latest public achievement. Be sure to answer 'Terrific.' This should get you through dinner. Now for the football field. It's 'touch' but it's murder. If you don't want to play, don't come. If you do come, play, or you'll be fed in the kitchen and nobody will speak to you. Don't let the girls fool you. Even pregnant, they can make you look silly. If Harvard played Touch, they'd be on the varsity. Above all, don't suggest any plays, even if you played quarterback at school. The Kennedys have the signal-calling department sewed up, and all of them have A-pluses in leadership. If one of them makes a mistake, keep still. . . . But don't stand still. Run madly on every play, and make a lot of noise. Don't appear to be having too much fun though. They'll accuse you of not taking the game seriously enough. Don't criticize the other team, either. It's bound to be full of Kennedys, too, and the Kennedys don't like that sort of thing. To become really popular you must show raw guts. To show raw guts, fall on your face now and then. Smash into the house once in a while, going after a pass. Laugh off a twisted ankle, or a big hole torn in your best suit. They like this. It shows you take the game as seriously as they do.

"But remember. Don't be too good. Let Jack run around you now and then. He's their boy. . . ."

8 ★ McCARTHYISM: THE ISSUE THAT WOULD NOT DIE

The year 1954 should have been the happiest in Kennedy's life. He was newly married and he was coming into his own in the Senate. Actually, it was probbly the unhappiest.

Although very much in love, the young couple found adjustment difficult under the trying circumstances of a politician's life. Kennedy was often away in Massachusetts or elsewhere on political errands. Jacqueline confided to a reporter that sometimes when he was home he was so wrapped up in his work that she might "as well be in Alaska." The couple bought a $125,000 house in Virginia, but Jacqueline at times felt rather lonely there.

A more grievous situation was Kennedy's health. Friends at the wedding had worried that he might not be able to kneel at the altar, but he had done so with aplomb and then had borne up well during three hours of shaking hands with hundreds of guests in the reception line. During 1954 the pain in his back became almost unbearable. He tried a number of recommended remedies but nothing seemed to work. To ease his pain, he installed a rocking chair in his office and a couch for lying flat, but still to little avail. By the summer of 1954, he was continuously on crutches. As if all this were not enough, there was always the prospect of malarial attacks; he had suffered from one only a few weeks before his marriage.

The worst aspect of 1954, however, was the drift of things

in the Senate. It was clear by mid-1954 that the upper chamber was headed for a showdown over McCarthy and his tactics. A showdown over McCarthy would also mean a showdown for Kennedy. He had evaded the McCarthy issue in his 1952 campaign and ever since. Now both friends and foes were waiting to see which way Kennedy would jump when forced off the fence. Market-basket liberalism had been enough to show his progressivism in the House; but not in the Senate. Now he would be tested on the grounds of ideological liberalism embracing individual freedom as well as social welfare. "Democracy," Maury Maverick said, "equals groceries plus liberty." There was no question where Kennedy stood on groceries; but where did he stand on civil liberty? Kennedy knew he was under the scrutiny of liberals to whom McCarthyism had become the most crucial of all issues.

Kennedy and the Liberals

By 1954, liberals in Massachusetts felt they had some justifiable suspicions about Kennedy. First of all, they were concerned about his family and friends. His father may have been a New Dealer under Roosevelt, but he had also made his millions through financial speculations, and he was close to Joe McCarthy, and to Herbert Hoover, Robert A. Taft, and other conservatives and isolationists. Brother Bob worked for McCarthy. Kennedy's closest friends seemed to be mainly conservative. Some liberals assumed that because these people were close to Kennedy they necessarily determined his political viewpoint.

Liberals were troubled also by some of Kennedy's political allies. The New Bedford *Standard-Times* was still solidly in his corner, and there was the special case of the Boston *Post*. Published by John Fox, and avidly pro-McCarthy, the *Post* had supported Kennedy in 1952 and still said nice things about him occasionally. So did many respectable and reliable papers, but liberal distaste for the *Post* was so great that the other papers were overlooked. Then, too, Kennedy had republished in the *Congressional Record* a series of articles by Fox on communism that were a veiled summons to preventive warfare against Russia.

Some liberals also remembered unhappily Kennedy's remarks about the Supreme Court decision in the Christoffel case. As a member of the House Labor Committee in 1947, Kennedy had called for perjury charges against Harold Christoffel, who was a leader of the notorious Communist-dominated strike against Allis-Chalmers early in 1941.

Although Kennedy's call for an indictment had been rather hasty, he was vindicated when Christoffel was convicted of perjury and sent to jail. Later, however, the Supreme Court, in a five-to-four decision, set the verdict aside on the grounds that the Labor Committee lacked a majority in attendance when Christoffel committed perjury. This decision was greeted by Kennedy, in a joint statement with a conservative Republican congressman, as "most regrettable" and a "travesty on justice." Christoffel was subsequently retried and successfully jailed, but Kennedy's remark about the Supreme Court disturbed those who saw in the courts the last bulwark against violations of due process.

Kennedy, moreover, had not hidden his disesteem for liberals who seemed to follow what he considered a doctrinaire "line." During the 1952 election, John P. Mallan, then a teaching fellow at Harvard, and more recently a Smith College professor and a Massachusetts government official, had reported in the *New Republic* on a seminar at the university that Kennedy had addressed two years before, in 1950. According to Mallan, the Congressman had said, among other things, that he could see no reason why we were fighting in Korea, that he felt not enough had been done about communists in government, that he rather respected Joe McCarthy and thought "he knew Joe pretty well, and he may have something," and that he had no great respect for Dean Acheson or indeed almost any member of the Fair Deal Administration. Friends of Kennedy contended that Mallan had taken these points out of context, that some of them were exaggerated, and that Kennedy himself overemphasized them to arouse his academic audience, but enough truth remained in the report to put liberals even further on guard. One political scientist who was then in the seminar as a graduate student reports in retrospect that Kennedy at the meeting had struck him as "an ambitious and likable young poitico on the rise" who reacted to the McCarthy issue with "nonchalance and minimal concern." "It appeared to me that he quite sincerely thought the problem of rent control was considerably more important (because of his constituency) and more worthy of his attention than was this rather abstruse and philosophical concern which was so exercising us intellectuals. . . . His pitch was not philosophical but mainly practical—he was out to serve his district and to get reelected on the basis of his record of service. He did not preclude the possibility that the constituency interest could be and should be reconciled with some conception of a broader national interest. Yet there was very little beyond 'district' which he appeared to have found attractive.

"There was, in fact, little of what he said which could be used to identify him as a partisan Democrat. He appeared to be not very interested in the party as a vehicle through which broader political values could be realized; rather the party was a label which was the most expedient to run under in his district. . . ."

Another member of the seminar remembers it the same way but from a different perspective. "Certainly Kennedy's judgments on McCarthy were more personal and political than ideological. Indeed, one of the striking and refreshing things about Kennedy at that time was that he did not look at political issues through the stereotyped lenses which we young Harvard liberal intellectuals used. In this respect, and in retrospect, it seems to me that Kennedy may then have been ahead of his times. The language of politics which he was talking, as a still young representative, is common today but it was new then in an era still dominated by the political semantics of the New Deal–Fair Deal."

As if being burned by the Harvard incident was not enough, Kennedy was again indiscreet in an interview with Paul F. Healy of the *Saturday Evening Post*, soon after becoming Senator. Noting that Kennedy resisted any effort to tag him with an ideological label and that he was annoyed by letters that chided him for not being a "true liberal," Healy quoted him as saying:

"I'd be very happy to tell them that I'm not a liberal at all. I never joined the Americans for Democratic Action or the American Veterans Committee. I'm not comfortable with those people."

Organized liberalism in Massachusetts had long been beleaguered in state politics. The Republican Boston *Herald* flayed it for its economic and social policies; the Democratic Boston *Post* attacked it for its strong stand on civil liberties. Office seekers sought quiet liberal support but not open endorsements. Any time a statehouse legislator had nothing better to do, he baited the Massachusetts Civil Liberties Union or the state chapter of Americans for Democratic Action. The crowning blow came late in 1953, when former Congressman Foster Furcolo, presented to an ADA convention as one who had achieved a fine liberal record in Congress with ADA support, proceeded to deliver a keynote address in which he told the state ADA that it was a hindrance to the liberal efforts of the Democratic party and should disband.

Was Kennedy, liberals asked, just another state politician who saw liberalism as only a bread-and-butter proposition? The remark reported in the *Saturday Evening Post* seemed to give the answer. Indignant letters came to the Senator's office.

Answering an inquiry from the secretary of a local AVC chapter in Massachusetts, Kennedy wrote that he could not remember making such a comment about the veterans group. He had not joined AVC, Kennedy explained, because he felt after the war that progressive-minded World War II veterans would have more influence in politics if they joined established veterans' groups and tried to direct them along lines beneficial both to the veterans and the public, instead of joining an exclusively World War II veterans' group that could not develop a large-enough membership to make its influence felt. Kennedy added that he had discussed the matter as far back as 1945 with Charles Bolte, a founding father of AVC.

An ADA housewife in a Boston suburb was outspoken. "You don't have to join ADA or the AVC," she wrote, "but why do you express your discomfort about associations which you not only accept, but which you court when they can do you any good? I don't know whether you will ever develop a 'political philosophy'; however, it would seem to be a good idea for a United States Senator to renounce opportunism for a certain degree of consistency. As one of the people with whom you 'are not comfortable' may I say that I have talked to many people who are uncomfortable about you."

He hoped, Kennedy replied, that ADA did not intend to base its attitude toward him on a statement appearing in a magazine. "We both have known that my record was not in accordance with the program of ADA on all occasions, but I never did believe that uniformity of opinion was what that organization required." He noted that his correspondent had objected to getting form letters on his policy views. Did she prefer that he write different letters expressing different viewpoints to constituents who take the opposite view on a particular question?

"I cannot hope to say anything in this letter which can make your friends or yourself more 'comfortable' about me, for that is a question that is wholly within your judgment; but I do appreciate the frankness with which you wrote."

Whatever his differences with ADA, Kennedy was ready to defend it, too. He wrote a Boston insurance man who was livid over the Senator's "sponsorship" of an ADA function that he was not a sponsor of ADA but of an ADA dinner in memory of Franklin D. Roosevelt at which his colleague Senator Herbert Lehman was a guest.

"I do not agree with many of the positions taken by ADA," he said, but "I cannot find any evidence that would justify your assertion that the ADA has not always been a strongly anti-communist organization. . . ." It was wrong, he added, to blur over specific matters with general charges.

On the Fence

When Kennedy first came to the Senate in January 1953, McCarthy was nearing the zenith of his career. For three years, he had bedeviled the Truman administration and the Democratic party with charges of laxness on security measures and even of procommunism. He had called General George C. Marshall "a man steeped in falsehood" and part of a "conspiracy on a scale so immense as to dwarf any previous such venture in the history of man." He had made reckless charges against individuals and had failed notably to back them up.

His Republican colleagues had looked on, half in loathing at the Senator's dishonesty and vulgarity, half in sheepish admiration of the trouble he caused Democrats. A man of the apparent integrity of Robert Taft held that "the procommunist policies of the State Department fully justified Joe McCarthy in his demand for an investigation." On the other hand, several Republican Senators, including Margaret Chase Smith, of Maine, and George D. Aiken, of Vermont, had submitted an anti-McCarthy manifesto in the form of a "Declaration of Conscience," but this had led to naught. By 1952, Republicans were scrambling all over one another to enlist McCarthy's help in the election, and Dwight Eisenhower, campaigning in Wisconsin, had dropped a defense he had planned to make of George Marshall, his old comrade in arms, apparently to escape a clash with McCarthy.

Some Republicans had predicted that a victory for their party would be the best way to deal with the Wisconsin Senator. "McCarthyism would disappear overnight if Eisenhower were elected," asserted the independent Washington *Post* in March 1952. Such hopes were quickly dashed. Soon McCarthy, now chairman, and, in effect, dictator, of the Government Operations Committee and of its investigations subcommittee, was actually sharing with Eisenhower power over foreign policy and military administration. Few Americans—and certainly no senator—made Eisenhower so sick at heart as McCarthy, though the President avoided an open break. In the end, McCarthy was to deliver a formal apology to the American people for having endorsed Eisenhower for President.

The struggle spilled over into every corner of American politics, and in no state more than in Massachusetts. For there on one side were civil libertarians—some entrenched in academic halls, many of them Democrats—and high-minded Republicans appalled at McCarthy's destructiveness to their country and party; on the other, "practical" Republicans who saw McCarthyism as a bridge to groups who had been "captive" to the Massachusetts Democracy, and Democrats, particularly the Irish, who seemed to be attracted to McCarthyism. Each party was sharply split over the issue, and so were the press, the clergy, and the bar. Probably in no single area of the country could more open and violent feeling for McCarthy be found than in Boston. It was strongest in areas such as Kennedy's old congressional district, where it tied in with Catholic hostility to communism; with immigrants' hatred for Russian control of their countries, as in the case of the Polish-Americans; and with low sensitivity to the civil-liberties tradition.

"How do people feel about McCarthy these days?" Senator Lodge once asked Governor Dever.

"Your people don't think much of him," answered the Democratic Dever, "but I'm afraid mine do."

Kennedy's mail mirrored the deep rifts among his constituents. "Surely when you received that degree from Notre Dame," a woman wrote from a western Massachusetts mill city, "the Holy Ghost should have descended upon you and enlightened you! Therefore I cannot understand why you are not completely behind Senator McCarthy and overjoyed at being able to work with him on a committee so vital to our nation's welfare."

She mentioned a talk McCarthy had recently given at Smith: "He left that jeering ill-bred group of girls with something to think about. . . . And believe me not one of the six Sullivan girls will attend Smith College if that's what they turn out there!!"

From a noted professor at Harvard Law School came an eloquent plea in the wake of a McCarthy foray into Boston: "The issue, as I see it," he wrote Kennedy, "does not turn upon the morality, the legality, or the wisdom of the position which the two witnesses [before McCarthy] took. It turns rather upon the responsibility of the Senate to see that the processes of government are not abused and degraded by one of its members. What was exhibited to the New England community by television and radio was a spectacle of governmental power being exercised with truculent brutality. . . .

"When legislation transgresses constitutional limits," his letter went on, "the courts are authorized to declare it unconstitutional. . . . The Supreme Court, however, has indicated that it is not vested with extensive powers to control the conduct of legislative investigators. As a consequence the community lacks the usual safeguards by which decency is secured. Those safeguards, accordingly, must be provided by the Congress itself, and if the Senate puts loyalty to one tyrant among its members above its responsibilities to preserve decency in government there will be no security for tradition.

"Surely it is better that two small and misguided radicals who have publicly identified themselves and admitted the folly of their earlier ways should go free than that the Senate, by responding to Senator McCarthy's wishes, should endorse his indecencies, and thus bring our government into a contempt far larger and more destructive than that of the two witnesses."

How did Kennedy deal with these competing views? In his correspondence he straddled the fence. McCarthy's investigation of the trade of certain allies with Red China served a useful purpose, he wrote a Boston newspaperman. (This report on trade by the McCarthy subcommittee, for which his brother Bob was largely responsible, was characterized by Arthur Krock as "an example of Congressional investigation at the highest level. . . .") But, said Kennedy, "other inquiries which have been reported in the press would not appear to have produced results of sufficient value to justify the bitter controversies raised by the methods employed."

"I appreciate knowing of your support of Senator McCarthy," he wrote a Fitchburg woman. "I have always believed that we must be alert to the menace of Communism within our country as well as its advances on the international front. In so doing, however, we must be careful we maintain our traditional concern that in punishing the guilty we protect the innocent." To the Harvard Law School professor, he wrote: "Inasmuch as I am a member of the full Committee on Government Operations, I have in the past given some consideration and raised some questions concerning the contempt citations requested by Senator McCarthy. In such cases, however, I have relied upon legal, primarily constitutional grounds. A citation for contempt is in itself a matter largely of legal form, which has little or no relation to our dislike of the methods employed by the committee chairman or our sympathy for the difficulties encountered by the witness. To attempt to take a position whereby contempt citations would be refused against those who had no legal basis for conduct which is contemptuous by definition would be to attempt to overthrow all past precedents of the Senate and raise serious doubts as to the long-range implications of such a stand." To Kennedy, the problem seemed essentially a legal rather than a moral one, and it was on the legal aspect, he implied politely, that he would especially appreciate the professor's advice.

When pressed, Kennedy could make a choice. Since the stakes—national security—were so high, he wrote a student at Oberlin, "we must resolve every doubt, in the case of government employees and defense workers, in a manner which will insure the greatest security to our country." To a Cambridge correspondent, however, he said that he favored Senate Resolution 16, which would permit the Senate under certain circumstances to discharge a committee from further pursuing certain investigations. He also supported Senate Concurrent Resolution 10, he said, which would assure a number of personal rights to committee witnesses and would subject to disciplinary action and to censure any member of Congress failing to observe the requirements.

Kennedy evaded the issue but he did not contradict himself; he took pains to remind the libertarian of the needs of security and the McCarthyites of the claims of liberty and due process. He was apparently unsure of exactly where he stood between the (ostensibly) competing claims of security and liberty. What he did know was that the controversy was getting out of bounds. The intensity of the struggle offended him; he could not throw himself into the battle as so many Americans and even his fellow senators were doing. He was consistent in his noncommitment, but to many this was just another way of saying that he was shilly-shallying.

"Please explain your inconsistencies, Senator," a pro-McCarthy Bostonian wrote on the envelope of a letter. Giving the usual pro-and-con answer, Kennedy went on to say a bit sadly, "The storm that has swirled about Senator McCarthy's head has caused many level-headed individuals to become emotionally upset and violent pro and anti attitudes have been struck. . . ."

"The Honor and Dignity of the Senate"

The very storm that Kennedy deplored made a showdown inevitable. He could take a compromise position in letters to correspondents, but how would he vote when the showdown came? The Senate record is clear. On almost every policy issue involving McCarthyism, Kennedy voted against McCarthy. Yet on the issue of McCarthy himself, Kennedy took no stand.

During his first year in the Senate, Kennedy's personal relations with McCarthy were not close, but they were amicable. The Wisconsin Senator had been a friend of Joseph P. Kennedy for some time, visiting him in Hyannisport and talking with him on his yacht, and the son had known him primarily through his father. Although Kennedy was appointed to McCarthy's Government Operations Committee, the members did not meet as a full unit often enough to bring the two men into frequent contact in the Senate—it was the committee's subcommittee on investigations that conducted the notorious hearings. Bob Kennedy worked for the subcommittee from January to August 1953, when he resigned following altercations with Roy Cohn; he was reappointed as counsel for the Democratic minority when it returned in 1954 after boycotting McCarthy. But Bobby was never one of McCarthy's intimates.

When Irwin Ross, a reporter for the New York *Post*, asked Kennedy in 1953 what he thought of McCarthy, he answered: "Not very much. But I get along with him. When I was in the House, I used to get along with Marcantonio and with Rankin. As long as they don't step in my way, I don't want to get into personal fights."

In his first vote on a McCarthy issue—the appropriation of funds for McCarthy's investigations, January 1953—Kennedy went along with him, as did virtually every other senator. A year later, the Senate again granted its investigator in chief a substantial sum, with only Senator William Fulbright, of Arkansas, voting "no." "The truth is," Richard Rovere has aptly said in reporting this incident, "that everyone in the Senate, or just about everyone, was scared stiff of him. Everyone then believed that McCarthy had the power to destroy those who opposed him, and evidence for this was not lacking. Evidence was not conclusive, either, but politicians cannot afford to deal in finalities and ultimate truths; they abide, by and large, by probabilities and reasonable assumptions and the law of averages. . . ." And the fact was that McCarthy had campaigned against the reelection of four Democratic senators, and every one had been defeated.

Kennedy was not scared stiff of McCarthy, but he did respect his power to make trouble in Massachusetts if he set his mind to it. Kennedy was not worried about his own reelection, which would not come up until 1958 anyway, but he hated being directly involved in the violent controversy that followed McCarthy wherever he went. As he said later in a speech on the censure motion which was never delivered, "I am not insensitive to the fact that my constituents perhaps contain a greater proportion of devotees on each side of this matter than the constituency of any other Senator. . . ."

Still, when issues arose that were widely viewed as tests of a senator's position on McCarthy, Kennedy voted against the Wisconsin Republican. Two such tests that came early in his first year involved Senate confirmation of presidential appointments that McCarthy heartily opposed. One of these was Eisenhower's nomination of James B. Conant, former president of Harvard, as ambassador to Germany. Kennedy supported the nomination. His position was made easier in that Saltonstall also strongly supported Conant, an old Harvard classmate of his, but harder in that Conant had been accused by John T. Flynn and others of hostility to parochial schools. A few weeks later, Kennedy was one of seventy-four senators who voted to confirm Charles Bohlen —whom McCarthy had fought—as ambassador to Russia.

When it came to voting on plums for McCarthy's good friends, Kennedy would not go along. At the beginning of the 1954 session, Kennedy was one of a liberal bloc of twenty-five senators to vote against the appointment of McCarthy's friend Robert E. Lee to the Federal Communications Commission. McCarthy was so committed to this appointment that, according to friends of the Massachusetts Senator, he never spoke to Kennedy again. In June 1954, Kennedy voted with many other Democratic senators in favor of a move, in effect, to declare that R. W. S. McLeod, who had been making pro-McCarthy speeches while running the State Department's security program, came under the Hatch Act, which regulated political activity by government employees, and hence was not authorized to make political speeches. (In 1957, he voted with the minority of twenty against the appointment of McLeod as ambassador to Ireland.)

The Boston Post and other Massachusetts McCarthyites had been viewing Kennedy's votes with growing alarm. He "voted with the crew who are out to get R. W. Scott McLeod, who has been cleaning the communist coddlers out of the State Department," the Post charged. "Senator Kennedy hasn't discovered that cleaning communists out of government is not a party matter. If he wants to maintain his political viability he ought to consult a few solid and loyal Democrats in Massachusetts who are every bit as determined to clean communism out of government as is Senator McCarthy." But two months later, Kennedy led the fight in committee against another friend of McCarthy, former Senator Owen Brewster of Maine, whom McCarthy wanted to install as the committee's chief counsel.

All these issues swirling around McCarthy came to a head in August 1954. Kennedy voted against an immunity bill designed to compel waiver of a witness's rights under the Fifth Amendment, as he had also voted against a similar bill the year before. In neither case, however, was the vote recorded, and Kennedy was not one of the ten senators to stand up to be recorded against the bill. A week after opposing the immunity bill a second time, Kennedy voted to cite Corliss Lamont for contempt of Congress. In committee, however, Kennedy had fought the citation; he charged that McCarthy was attacking Lamont on the basis of his writings and that this was unconstitutional. McCarthy was disconcerted for a moment. At this point, a Democratic senator said: "When somebody walks like a duck, flies like a duck, and quacks like a duck, it's pretty certain he is a duck." While the press waited outside the door, Kennedy stood his ground; finally the committee agreed to ask the Justice Department to comment on the constitutionality of citing Lamont. Eventually, that agency adjudged it constitutional, and then Kennedy voted for it in the Senate. Among the Senate liberals Senators Hubert Humphrey and Stuart Symington, for example, also approved the Lamont citation.

At this time, the Senate was considering measures to strengthen efforts against domestic communists. Kennedy voted for an amendment to the Subversive Activities Control Act to establish a commission to recommend a co-ordinated program for security screening of persons in defense activities, and to eliminate duplication in existing programs. Designed as a substitute for harsher anticommunist measures that were pending, the amendment failed. A few days later, Senator Humphrey, who had voted for the substitute, took the floor with a speech that surprised many present.

"I am tired of reading headlines about being 'soft' toward communism," the Minnesota liberal exclaimed. "I am tired of reading headlines about being a leftist." It was time, he said, "to come to grips with the Communist issue." He favored a simple proposal—to outlaw the Communist party. This proposal passed with the support of every senator on the floor, including Kennedy. McCarthy watched the proceedings sardonically. When he lived on a farm as a boy, he told the Senate a few days later, he had to dig out skunks that were killing chicks. "It was a very unpleasant job. It could not be done by passing a resolution against skunks. The nice little boys could pass a resolution against skunks, but the nice little boys did not help us dig them out. It was an unpleasant task; and sometimes after we got through, we were not too welcome sitting next to our friends in church. . . ."

When McCarthy said this he was already on the run. The Senate had had about enough. On July 31, after the electric drama of the televised Army-McCarthy hearings, Senator Ralph Flanders had brought in a resolution of censure: "*Resolved,* That the conduct of the Senator from Wisconsin is unbecoming a Member of the United States Senate, is contrary to senatorial traditions, and tends to bring the Senate into disrepute, and such conduct is hereby condemned." Kennedy sat through most of the tempestuous debate in the Senate but spoke only once. This was to correct a misstatement by a pro-McCarthy senator about the Annie Lee Moss case; Kennedy remarked parenthetically that he felt that there were "no adequate grounds for censure in the Annie Lee Moss case because of the questions asked by the junior Senator from Wisconsin" but that some of the committee counsel's interrogation was not adequately based.

Kennedy decided to vote for the censure resolution but not on Flanders' terms. In a speech prepared for delivery but never given, Kennedy carefully distinguished his position from that taken by the liberal bloc. The issue involved "neither the motives nor sincerity of the Junior Senator from Wisconsin," he said. "We are not asked to vote for or against Senator McCarthy." Kennedy did not feel free, he said, to base his vote on the "long-past misconduct" of McCarthy, to which neither he nor Flanders had publicly objected at the time. Nor could he vote for censure in order to conciliate foreign opinion.

"The hostility showed to Senator McCarthy by those outside the United States is not, in my opinion, altogether the result of his own actions, however serious they may be, but rather because he offers an easy mark to those who wish to attack the prestige and power of the United States. Even if Senator McCarthy were removed from public life, those same forces would speedily fill the void left by his passing. . . . It is because we are the leaders of the Free World that we receive this ceaseless hostility, rather than because of any single man or any single action." Kennedy did not agree either that McCarthy had split the country wide apart. "Indeed, I think the action we are about to take, precipitated as it has been by the Senator from Vermont, will have serious repercussions upon the social fabric of this country and must be so recognized."

Still he would vote for censure. Why? Because McCarthy had attacked the honor and dignity of the Senate. Kennedy described in detail the abusive language and threats of reprisal used against the Army by Roy Cohn and acquiesced in by McCarthy. As chairman, McCarthy must take responsibility for a staff member's acts, even though the censure motion "is more concerned with the dignity and honor of this body than with the personal characteristics of any individual Senator."

"Thus the Senate is again faced with the necessity of reasserting its honor and dignity in the face of any abuse of those privileges affirmed by one of its members," Kennedy went on. But he insisted again that this was the only basis of his decision, that broader issues were not involved. "Our action today, as in the previous motions of censure adopted by this body, does not involve the vindication or condemnation of an individual Senator. It does not involve his views and objectives in years gone by"—only the dignity and the honor of the Senate.

But there was to be no showdown in the Senate that day on Flanders' resolution of censure. Senate Majority Leader, Republican William Knowland, hotly opposed to the resolution, moved the establishment of a select committee to consider the charges. The idea was a godsend to Saltonstall, for it would probably postpone the need for a stand on his part until after his coming election contest with Foster Furcolo. A liberal group opposed the move because it feared that the psychological moment to chastise McCarthy would be lost. Kennedy and Saltonstall were among the seventy-five senators who favored Knowland's postponement measure, which would also mean a postponement of Kennedy's own speech. Some liberals, like Wayne Morse, who voted with the majority did so partly on the grounds that McCarthy had the right to answer charges with aid of counsel before an investigating committee. A liberal bloc of twelve senators opposed postponement, arguing that McCarthy's rights could be fully protected in censure deliberations in the whole chamber. Among this group of twelve were Lehman and Fulbright, who had over the years done battle with McCarthy, and Douglas and Humphrey. Both Douglas and Humphrey favored an immediate showdown, although they had to face election contests in the fall.

"A Reasonable Indictment"?

There would be a showdown—but Kennedy was not to be part of it. He had sat through the debate on McCarthy in increasing physical distress. As soon as the Senate recessed, he went to Hyannisport for rest; still he felt no better. He could stand the pain no longer. For some time, drastic surgery had been considered, but doctors were reluctant to undertake a perilous operation unless it was imperative.

Before Kennedy could go to the hospital, however, there was one more unpleasant incident to conclude the general unpleasantness of the politics of 1954. During the fall, Saltonstall and Furcolo were going at each other with hammer and tongs in the race for the Senate. Kennedy's loyalties were sharply divided. He had worked closely with Saltonstall in the Senate on the New England program and help for Massachusetts, and he liked the old blue blood personally. With Furcolo, an aggressive, attractive Yale man and now state treasurer, Kennedy's relations had long been on rather distant terms. Furcolo was a Democrat and headed the state's campaign ticket, but Kennedy felt that Furcolo had refused to help him in 1952 because of fear of alienating Lodge supporters. Now Furcolo felt that Kennedy refused to help him because of the risk of alienating Saltonstall. The Furcolo forces were edgy because Kennedy had long played up his bipartisan co-operation with Saltonstall. Indeed, in September, just at the point when Furcolo was denouncing his opponent for doing too little for Massachusetts, Kennedy and Saltonstall issued a joint communiqué listing the achievements of the New England bloc and playing up their own co-operation.

So the stage was set for an open breach. It came one night after Kennedy had been persuaded to endorse the whole Democratic ticket, including Furcolo, in a joint television appearance in Boston. Kennedy flew up from Hyannisport despite a fever. A few minutes before the two men were to go on the air, along with Robert Murphy, candidate for governor, Furcolo looked over the script and complained to Kennedy that his endorsement was not strong enough. Kennedy's nerves were already stretched taut because he had been sitting in the studio over an hour waiting for Furcolo to arrive.

"Foster, you have a hell of a nerve coming in here and asking for these last-minute changes," Kennedy said heatedly.

"Jack, it's not an outright endorsement," Furcolo protested.

After a short altercation, Kennedy reached for his crutches and hobbled out of the studio and into a men's room. The studio was in an uproar. Murphy went out and pleaded with Kennedy to return, and at the last minute he did so, but he omitted any specific reference to Furcolo. He gave his endorsement simply to Murphy and the Democratic ticket. Banner headlines a few days later proclaimed a split between the two Democrats. Many in Massachusetts considered the rivalry in part a sign of the mutual suspicion between the Irish and the Italians.

The next day, Kennedy entered the hospital for surgery on his back. He remained there several months. He was still in the hospital when the censure motion finally came to a vote, on December 2. He was listed as "absent by leave of the Senate because of illness." The verdict went against McCarthy, 67 to 22, with only a small band of Republicans, and not a single Democrat, staying with him. The main basis of the censure had been changed, however, from the long-standing charges against McCarthy for general misconduct to a list of specific statements he had made about members of the censuring committee.

The verdict was in on McCarthy, and he never again would be a power in the Senate. But, in later years, some brought in a verdict against Kennedy. It was charged that he had been weak and evasive about McCarthy and about McCarthyism and should have officially notified the Senate as to his stand on censure even though he could not leave the hospital to vote, or he could have had his vote "paired" with that of another absent senator planning to vote the other way, as did all the rest of the absent senators.

What are the facts on the verdict against Kennedy?

On the one hand:

1. On motions involving McCarthy's own perquisites, such as funds for investigation committees, Kennedy voted for McCarthy, as did almost every other senator.

2. On issues that seemed to Kennedy to involve the drawing of a fine line between the claims of individual liberty and the claims of national security, Kennedy gave priority to the latter.

On the other hand:

1. On clear issues of civil liberties, Kennedy voted against McCarthy.

2. On appointments McCarthy favored, Kennedy voted against him.

On the one hand *and* the other hand:

1. In blocking the Flanders motion, Kennedy voted against the liberal anti-McCarthy bloc and in favor of setting up a censure committee. According to Washington observers, the Flanders motion might well have failed; the committee did censure McCarthy, and the censure stuck in the Senate, with heavy cost to the Wisconsin Senator. But a majority vote against McCarthy in August, if it could have been mustered, might have been at least as damaging.

2. If censure had come to a vote in August, Kennedy

would have spoken and voted for it, on the narrow basis of the "honor and dignity of the Senate."

3. Kennedy was ill and did not, and physically could not, vote on the final censure, nor did he give any indication of his views. It is almost certain that if present he would have voted for censure, on the same narrow grounds as he had planned to do in August. However, he did not take a public stand from 1950, when McCarthy first made McCarthyism a public issue, to 1954, when the Senate finally voted censure, or, indeed, for a long time thereafter.

So much for the record. The fact remains that nothing has caused Kennedy more trouble in recent years than his failure to vote on the final censure. During his quest for the vice-presidency and later the presidency, a sharp question from the audience on the McCarthy issue was the one thing that could ruffle his ordinarily immaculate composure. His mixed record on McCarthyism was the number-one issue for most liberals, and some of these had influence in national conventions. McCarthyism, in short, years after McCarthy's death, was the "issue that would not die." The whole eposide raises three important questions:

Why did Kennedy take the censure stand that he did? How does he feel about his stand now, and about the liberals' criticism of it? How has he dealt with the issue in the years since?

The first question is the most crucial of the three—and its answer the most difficult. Anti-McCarthy senators followed, in general, two different lines of attack on McCarthy. Flanders, a mild-mannered Vermont Republican who was slow to boil but could boil hard, felt that McCarthy posed a supreme moral issue. His censure resolution was no legal document, but an expression of outrage. The liberal bloc supported him on these grounds, as well, of course, as on other grounds.

The other anti-McCarthy line, finally taken by the censure committee itself, was a more legalistic and technical one. McCarthy had violated the proprieties and written and unwritten rules of the Senate. He should be curbed as a lawbreaker, but only after all due procedures were followed. Giving McCarthy the benefit of the doubt, the censure committee rejected charge after charge brought in by Flanders and the liberals. They could not ignore, however, McCarthy's dishonorable treatment of senators and Senate committees.

Of the two approaches, Kennedy preferred the second. Always a bit detached and emotionally uncommitted, he tended to view McCarthy more as a procedural problem than a moral one.

In a way, this is curious, because McCarthy symbolized everything Kennedy personally detested. Vulgar, bullying, crude, cynical, dishonest, McCarthy represented the mucker element in politics that Kennedy had fought in Massachusetts. McCarthy sneered at the traditions, orderly procedures, and senatorial good manners that Kennedy valued so highly. The Senator from Wisconsin was, indeed, a rule breaker and hence a subversive. But nonetheless Kennedy never spoke up for or against McCarthy; he voted his conviction on issues of McCarthyism and let it go at that.

Why, then, did Kennedy take such a narrow position on a matter that to many Americans—Democrats and Republicans, conservatives and liberals—was the transcendent moral issue of their time?

One reason was his view that since the main indictment of McCarthy turned on his contempt for due process and fair play, any counterattack on McCarthy must scrupulously conform to proper procedures. "We had all voted to seat McCarthy," Kennedy says today. "We had voted him funds. Any question up to January 1953 should have been fought over when he came in. There is an old doctrine in equity law that 'he who doesn't speak when he should speak therefore loses the right to speak.' McCarthy, after all, had been elected by the people of Wisconsin in the fall of 1952—he was their choice to represent them in the Senate. The Senate had acquiesced by seating him, making him chairman of the committee, giving him funds. If there was any objection to his conduct prior to 1953, the fight should have been made in January 1953 when he was seated." As for the Flanders approach, Kennedy felt that McCarthy was entitled to a specific indictment, not just disapproval. "Hell, if you get into the question of just disapproving of Senators, you're going to be in some difficulty. . . . We have never exercised our judgment on our peers very vigorously, and it's probably just as well."

This view of Kennedy's, that the McCarthy situation required due process, also was behind his failure to make his position known at the time of the final censure. The Senate was acting like a jury, and no juror, Kennedy feels, can cast his ballot from a hospital sickbed—especially when the charges were not the original Flanders indictment or the Cohn-Schine affair but McCarthy's treatment of a committee that was sitting while Kennedy was in the hospital.

Another reason, however—perhaps a more important reason for Kennedy's mixed stand on McCarthy—was much more personal. His brother Bob was a member of the McCarthy staff; his father was a friend of McCarthy. The Senator had opposed Bob's going to work for the committee, but his father, then serving on the Hoover Commission, wanted Bob to get into government and had no objections. "So I was rather in ill grace personally to be around hollering about what McCarthy had done in 1952 or 1951 when my brother had been on the staff in 1953," Kennedy says. "That is really the guts of the matter."

But what Kennedy sees as a decisive reason for his stand may still not be the basic one. Was it political expedience? Certainly to some extent. While not unduly concerned about his prospects in 1958, he could never forget the intensity of the pro-McCarthy feeling back home, nor would his McCarthyite correspondents allow him to. But again, his stand reflected the pressures in him more than those on him. The civil-liberties creed was not part of his family tradition or his early environment. It was something he had met in later years, mainly at Harvard, and even then the great questions of the time were not civil liberties, but economic and social reform at home and intervention abroad.

Kennedy's judgment today on his McCarthy stand illustrates the fundamental attitudes that separated him from the libertarians for whom McCarthyism was the supreme issue: "The whole McCarthy episode must be judged in the perspective of the atmosphere which has always prevailed in the Senate, where most members are reluctant to judge personally the conduct of another. Perhaps that was wrong in McCarthy's case—perhaps we were not as sensitive as some and should have acted sooner. That is a reasonable indictment that falls on me as well, although I was completely out of sympathy with McCarthy and had no close relationship with him, particularly after I voted against him on several occasions."

Such was Kennedy's "reasonable indictment" of his McCarthy position from the perspective of five years. How has he dealt with the issue in the intervening years?

He could not ignore it—for the liberals would not let him, nor would the journalists. It was a rare press interview or television panel on which the question was not asked. He evaded an answer when he returned to the Senate in the spring of 1955. A few weeks before the 1956 convention, he indicated approval for the censure action of the Senate. But it still seemed a straddle to some, and, following publication of *Profiles in Courage,* reporters passed around the remark that Kennedy should have shown less profile and more courage. Mrs. Roosevelt, in particular, was critical of his position. White House decisions, she has said, should not be in the hands of "someone who understands what courage is and admires it, but has not quite the independence to have it." Why had he not gone on record when he returned to the Senate? she demanded of friends of Kennedy who interceded for him. "I think McCarthyism is a question on which public officials must stand up and be counted," she told them. "I cannot be sure of the political future of anyone who does not willingly state where he stands on the issue." It was not enough, she said, to uphold the vote of the Senate. "I believe that a public servant must clearly indicate that he understands the harm that McCarthyism did to our country and that he opposes it actively, so that one would feel sure he would always do so in the future."

It is questionable whether Kennedy at this time truly understood the intensity of the liberals' commitment to civil liberties. To them, freedom of speech and of conscience were not simply worthy policies to be placed on a par with other desirable principles of government. They occupied the very summit of the liberals' hierarchy of values. And they held a fixed position there. It was all right to experiment on social and economic matters, liberals felt, but impermissible to tamper with the basic liberties of the Bill of Rights, for only if those liberties remained secure could the free processes of government remain open for the detection and correction of error. The American civil-liberties heritage was a faith, renewed through time by Socrates and Milton, John Stuart Mill and Justice Oliver Wendell Holmes; indeed, it was a fighting faith for which many a man would die if necessary. And rarely had civil liberties in America been so threatened, liberals felt, as by the ruthless thrust of McCarthyism.

The question was still bobbing up when Kennedy made a campaign tour of McCarthy's home state of Wisconsin in April 1959. At a Press Club Gridiron dinner for Kennedy, costumed reporters sang, to the tune of "Clementine":

"Where were you, John—where were you, John,
   When the Senate censored Joe?"

At McCarthy's home town of Appleton, where there is now a memorial to the late Senator, who died in 1957, a questioner in the audience asked Kennedy to comment on Mrs. Roosevelt's judgment that he had been soft on McCarthyism. With some irritation he said that his civil-liberties record was clear and "I am not ready to accept any indictment from you or Mrs. Roosevelt on that score." Later that year, in writing a newspaper review of Richard Rovere's *Senator Joe McCarthy*, he mentioned that the nation had "recovered its health" from the "McCarthy contagion" and that Rovere could expect the "usual stream of abusive, venomous letters from the still-vibrant cult of McCarthy admirers." (Kennedy himself received such a letter on his review from a St. Louis man who said that in praising the book he had become a discredit to the Catholic Church. It must be pointed out, however, that the attitude of American Catholics was by no means always pro-McCarthy; indeed, the liberal Catholic magazines *Commonweal* and *America* had early taken a strong anti-McCarthy stand, as had many individual Catholics, in particular, leading Catholic intellectuals.) Still, Kennedy had not made the flat denunciation of McCarthy that liberals demanded.

Why not? Partly out of sheer pride or stubbornness; he does not want to give the impression of taking flight from a position that he feels was a considered one. Partly out of a sense of futility; he, too, is aware now that the issue will not die. Partly out of political expediency; he has chosen to occupy a place on the liberal side of center in American politics and has left the more adventurous civil-liberties frontiers to Humphrey and Stevenson, who have staked out the territory. But mainly because the old pressures within him are still operative to some extent, even though on concrete civil-liberties issues, such as the loyalty oath required of students requesting federal loans, he has taken a strong civil-libertarian position.

The central clue to Kennedy's position on the question is this: He was shaping his liberalism by fits and starts, out of his experience with concrete problems. He had been willed the heritage of economic liberalism, "the groceries," but not the heritage of liberty. He had never found a ready-made philosophy of liberalism that encompassed the vital combination. Kennedy recognizes this today.

"Some people have their liberalism 'made' by the time they reach their late 20's," he said almost wistfully. "I didn't. I was caught in cross currents and eddies. It was only later that I got into the stream of things." The McCarthy era, in the long run, may have contributed to the maturing and deepening of Kennedy's own liberalism. But if so, neither he nor the liberals would admit it.

9 ★ THE ANATOMY OF COURAGE

During the summer of 1954, as a showdown was nearing on McCarthy, Kennedy was approaching a hard decision of his own. His back was hurting almost all the time now. He had talked with specialists of the Lahey Clinic and elsewhere but the doctors disagreed on what course to take. At least one regarded the indicated operation as too risky to undertake. But the pain and the nuisance were becoming intolerable; Kennedy decided to go ahead. The operation was postponed several times as test after test was made. Then he entered Manhattan's Hospital for Special Surgery, where on October 21, 1954, surgeons performed a double fusion of spinal discs in a long operation.

For weeks, Kennedy lay flat on his back in this hospital. The room was dark; he could not sit up to read; only his wife and other immediate members of the family could see him. The pain was severe and almost incessant. He slept a good deal, but for the first two weeks he was awakened every half hour for blood tests. There were frightening episodes. On one occasion he was given a blood transfusion, and, while Jacqueline watched in horror, his face suddenly swelled and puffed out from an adverse reaction.

Worst of all, he was not getting better. The wound in his back continued to drain. October slowly gave way to November and November to December, and he stayed in a slack, painful condition. His doctors decided, however, that he might recuperate better in Florida. Late in December, attended by his wife and a nurse, he was bundled in blankets on a stretcher, taken out of the hospital, and flown to Palm Beach. He was able to have Christmas with his family. But by January his improvement was so slow that another operation was ordered. In mid-February he flew up to his New York hospital. Again the last rites were said and again surgeons labored for hours while members of his family prayed outside. The plate was removed from his spine, and this time recovery was more rapid. On February 25, he triumphantly walked out of the hospital and, accompanied by Jacqueline and Teddy, flew back to Florida for a long convalescence.

Grace in a Vacuum

Lying for six months on his hospital bed in New York and Florida, Kennedy needed a very different kind of courage now from the kind he had needed in the South Pacific. Then, at least, he had not been helpless; he could keep moving from island to island. But now he was entirely dependent on others, on his wife and nurses for little personal things, on his father to issue medical bulletins, on his office to handle legislation and politics. McCarthy was being censured, Congress was convening again, committees were meeting, politicians were already talking about the 1956 elections, but Kennedy, usually so restlessly active, was out of the stream of affairs. Hemingway defined courage as "grace under pressure," but this situation required something more demanding, grace in a vacuum, where there was little to cling to.

So candid about most other aspects of his life, Kennedy today will say little about his emotional response to the long hospitalization. When pressed one time, he said simply, "I was just darned sick," and let it go at that. He may have felt—certainly he would have had a right to—that he had had more than his fair share of illness and hospitalization. He was underweight during much of his childhood. He had a severe case of jaundice, and then a severe recurrence, about the time he entered college, and he had to take liver injections. He built his weight up at Harvard—he weighed 156 in 1937—so that he could play football, only to suffer a back injury in scrimmage. As a youth he stayed for many weeks in Arizona building up his strength. Rejected by the Army, he again went in for a health regimen and got into the Navy. But in the Pacific his back injury was aggravated by the PT-boat crash, he got a severe case of malaria, he went through another operation, and his weight dropped over thirty pounds.

At the same time, he has never given the impression of

physical weakness. Year after year, he has driven himself at a relentless pace. For years his typical week has consisted of legislative work in Washington for four days and politicking in Massachusetts or elsewhere for three. There is nothing so fatiguing as months of campaigning, but Kennedy has been doing it for years. Some of his friends have a theory about his illnesses—they are nature's way of compelling Kennedy to rest in bed for a few days and hence to take a respite from the strenuous life that he otherwise usually refuses to take.

A trying aspect of Kennedy's medical background has been the flood of rumors accompanying any hospitalization or health treatments. Following his back operation in 1954, stories floated around that he had incurable cancer, tuberculosis, or some other serious malady. Things had got off to a bad start when successive bulletins after the operation described his condition as "excellent," then as "reasonably good," and finally as "fairly satisfactory." His father issued a statement scotching "unfounded and disturbing rumors that are being circulated especially in Washington." A photographer snapped a picture of the Senator, looking pale and gaunt, as he was carried on a stretcher out of the hospital. And the estimate, originally only two months, of the period before Kennedy would return to Washington was extended time after time.

Nor would the rumors die. In 1959, five years after the operation, stories began to circulate that Kennedy had Addison's disease. A degenerative disease of the adrenal glands, this malady was often fatal, but today it can be fully and permanently controlled by drugs like cortisone, just as diabetes is by insulin. As the rumors spread, Kennedy stated in an interview: "The facts are these. . . . During the war I contracted malaria in the South Pacific, along with water exposure and a series of fevers. Diagnosis showed that this stress was accompanied by a partial adrenal insufficiency, though there was no tubercular infection or other serious problem.

"From 1946 through 1949 I underwent treatment for the malaria—the fevers ceased—there was complete rehabilitation and I have had no special medical care, no special checkup, no particular difficulty on this score at all, while meeting a very full schedule of committee work, Senate responsibilities and speaking engagements."

While Kennedy's adrenal insufficiency might well be diagnosed by some doctors as a mild case of Addison's disease, it was not diagnosed as the classic type of Addison's disease, which is due to tuberculosis. Other conditions, often not known, can cause inadequate functioning of the adrenal glands. As in Kennedy's case, this can be fully controlled by medication taken by mouth and requires a routine endocrinologic checkup as a part of regular physical examinations once or twice a year.

His back has, however, continued to give Kennedy trouble. He tried a number of treatments without much improvement. In the fall of 1955, he encountered a New York City doctor who specialized in the use of novocain to treat muscular spasm. Injections of novocain, according to Kennedy, relax the spasm and permit blood to flow in; otherwise his muscles might stay in spasm for years and gradually stiffen.

According to this doctor, there have been no "sequellae" to the back operation and today "his back is entirely well. . . . Senator Kennedy has tremendous physical stamina. He has above-average resistance to infections, such as influenza. The outstanding vigor with which he meets an incredibly demanding schedule, often seven days a week and with the briefest of vacations (only once as long as two consecutive weeks in the past four years), is clear evidence of his fine physique and remarkable vitality."

Kennedy feels, however, that no statements will put the rumors to rest. They are inherent in a campaign situation. The best way he finds to answer them is by keeping up his strenuous physical schedule. Anyone interested in his condition, he says, can try the pace of his next barnstorming tour. Meantime, he plays golf, swims with long, sure strokes, carries his two-year-old daughter on his back. Until recently, at least, he occasionally wore a light corset. In bathing trunks he looks strong and fit; the operation cut is hardly visible.

"Profiles in Courage"

Once Kennedy was out of immediate danger from his operation, his aides began to worry about his mental state. How would he take this prolonged inaction? They did not need to worry. As soon as he could read and write, he got to work on a problem that intrigued him—political courage displayed by noted American legislators. It was not a new subject for the Senator; earlier in the year, before his hospitalization, he had done a little research and writing on the problem. Actually, his interest in political courage ran back at least fifteen years, to the time when he was writing *Why England Slept* and returning again and again to the failure of most English politicians to defy public opinion and rearm Britain while there was yet time. But now he had a long opportunity to write and think.

For the Senator, writing a book in a hospital bed was no great problem. Alerted to his needs, the Legislative Reference Service of the Library of Congress sent him cartons of books. In Washington, Sorensen acted as literary amanuensis, digging up factual material, checking with historians and other experts, going over drafts. Arthur Krock, an old family friend, and several others advised on examples of courage that should be included in the book; Krock in particular contended that Senator Taft deserved a chapter because of his unpopular stand against the Nürnberg trials, and Kennedy agreed. Jules Davids, a Georgetown University professor, and James M. Landis, prominent New Dealer and former Harvard Law School dean, long a close friend and now legal adviser to the Senator's father, helped a good deal in the preparation of several chapters.

But the brunt of the writing fell on Kennedy himself, lying in his bed in a ground-floor room or sitting out by the pool in front of the big stucco house in Palm Beach. In his loose, widely spaced hand he wrote on heavy white paper in a red stiff-covered "minute book" of the type used in law offices. Progress was slow. His thoughts in writing, as in conversing informally, would race ahead of his power to get the words out as he wished them to appear; he paused often to cross out sentences and paragraphs and make additions in the margins. He dictated the second draft to a secretary.

Slowly the examples of political courage piled up. The first was John Quincy Adams, whose struggles with the Federalist party had fascinated Kennedy long before he had entered the Senate. Another New Englander, Daniel Webster, Kennedy included for his support of Clay's compromise between the North and South, although Kennedy acknowledged that Webster was not as illustrious as he looked, for he had demanded and accepted retainers from the Bank of the United States. One of the most notable essays dealt with Edmund Ross, of Kansas, who said—rightly—that he had looked down into his political grave when, over the bitter protests of his constituents, he saved President Johnson from impeachment. And one of the most moving told of George W. Norris, of Nebraska, whose greatest act of courage was described as not his filibuster against President Wilson's Armed Ship Bill in 1917, but his support in 1928 of Al Smith, a Catholic, a "wet," an urbanite, and a Democrat, in a state that was none of these things. The inclusion of the progressive Norris also made for a nice balance to that of the Republican Taft, the only other twentieth-century politician to receive star billing.

Harper & Brothers, which had turned down *Why England Slept* sixteen years before, accepted this manuscript with alacrity. Their main concern was that the chapters seemed a bit stiff, and at the editors' suggestion, Kennedy wrote short anecdotal beginnings for most of the chapters. Allan Nevins, the eminent Columbia University historian, not only did a critique of the manuscript, but contributed a foreword that described the book, with its binding together of history, practical politics, and public morals, as a "real public service." Early in 1956, Harper brought the volume out under the title *Profiles in Courage*. Kennedy dedicated it to his wife.

The book was an instant and brilliant success. Accorded lead reviews in newspapers and magazines across the country, it drew high praise from most critics. It shot to the top of the best-seller lists and stayed there for many months. It was translated into Spanish, Turkish, Japanese, Arabic, Indonesian, Vietnamese, and Telugu. Readers seemed delighted and surprised that a politician—even a politician in the United States Senate—could be so literate. "That a United States Senator, a young man of independent means with a gallant and thoughtful background, should have produced this study is as remarkable as it is helpful," wrote editor E. D. Canham of the *Christian Science Monitor*. "It is a splendid flag that Senator Kennedy has nailed to his mast. May he keep it there!"

Since both author and subject were good copy, the short biographies of men of courage served double and even triple duty. Some were published in magazines as separate articles and one or two of these appeared in magazine digests. The book also served as an almost inexhaustible reservoir of anecdotes, historical facts, and ideas for Kennedy's future speeches.

The grand climax came more than a year after publication, when *Profiles in Courage* was awarded the Pulitzer prize for biography. No other honor has meant so much to Kennedy as this recognition of intellectual and literary distinction. (The $500 prize the Senator turned over to the United Negro College Fund.) It may well be, too, that the award had a small but discernible effect on his political popularity and presidential appeal. In January 1957, the Gallup Poll had asked people their preference if the choice for the Democratic presidential nomination narrowed down to Kefauver and Kennedy. The outcome was 38 per cent for Kefauver and 41 per cent for Kennedy. Four months later, in answer to substantially the same question, the returns split 33 per cent to 45 per cent in the same order. Since the only relevant and significant event in the four-month interim was the Pulitzer award, it seems possible that literary honors carry more weight with the public than has been commonly thought.

There was one jarring note. Some doubted that any United States senator could produce a book of literary merit. Soon after publication, a rumor began to circulate that Kennedy's book had been entirely ghost-written by Sorensen or some other assistant. It was strange that this rumor went as far as it did, since Kennedy had, of course, already written a best seller at the age of twenty-three, and no one charged that *Why England Slept* was ghosted; but the latter had been pretty much forgotten by 1956. To be sure, he had had more help in the preparation of *Profiles in Courage* than authors customarily have, because of his illness; nonetheless, he wrote his own book. Kennedy was annoyed but could do nothing about the anonymous whispers. After the Pulitzer award, however, Drew Pearson repeated the charge on the Mike Wallace television program. Kennedy threatened to take action, and after going over the original manuscript and drafts, Pearson stated that Kennedy was author of the book. Still the rumors lingered on. As late as March 1958, Kennedy invited Senator Richard Neuberger, himself a professional writer, to drop into his office some time and look over the manuscript. He knew this was unnecessary as far as Neuberger was concerned, but he wanted the Oregon Senator to be able to speak on the matter with complete authority.

The Meaning of Courage

Kennedy's profiles of courageous politicians were sandwiched between opening and closing essays on the meaning of political courage in general. These were the most important part of the book. Drawn from the Senator's own experience as well as from his researches, the essays dwelt on the practical problems and complex aspects of political courage. Because this quality is to Kennedy the "most admirable of human virtues," because his own career has seemed to some full, and to others empty, of political courage, and because he has thought about this quality in relation to political success, his views may throw some light on his own career and prospects.

Kennedy began by quoting Walter Lippmann's statement that successful democratic politicians are insecure and intimidated men who advance politically only as they "placate, appease, bribe, seduce, bamboozle, or otherwise manage to manipulate the demanding threatening elements in their constituencies." Kennedy denied this. Innumerable obscure acts of political courage, he said, took place almost daily in the Senate chamber. Any decline had been less in the Senate than in the public's appreciation of the nature of the Senate as a legislative chamber and the need for compromise and balance. People simply did not understand the "terrible pressures" that discouraged acts of political courage.

What were these terrible pressures? One was the legislator's human desire to get along with his fellow members of the club, not to follow lone-wolf tendencies that might embarrass his colleagues. "The way to get along," Kennedy said he had been advised when he entered Congress, "is to go along." But to the Senator, going along was more than just good fellowship; it was also the essence of compromise, the compromise that "prevents each set of reformers—the wets and the drys, the one-worlders and the isolationists, the vivisectionists and the anti-vivisectionists—from crushing the group on the extreme opposite end of the political spectrum." He wrote:

"The fanatics and extremists and even those conscientiously devoted to hard and fast principles are always disappointed at the failure of their Government to rush to implement all of these principles and to denounce those of their opponents. But the legislator has some responsibility to conciliate those opposing forces within his state and party and to represent them in the larger clash of interests on the national level; and he alone knows that there are few if any issues where all the truth and all the right and all the angels are on one side."

The second pressure against courage was the desire to be re-elected. This was not necessarily a selfish motive, for politicians going down to defeat in defending a single principle would not be on hand to fight for other principles. Defeat, moreover, was not hard simply for a senator, but for his friends and supporters who had sacrificed for the cause and even for his wife and children. After all, only in totalitarian countries were persons expected to sacrifice all—even their careers—for the national good. Dwelling on this point, Kennedy defended the lot of the harassed politician. "In no other occupation but politics is it expected that a man will sacrifice honors, prestige, and his chosen career on a single issue.

"Lawyers, businessmen, teachers, doctors, all face difficult personal decisions involving their integrity—but few, if any, face them in the glare of the spotlight as do those in public office. Few, if any, face the same dread finality of decision that confronts a Senator facing an important call of the roll. He may want more time for his decision—he may believe there is something to be said for both sides—he may feel that a slight amendment could remove all difficulties—but when that roll is called, he cannot hide, he cannot equivocate, he cannot delay—and he senses that his constituency, like the Raven in Poe's poem, is croaking 'Nevermore' as he casts the vote that stakes his political future."

The third and strongest pressure was the pressure of a politician's constituency—the interest groups, organized letter writers, and voters as a whole. And the demands from these forces were complex and conflicting. Only recently, two groups had called him off the Senate floor, the Senator related—one a group of businessmen seeking to have a local federal installation closed as unfair competition for private enterprise; the other, a delegation from the employees in the installation who were worried about their jobs. Such spokesmen might represent only a small percentage of voters, but, still, they were the articulate few whose views could not be ignored and who comprised the greater part of a politician's contacts with the whole electorate.

It was easy enough for idealists to preach that politicians should ignore such pressures, the Senator went on, but it was not easy for practical men in office. And even if politicians could withstand such pressures, a crucial question arose—did they have any *right* to do so? Should not a senator speak for his state, especially in a chamber where other senators would work for their states? Was there not some responsibility to the political party that put him in office? Above all, should he not, in a democracy, respond to his constituents' views, even if he personally differed with them?

To these questions Kennedy had some interesting answers. Parties, to be successful, needed independence and variety in their leaders as well as loyalty and unity. Local and state interests should be served but not at the expense of the national interest. As for responsibility to constituents, this, Kennedy admitted, was a more difficult problem. But he would not accept the narrow conception of the role of a United States senator that was implied. Had the people of Massachusetts sent him to Washington to serve merely as "a seismograph to record shifts in popular opinion"? No—such a view of democracy actually put too little faith in the people, for it assumed that they wanted lawmakers to act in slavish obedience to public opinion (even if it could be measured, which it could not), whereas actually the people wanted their leaders to act with courage.

"The voters selected us, in short, because they had confidence in our judgment and our ability to exercise that judgment from a position where we would determine what were their own interests, as a part of the nation's interests," Kennedy concluded. "This may mean that we must on occasion lead, inform, correct, and sometimes even ignore constituent opinion, if we are to exercise fully that judgment for which we were elected. . . ."

It was an ingenious way of reconciling leadership and democracy. How usable was it? And what light, if any, did it throw on Kennedy's own behavior as a politician?

One difficulty is that voters rarely give much indication of choosing candidates on the basis of character or leadership potential. Personality, charm, friendliness—certainly these are winning qualities in politicians; probably, too, their "sincerity" and their training, possibly also their air of conviction and acquaintance with issues. But beyond this, character and leadership are rather intangible qualities. Moreover, men who later display striking leadership often give little indication at election time that they will behave this way. Probably it was hard to foresee in 1916 that Wilson would lead the country into war and then assume the moral leadership of the world in fighting for a League of Nations. Certainly few could have known in late 1932 that Franklin D. Roosevelt would display the courage and vigor that he did display only a few months later.

Kennedy's reconciliation of democracy and leadership, in short, was more an expression of faith than a statement of historical fact. But as an expression of faith it had its own importance, for he was saying that a courageous politician must act with the conviction that the people *do* want leadership, that they will re-elect politicians who vote according to inner conviction. Sometimes such faith would be crushed; the courage of some of Kennedy's heroes, after all, had not been vindicated at the polls. But the courage of many others had.

Everything turned, then, on the willingness of the people to support in fact—that is, at the polls—the courage and independence that they praised in theory. And this capacity to support courage in turn depended on certain qualities of the electorate. All about us, Kennedy said, politics was saturated with expensive public-relations operations and mechanized mass communications that threatened to stifle independence and unorthodoxy. "And our public life is becoming so increasingly centered upon that seemingly unending war to which we have given the curious epithet 'cold' that we tend to encourage rigid ideological unity and orthodox patterns of thought. And thus, in the days ahead, only the very courageous will be able to take the hard and unpopular decisions necessary for our survival in the struggle with a powerful enemy. . . ."

There were some who said later that Kennedy wrote *Profiles in Courage* as an act of contrition, even as unconscious self-indictment, because of his failure to take a position on the McCarthy censure. The book might give him some solace for not standing for McCarthy, a priest in Pennsylvania wrote the Senator, but he had lost the support of "the most effective Catholic group." Others held that the key argument in *Profiles* was a damning indictment of the main tendency of McCarthyism—the stiffling of unorthodox thought. The ultimate source of political courage in a nation, Kennedy was saying in his book, lay in the extent that independence, unorthodoxy, and dissent were tolerated among the people as a whole. This conclusion was of particular importance, for he was arguing that the toleration of unorthodoxy is a matter not merely of democratic rectitude, but a matter of democratic survival. But each man has his own definition of nonconformity and of courage, and chooses the times to display it.

Kennedy's book was, perhaps, both of these things to a minor extent, but essentially it was simply a phase in his intellectual and political development. His work on courage helped emancipate him from a narrow conception of a politician's responsibilities to his district. It opened up vistas of political leaders who were willing to defy public opinion in their states and districts because there was something much bigger—a moral principle or the welfare of the whole nation —for which they would fight and even face defeat.

10 ★ VICE-PRESIDENTIAL POLITICS

Something like a hero's welcome greeted Kennedy when he returned to Washington on May 23, 1955, after seven months' leave. Family and friends crowded around him at National Airport, where he had flown in from Palm Beach with his wife and his sister Jean. Jubilantly, Reardon and Sorensen drove the couple to the Capitol, briefing Kennedy on the way about the latest political and legislative gossip. When the Senator posed for newsreel and television cameramen on the Capitol steps, tourists grabbed his hand, and a delegation of textile workers from the South that was passing by stopped to cheer him roundly.

Secretaries rose to applaud when he entered Room 362 in the Senate Office Building later. His inner office he found full of reporters. Amid the letters and telegrams of greeting piled on his desk stood an enormous basket of fruit bearing the tag, "Welcome home" and signed "Dick Nixon."

Kennedy was in good form. He said he had tried to keep in touch with Congress by reading the *Congressional Record*. "An inspiring experience," he added. Asked by a newsman whether Eisenhower's popularity remained high, he flashed a broad smile. "It seems to be holding up pretty well—in Palm Beach, anyhow." He went on to get a few licks in at the President. Eisenhower, he said, had "guessed short" on Russian military strength. The recent decisions to cut the Army and Air Force were wrong. He felt, though, that the

Democratic party would have to present an effective and positive program in 1956 rather than follow Harry Truman's advice of pin-pointing attacks directly on the President.

"I threw my crutches away two days ago," he told the reporters, who noted that he looked strong and fit under his dark golden tan and hair slightly bleached by the Florida sun. He had ignored a wheel chair and pair of crutches that were in readiness at the airport, and he insisted on walking from the Capitol to the Senate Office Building. Reporters noted also, though, that he had limped a bit in climbing the Capitol steps and seemed to favor his left leg as he strolled through the little Capitol park with Jacqueline. Kennedy indicated that he would take it easy for a while by living at the nearby Congressional Hotel and using an office only a few yards from the Senate chamber.

When Kennedy entered the upper chamber the next day, the Senators rose in a body to applaud him. "We are glad to see you, Jack," declared Democratic leader Lyndon Johnson. "Those of us who have gotten to know him have for him a very warm and high place in our affections," Republican leader William Knowland added. In a few minutes, Kennedy was voting with his Democratic colleagues in an unsuccessful effort to override a presidential veto of an increase in pay for postal workers.

Despite his plans to take it easy, Kennedy plunged back into a heavy schedule—appearances at Assumption College in Worcester and at a Jefferson-Jackson Day dinner in Boston, dedication of a new home for the aged in East Boston, introduction of the Italian Ambassador at a Boston dinner, and attendance at his fifteenth reunion at Harvard. A presidential election year was coming up, and the political pot was beginning to boil.

Fight for the Electoral College

The year 1956 was to see Kennedy's debut as a national politician. Shortly before that debut, there occurred an episode that was closely related to his national ventures of both 1956 and 1960, but it was a relation that few at the time—perhaps not even Kennedy—could perceive. The episode involved an attempt by conservative Democratic and Republican senators to change the method of electing the President and Vice-President, and Kennedy's role in blocking the effort. Politicians usually cultivate their immediate political interests and rarely are asked to defend the constitutional system protecting those interests. It is even rarer for a politician to take a commanding role in such a defense.

The legislative situation was as follows: for years a number of senators, including Henry Cabot Lodge, had been trying to overcome the failings of the Electoral College. The most popular proposal was to abolish the Electoral College as such and to give each presidential candidate the same proportion of the electoral votes of a state as he won of its popular vote. (For example, a candidate winning two thirds of New York's popular vote would win two thirds, or thirty, of its forty-five electoral votes, rather than *all* the electoral votes, as at present.) The leading spokesman for this proposal in the 1956 session was Senator Price Daniel, a conservative Texas Democrat.

This reform had never made much progress, however, and Daniel and his friends looked around for allies. They found support in another group backing a wholly different reform. This group would allow state legislatures to adopt a system giving one electoral vote to the leading presidential candidate in each *congressional district* (with the remaining two electoral votes going to the candidate winning the whole state). Champion of this proposal was Senator Karl Mundt, conservative South Dakota Republican. The way the two groups got together was simple: they jammed the two totally different bills into one ungainly package and presented the result to the Senate as a proposed constitutional amendment.

The technicalities barely cloaked a power struggle of considerable importance. Conservative senators had long been concerned about the "winner-take-all" feature of the Electoral College, which gave all a state's electoral votes to the presidential candidate winning the most popular votes in the state. The result, they argued, was to compel candidates to strive mightily for the support of potent minority blocs and pressure groups—Catholics, Jews, Negroes, labor, nationality groups—that might swing the state's whole bloc of votes either way. And since the big, populous, industrial states such as New York, California, and Illinois "teemed" with such blocs, the Daniel and Mundt groups in fact were hoping to make the President less responsive to liberal voting alignments.

The issue was complex, involving a complicated feature of the world's most complicated political system. But the Daniel-Mundt conservative coalition was able to dress up its proposal to lure a wide range of supporters. Northern Democrats were told that the proposal would give them permanent control of the White House, Southern Democrats that it would give them greater influence in their party, liberals that third parties would be treated more fairly, conservatives that liberal voting blocs would be curbed, Republicans that they would pick up more strength in the South. The proposal was also able to capitalize on widespread discontent over the failings of the Electoral College, which had been likened to the human appendix as useless, unpredictable, and a possible center of inflammation. By March, a bipartisan group of fifty-one senators had joined Daniel and Mundt in cosponsoring the measure. With such strong initial support, the bill seemed almost sure of gaining the two-thirds vote necessary for a constitutional amendment.

The more that hardheaded liberals scrutinized the Daniel-Mundt measure, the more alarmed they became. It was clearly intended to erase the "winner-take-all" feature of the Electoral College, which however strange in appearance, had the effect of forcing presidential candidates to appeal to the big states and their urban population. If the Senate, and even the House, overrepresented rural and conservative voters, why should not the President overrepresent the liberal groups? Liberals were even more concerned about the Mundt provisions, which allowed electors to be chosen in congressional districts. These districts were already gerrymandered to overrepresent rural, conservative voters, and they could be distorted even more by the state legislatures that drew congressional district lines and that were themselves products of gerrymanders by rural conservatives.

Kennedy had disliked the Daniel measure when it previously had been sponsored by Lodge; the new plan seemed even worse. He was fortified in his suspicion by a letter from his old American government professor at Harvard, Arthur Holcombe. "Under present conditions the preponderant influence of the big close states on the executive branch of the government checks the disproportionate influence of the small and often more one-sidedly partisan states in the Senate," Holcombe wrote. Lessening the influence of the big close states, he felt, would seriously upset the balance of our political system.

Kennedy decided to spearhead the counterattack on Daniel-Mundt. The prospects were uninviting. Not only had the proposal won wide support in Congress and the press, but it had the aroma of moderate, bipartisan reform. Too, the objections were hard to dramatize. Seemingly so technical and complex, the Electoral College could not easily be pictured as in reality an important part of what Kennedy called the whole solar system of governmental power.

Kennedy's tactic was simple—so simple that a more cynical politician could have overlooked its possibilities. He mastered the subject thoroughly, gained the Senate floor early and often, argued with his opponents at every opportunity, and finally outdebated and outvoted them. He had powerful support from Lehman and from Douglas, who produced statistics showing in devastating detail the extent to which congressional districts had been gerrymandered. But otherwise he fought the battle almost alone.

With statistics, with a command of American history and constitutional precepts, with cold reasoning, even sometimes with little flashes of wit, Kennedy opened holes in his opponents' arguments. Politely he interrupted them to correct their figures or their reasoning. He took the initiative from Daniel early in the debate and never lost it, largely by the simple device of holding the floor. He readily yielded the floor for questions and took on the Senate's best debaters. Since political machinery is a subject on which every politician feels expert, many senators took part. Like a boy fighting off a swarm of bees, he had to handle attacks from all directions, and from both sides of the aisle.

Lehman and Douglas centered their objections on the danger of the Daniel-Mundt plan to the big cities. Kennedy used all the arguments available, and dwelt especially on the "shotgun wedding" that had brought Daniel and Mundt together and the "hybrid monstrosity" that had resulted. Kennedy had one great strategic advantage: defense of the *status quo* in this case was the liberal position, while it was the conservatives who wanted change. Hence, Kennedy could cite the Constitution, history, and the Founding Fathers in his own defense. He also divided the opposition by arguing that the Daniel-Mundt Bill was actually a threat to all the groups —conservative and liberal Republicans, Northern and Southern Democrats—that it was supposed to help.

"Not a single sound argument," he told the Senate, "has been put forth for adoption of this radical change which is demanded by no State, which had been discredited in the past and which promises only doubt and danger for the future. . . . I know of no other step which could be taken to disrupt more thoroughly and more dangerously the American constitutional system."

The Senate vote vindicated Kennedy's leadership and tactics. Not only did the Daniel-Mundt Bill fail to muster the necessary two-thirds support, but no less than ten of the original sponsors—nine Republicans and one Democrat—deserted the bill to which they had once lent their names. Kennedy's emphasis on the makeshift and ramshackle aspects of the bill, rather than on its conservative aspects, was justified by the fact that half the deserters represented smaller states and at least half were conservatives.

"Your leadership in that battle was most skillful and decisive," Douglas wrote him later. Although Arthur Krock grumbled over Kennedy's "sometimes flimsy material," other newspapers and many senators credited him with the rare achievement of winning the battle in debate. Certainly his command of his material and his conduct on the floor had immensely boosted Kennedy's stock among the political leaders who make up the Senate.

Melee in Massachusetts

Kennedy's handling of the Electoral College fight was all the more significant in view of a hot political battle that was brewing back home at the time. By March 1956, the Senator's power and prestige in his own state were under severe challenge.

Kennedy had long before decided on his choice for the presidential nomination: Stevenson again. While he was not hopeful about the chances of any Democrat against Eisenhower, he felt that Stevenson, more than any other Democrat, had the capacity, experience, and moderate philosophy necessary for the job. Stevenson was also the front runner in early 1956, although Estes Kefauver was likely to contest with him. Kennedy had pleasant working relationships with Kefauver, but like most of his colleagues he did not rate the Tennesseean as of presidential quality.

There was some talk early in 1956 in Massachusetts that Kennedy would be a fine running mate for Stevenson. For example, a Democratic leader in the western part of the state, on his own initiative and without clearing with Kennedy, had announced his own candidacy for delegate to the national convention on a pledge to support Stevenson and Kennedy. The Senator, while undecided as to his own candidacy, was eager to control the Massachusetts delegation as much as possible in order to have some chips to throw Stevenson's way in the great game scheduled for Chicago in August.

The stumbling block was John McCormack. The Majority Leader was cool to Stevenson for a number of reasons, one of which was a realistic view that Stevenson could not win. The veteran legislator had no candidate of his own; what he wanted was control of delegates at the convention. Now in his twenty-eighth year in the House, he disliked the notion of sharing power with a thirty-nine-year-old Boston green blood. Always a hard party worker and long considered the federal patronage dispenser for the state, McCormack had more influence among top Democratic circles than Kennedy, who had relied on his own appeal to the voters rather than working closely with the party organization. Indeed, many Democrats viewed Kennedy as a lone wolf who liked to play the Republican side of the street.

The stage seemed set for a tussle between the Majority Leader and the Senator. Matters came to a head when William Burke, a vehement supporter of McCormack, was elected chairman of the state Democratic committee at the end of 1955. Kennedy and McCormack had some liking and respect for each other, but Burke was of a very different cut. He was a long-time crony of Jim Curley; Collector of Customs in Boston under Roosevelt; more recently a gentleman onion farmer in the western part of the state. The big, bald politico had a dubious reputation as a wirepuller and bully. Also joining the McCormack forces were Fox of the Boston *Post,* now completely on the outs with Kennedy, and Curley himself, who still sought revenge against the man who had "betrayed" him during his time of anguish. Egged on by his supporters, McCormack considered running as a favorite son in the presidential primary scheduled for April. With Burke as chairman, such a combination, if uncontested, would have produced a delegation not only favorable to McCormack, but hostile to Kennedy and Stevenson.

Getting wind of this plan, Kennedy told McCormack and Burke that he would run as a favorite son himself unless they agreed to compromise on the membership of the delegation. In return, Kennedy agreed not to oppose Burke as chairman, at least for a time. McCormack and Burke agreed to this proposal. Kennedy and McCormack sat down together, and after some haggling they were able to agree on a unity slate.

Harmony was not to last long. Stevenson leaders in Chicago, with whom Kennedy was keeping in close touch, were pressing for some expression of support by Massachusetts voters. Burke and Fox could not resist a chance to boom McCormack and batter Kennedy and Stevenson. The unity slate meant that they could not fight for delegates at the April primary, but the April ballot would also have a space where voters could write in the name of the man they preferred for President. Why not get a big write-in vote for McCormack? While Burke bustled around the state and McCormack stayed out of the way in Washington, Fox converted the *Post* into a propaganda sheet for the old war horse.

Fox had some scores to even. With rising indignation he had watched Kennedy's votes against McCarthyism and his shift to a more liberal position. What had happened to the man he had endorsed in 1952? One episode in particular had annoyed him. After fruitlessly denouncing Harvard's toleration of "left-wingers" on its faculty, he had decided on a campaign to hit his alma mater where it would hurt—in the pocketbook—by setting up a committee to ask all alumni to withhold contributions to Harvard until it got rid of them. Fox had asked Kennedy to join the committee and Kennedy had refused.

As reports of McCormack write-in activities reached him, Kennedy tried to rally Stevenson supporters. But Kennedy and the Stevenson people had no chance against McCormack's popularity among the party faithful in Boston. Carrying his own city by a four to one margin, the Majority Leader piled up almost 30,000 write-in votes across the state, about 10,000 more than Stevenson.

It was a trouncing for the Illinoisan—and for Kennedy, too. The results meant not only that McCormack could ask the delegation to support him on the first ballot as a favorite son, but McCormack now had more say about where delegates would go on the second ballot. Kennedy had lost face and prestige and still could offer nothing to Stevenson at the convention. All he had gained from the fight so far was an expensive lesson in the Boston school of political hard knocks.

Then Burke made a mistake. Stevenson's supporters, he crowed, should have been in Princeton listening to Alger Hiss, who was making his first appearance after his release from prison. Kennedy had been aware throughout the winter of the opposition of McCarthyites like Fox. He had been aware that he confronted the old mucker element in Boston politics in the form of Curley and Burke. But now Burke's statement was not only a slap in the face; it meant that the opposition, aside from McCormack himself, was stained with McCarthyism. In one sentence, Burke had illuminated the fact that Curleyism and McCarthyism, which had been somewhat separate tendencies in Boston, were now joined in opposition to Kennedy's national ambitions.

Kennedy studied the situation. The weak point in McCormack's forces was Burke himself, who had earned the ill will of a host of party leaders over the years because of his political tactics. The portly onion grower was up for re-election in mid-May. If he could be knocked out of the chairmanship, Kennedy could reassert his influence over the delegation at the convention.

Unhappily, this plan demanded of Kennedy something he

had never done and was reluctant to undertake—moving into an internal party struggle with both fists flying. He had always managed to steer clear of such fights; he detested the murky maneuvers and petty name-calling that inevitably would be involved. A fight with Burke meant that both men would get dirtied, for Burke loved to pull his adversaries down to his own level. In one of the classic exchanges of Boston politics, he had once bellowed that he would grapple in the gutter with Paul Dever, to which someone replied quietly, "You would have to climb up, Bill."

But his dander was up, and Kennedy decided to move against Burke, to do so quietly, however, by putting pressure on members of the state committee. The Kennedy forces had helped elect some pro-Stevenson committeemen in the April primary, and now Kennedy and his people went to work on the neutrals. Mayors, state legislators, union officials, liberal leaders, ADA members, and others were asked to put pressure on the committee members in their districts. Kennedy toured the state making phone calls and paying visits on party leaders. He even held a breakfast meeting with Burke in Northampton to see if he would pull out, but to no avail.

In the Berkshires, Kennedy was rash enough to tell a reporter of his plans, and soon the battle was front-page news across the state. Former Governor Dever and a host of politicians lined up with Kennedy; McCormack announced that he was supporting Burke "1000 per cent." Then Kennedy began to experience gutter warfare. Burke announced that at the Northampton meeting Kennedy had offered to make him Democratic national committeeman in place of Curley if Burke would quit as chairman. Quickly picking up his cue in Boston, Curley charged that Kennedy was trying to bribe him to get off the national committee to make room for Burke.

"Well, he hasn't got money enough to buy me at any time," declared Curley in righteous, and phony, indignation. "I never took any money from him or his whole family, and I never will." Other Burke followers picked up the refrain —the millionaire Kennedy family was trying to take over the Democratic party.

For Kennedy, bringing his father and family into the picture was unbearable. Friends had never seen him so angry. Publicly, he hid his rage while he coolly set about to destroy Burke. As the committee meeting neared, Kennedy laid plans for the chairmanship battle with his usual attention to detail. To run against Burke, he dug up a city mayor, Pat Lynch, who could appeal to all factions. An elaborate "scenario" of six typewritten pages was prepared to guide the Kennedy forces through the correct parliamentary procedure and tactics at the coming election of a chairman. Burke's tactics were anticipated and alternative lines of action established. As a final precaution, guards were hired to prevent the Burke forces from physically taking over the election meeting. Kennedy coached his forces at a last-minute strategy conference.

The meeting was in the best Boston tradition. Burke and a group of burly henchmen forced their way past the guards and took their places in the hotel conference room. The guards came in to keep order and barely averted fisticuffs. It took an hour to elect a temporary chairman to supervise the balloting. As the room grew dense with smoke, committeemen waxed eloquent over procedural points. Anonymous men in dark suits moved about whispering in people's ears.

"Who are we voting on?" asked a man in a dark suit.

"Sit down—you're not a member," someone shouted.

"Just a point of order," the man said, and sat down.

Somehow a vote was finally taken, and the Kennedy forces won decisively, 47 to 31. Quivering with frustration, Burke told reporters that he would run against Kennedy for the Senate in 1958, and "let him try to go out and buy votes like he bought this election. He and his millions don't know what decency and honor mean." The election, announced Kennedy, marked the beginning of a new era for Massachusetts Democrats. The fight, he added carefully, had not been directed at Congressman McCormack.

Who but Kennedy?

Whatever its moments of high and low comedy, the battle over Burke marked a major turn for Kennedy. For the first time, he had thrown his full weight into a battle not for his own candidacy, but to get a grip on the party machinery. Friends had warned him that he had little to gain and much to lose, that he might even be jeopardizing his chances for re-election in 1958. But the Senator was now turning his attention to national party politics. He had gambled for more power over the delegation to Chicago and won.

He now had a moral influence over a batch of delegates —but how would he use it? The national party picture was obscure. Kennedy's best chance for the vice-presidential spot was on a ticket headed by Stevenson, but in the spring of 1956 the race seemed wide open. Kefauver had dealt Stevenson's prospects a heavy blow by beating him in Minnesota, and Governor Averell Harriman, of New York, was running hard.

Kennedy, moreover, was genuinely uncertain of his own best interests. His father flatly opposed his candidacy on the grounds that Stevenson would probably lose to Eisenhower, no matter who his running mate was, and if it was Kennedy, the result would then be laid to a Catholic being on the ticket, and hence the prospects of a Catholic running for President would be set back by decades. Sorensen and others on Kennedy's staff, however, urged him to run. They argued that a campaign, even if it failed, would project him onto the national scene. There was some grass-roots pressure, too; Massachusetts Democrats were organizing Kennedy-for-Vice-President committees, putting out leaflets, even ordering big Kennedy buttons.

Kennedy resolved the problem, for the moment, in his usual way—he made no decision but told Sorensen and other aides and members of his family to go ahead on their own.

It was a blinking green light—to go where? Sorensen and Reardon had the awkward problem of trying to organize support for a reluctant candidate, with the prospect that the decision ultimately would be made by one man whose identity they did not know. The only thing to do, they decided, was to build a strong case for Kennedy while quietly lining up support.

The main problem was the Catholic issue. Sorensen delved into voting records and came up with a detailed analysis claiming to demonstrate that a Catholic running mate would be a positive advantage to a Protestant candidate. Adorned with tables and footnotes, the long analysis argued that there *was* a "Catholic vote," that this vote was coming to a peak with the maturing of immigrant offspring, and that it was concentrated in the big electoral states (whose strength in the Electoral College, of course, Kennedy had just safeguarded in Senate debate). Stevenson especially, it was argued, needed this Catholic support, for Eisenhower had made inroads on the Catholic vote. A page of statistics showed how Stevenson had run behind local Catholic candidates in the previous election.

Later on, this intriguing document was quietly let out to reporters as an analysis drawn up by "backers" of Kennedy. The planting was done so skillfully that the *U.S. News & World Report* published the whole account, and *Time* a long summary of it, both on the eve of the convention.

By June, the Kennedy-for-Vice-President boom was on—to the extent campaigns for second place can be boomed. A strong backer was Connecticut's Governor Abraham Ribicoff, who, at the Governors' Conference in Atlantic City, urged his fellow chief executives to support a Stevenson-Kennedy ticket. Asked if Kennedy's religion would be a handicap, Ribicoff said: "Since 1928, the country has reached a deeper sense of maturity. Politicians are unimaginative when religious factors come up, but the people vote for a man on the basis of his character, personality and principles. I am for Senator Kennedy because of what he stands for. His religion doesn't enter into it. I think he would add strength to the ticket. He has always had a strong appeal for the independent voter. He did so in a year when Eisenhower carried Massachusetts in a landslide. He would have a wide appeal because he is a middle-of-the-roader. Southerners would like his position on most matters."

Other vice-presidential camps were active, too, by the spring of 1956. Defying the old political notion that a self-respecting politician has to be coaxed into accepting the nomination for second place, a dozen candidates were sniffing the political winds. So the Kennedy camp got busy with another lengthy analysis—this one of several dozen candidates, including some admittedly "preposterous" possibilities, in terms of certain tests. The tests were:

1. *Availability.* Thirteen possible candidates were dismissed as committed to their present job or running for something else—John McCormack, for example.

2. *Compatibility.* Must be consistently pro-Stevenson—ten candidates held ineligible.

3. *Marital status.* Should be married, and with no previous divorce—five candidates out.

4. *Veteran status.* "Not necessarily essential" but "strongly desirable"—eight candidates adversely affected.

5. *Geographical status.* Should come from large, balance-of-power states not too near Illinois—twenty-seven candidates dropped.

On the positive side, the report argued that Stevenson's running mate must have a background in national policy and politics, a record as a vote getter, a "moderate" philosophy like Stevenson's, a warm and sincere appeal on the "stump," enough money to finance most of his own campaign and good contacts to get more. Carefully and coldly, the report analyzed the pros and cons of the other candidates. Humphrey, for example, was summarized as "Strongly pro-Stevenson; married; young and healthy; not a veteran; state adjacent to Stevenson's (11 electoral votes); 8 years' experience in Congress; good vote getter; nationally known; considered active ADA'er to Stevenson's left; 'right' on farm issue and Taft-Hartley; good speaker and personality; not wealthy."

This merciless siphoning-out process came up with one ideal candidate: John F. Kennedy. "It would appear that the best of a good group is Senator Kennedy—young but not as young as [Frank] Clement (and nearly as old as Teddy Roosevelt when he was nominated Vice-President); now fully recovered from his spinal operation; holder of a brilliantly heroic combat record; married to a lovely wife; from the right kind of state in terms of size, location, and political tendencies; with more experience in Congress than Humphrey, Wagner, or Clement; author of a highly praised best-seller; widely known and popular; a proven vote-getter against big odds; a moderate Stevensonian philosophy; friendly with party leaders in all sections; 'right' on Taft-Hartley and acceptable on the farm issue; with a winning charm, particularly on TV; an able speaker; and independently wealthy, with close contacts with other contribution sources.

"He is not as experienced as [Clinton] Anderson," the report granted, "as oratorical as Clement or as pro-farmer as Humphrey—but he has by far the best combination of positive qualifications, the only one who can meet every specification posed, and the most 'winning' of all the potential running-mates." The reference to his being not as "pro-farmer" as Humphrey reflected awareness by the Kennedy forces that his opposition to more rigid price supports in the spring of 1956 had aroused some opposition on the part of farm groups.

All the hopes of the Kennedy-for-Vice-President camp turned now on Governor Stevenson's winning the presidential nomination. Kefauver dropped out following his primary defeat in California, and Stevenson seemed a sure winner. But the Governor was not showing his hand on the matter of his running mate. When Kennedy's brother-in-law Sargent Shriver managed to wangle a few minutes with Stevenson at the tail end of a plane ride to Chicago, he found him alert to the problems of a running mate but non-committal on the man. Stevenson asked bluntly about Kennedy's health and how his father, mother, and wife felt about his running. Reassured by Shriver on both these scores, he turned to the religious question. He had seen the Catholic analysis, Stevenson said, but he was not sure about the statistics. At best, such matters were only an "educated guess."

"In the final analysis," Stevenson said thoughtfully to Shriver, "it is not the political advantage of the vice-presidential choice that is crucial but the needs of the United States—who could best perform the duties and responsibilities of the job." Stevenson went on, "I hope the convention will give a good deal of deliberation to the vice-presidential question."

Shriver pricked up his ears. Would not the presidential nominee still pick his running mate? Stevenson was evasive but indicated that he would. He went on to say that Kennedy, with his clean, "All-American boy" appearance and TV personality, would be a splendid contrast to Nixon and his heavy, thick looks. Shriver brightened at this, but Stevenson went on to say that perhaps Humphrey could "give Nixon hell" better.

Shriver's report on this talk left the Kennedy camp more uncertain than ever. If Stevenson should *not* pick his running mate, it would be well to start organizing for a floor fight. Friends of Kennedy in Stevenson's headquarters warned Sorensen, however, that it would be best not to engage in extensive campaigning; clearly, the Governor did not want to find himself pressured into a choice he did not prefer.

Other reports from Chicago seemed more ominous. A story had reached the Stevenson camp that Kennedy had contributed to Nixon's campaign fund in the contest with Helen Gahagan Douglas; Sorensen hurriedly explained that it was the father, not the son, who may have contributed. What about the Senator's position on McCarthy? Stevenson people were saying that Kennedy was still being evasive on the matter.

The Kennedy camp decided to go ahead with some quiet organizing. Friendly governors, congressmen, and party leaders were asked to talk with their friends about Kennedy. A list of the fifty men closest to Stevenson was drawn up. As the convention neared, plans were laid for a central message room, distribution of material to delegates and the press, "spontaneous" cheering when Kennedy appeared on the rostrum, instructions for the convention orchestra, special contacts with congressional members of state delegations.

It was a shoestring operation, and the situation was too fluid for a definite convention program. But excitement was mounting. Kennedy, who was still letting his aides take the initiative but who was helping out when asked, had an understanding with Sorensen that the whole operation would be conducted on a nothing-to-lose basis and he would not be disappointed if he lost. By early summer, Sorensen wondered if Kennedy's hopes were rising.

"You're not going beyond our understanding, I hope," Sorensen said.

"Well, I must admit—I *will* be disappointed if I don't make it—from the time the convention decides on Friday until the time I leave for Europe Saturday morning!"

The First Hurrah

The Stevenson band wagon was rolling smoothly when the Democratic convention opened in Chicago's International Amphitheatre in mid-August 1956. Harry Truman tried to spike it by plumping for Averell Harriman, but the band wagon hardly slowed down. In its wake were a dozen vice-presidential hopefuls waiting for their own chance to move.

Kennedy got off to a good start the opening night thanks to his role as narrator in a propaganda film on the history of the Democratic party. His appearance on the rostrum afterward set off the convention's first demonstration, a placard-waving effort by the Massachusetts delegation that set off mild cheers throughout the hall. The delegates were not yet interested in running mates. Earlier, Kennedy was host at a breakfast for the entire New England delegation, and governors and party leaders rose to offer him solid support.

"I should invite you all to breakfast every morning," Kennedy said with a laugh.

A sudden call came to Kennedy from Stevenson's headquarters late the second night of the convention. Stevenson told the Senator that he might want him to give the nominating speech for him the next day. If the South were aroused by a civil-rights fight, however, Stevenson said, he might prefer a Southerner for the job to unite the convention. Kennedy had mixed feelings—was this a consolation prize for not being Stevenson's running mate? No, Stevenson said, he had not made up his mind. Two hours later, a call came from a Stevenson aide: "You're it. Go to it." The Senator and Sorensen toiled over a speech until six in the morning. After a few hours' sleep, Kennedy, speech in hand, took a taxi to the Amphitheatre. En route he rehearsed his remarks; Tom Winship of the Boston *Globe,* sitting next to him, thought he saw Kennedy clench his fists and whisper to himself, "Go!"

Kennedy made a valiant effort to do justice to his assignment. "We here today are selecting a man who must be more than something of a good candidate, more than a good politician, or a good liberal, or a good conservative. We are selecting the head of the most powerful nation on earth —the man who literally will hold in his hands the power of survival or destruction, of freedom or slavery. . . .

"The grand alliance of the West. that chain for freedom forged by Truman and Marshall and the rest is cracking, and its unity deteriorating and its strength dissipating. . . ."

But while he was paying fulsome tribute to Stevenson, Kennedy was wondering about his own prospects. The only concession he had got from the Stevenson forces was that they would consult with him before deciding on the vice-presidential nominee. As the hours passed, no such meeting seemed in the wind. Persistent rumors had it that Stevenson had narrowed his choice down to Kefauver or Humphrey. The Minnesotan was making a hit with delegations as he toured their caucuses, giving forth with pithy, humorous talks. Fearing that his selection as Stevenson's nominator was simply a consolation prize, Kennedy told New England delegates at another breakfast meeting that he had virtually abandoned hope of getting second place.

Delegates crowded around him at the head table. Was he really pulling out? No, said Kennedy, it was not a formal withdrawal.

The next day, Stevenson rolled to a big victory on the first ballot. Massachusetts gave him thirty-two of its forty votes; McCormack was able to deliver only seven and a half to Harriman. Kennedy had produced almost a solid delegation for Stevenson, but what would the Illinoisan do? The convention was soon to find out. Asking permission to make a short statement, Stevenson appeared before the wildly applauding crowd:

"The American people have the solemn obligation to consider with the utmost care who will be their President if the elected President is prevented by a higher will from serving a full term. . . ." Stevenson did not mention Eisenhower, twice stricken with illness as President.

"In these circumstances I have concluded to depart from the precedents of the past. I have decided that the selection of the Vice Presidential nominee should be made through the free process of this convention. . . ."

In his suite at the Conrad Hilton, Kennedy met late in the evening with aides and family. He had his staff, family, and assorted college and political friends with him, but he lacked the organization for a full-fledged drive among the fifty-three delegations. Little more than twelve hours remained before the balloting. Through the night, Kennedy and his people ransacked the city for delegates, most of whom had gone to bars or to bed. Far off in France, Joseph Kennedy started making phone calls to political leaders. Kennedy was able to reach some Southern delegations, who seemed favorable. The New England bloc was standing firm, except for New Hampshire, which had been for Kefauver since his primary victory there. Illinois was friendly. What about New York's fat bundle of ninety-eight votes? Tammany leader

Carmine De Sapio came to offer support after a first-ballot nod to Mayor Robert Wagner; so confused was the Kennedy headquarters that De Sapio quietly waited for a time before anyone recognized him.

What about the New York liberals? Earlier in the week, Kennedy had been around to see Mrs. Roosevelt, who had mightily helped Stevenson get the nomination. The former First Lady was gracious but a bit glacial. She immediately asked Kennedy where he stood on McCarthyism.

"She was hurrying to go downstairs," Kennedy remembers, "the room was full of Roosevelts and others—it was like eighteen people in a telephone booth. She was giving what I said only half attention because of the confusion. She was giving her views on McCarthy, not listening to what I was saying. My point to her was that, since I had never really been especially vigorous about McCarthy during his life, it would make me out to be a complete political prostitute to be champing and jumping to change, to denounce McCarthy when he was gone politically."

Even though Kennedy had stated to her that he approved the Senate's censure vote, this seemed to Mrs. Roosevelt inadequate. She wanted an acknowledgment of the damage McCarthy had done to the whole country, not just to the Senate. This acknowledgment Kennedy did not make. Now, with the vice-presidential fight on his hands, Kennedy knew that he could not hope for support from Mrs. Roosevelt or some of her fellow liberals.

In other ways it was a trying night for Kennedy. It was hard to find delegation leaders, and those he did find were often evasive and unsure of their delegations. He managed to reach McCormack, who talked for two hours about his problems with the platform committee while Kennedy sat tensely, feeling that time was running out. But McCormack was willing to second his nomination.

Meantime, Kennedy workers ranged through Chicago getting placards ready, leaflets printed, noisemakers, buttons, banners. Other vice-presidential aspirants were busy, too; a delegate could hardly cross the street to get a drink without being accosted. Kefauver had strength throughout the country; a half-dozen other candidates had tied up their home states. But everything was obscure. Never had a convention race been so genuinely "wide open."

Moving their command post to the Stock Yard Inn, just outside the convention hall, Kennedy & Co. settled down for the balloting. Sprawled on a bed, Kennedy watched the turbulent floor action on TV. The first ballot went about as expected: Kefauver got 483½ votes, Kennedy 304, followed by Albert Gore, Wagner, Humphrey, and the others. Ribicoff and Dever huddled with New York leaders on the floor amid a jostling crowd and pleaded frantically for New York's ballots on the next turn. New York came through; so did several more Southern and border states and parts of other delegations. Texas, spurred by Sam Rayburn, who like other Southerners had little love for Kefauver, left Gore and put a solid bloc of fifty-six votes into Kennedy's column.

At this point the candidate was in the tub. Torby Macdonald shouted in: "Sam Rayburn just swung Texas to you!" Kennedy rose dripping from the water, wrapped himself in a towel, and returned to the TV set just as Lyndon Johnson announced that "Texas proudly casts its vote for the fighting sailor who wears the scars of battle. . . ." Kennedy's name shot ahead on the second ballot, outdistancing Kefauver, 618 to 551½; he needed only sixty-eight more votes for the nomination. Kennedy, who had had two hours' sleep the night before, was now resting on his bed in his shorts. On the third ballot Kentucky came over with thirty more votes. Sorensen reached over to shake his hand: "Congratulations, Jack. That's it."

"No, not yet," Kennedy said. He began to dress calmly in front of the television screen.

The convention was in a tumult. Sam Rayburn, the chairman, pounded for order. Eagerly waving their Kennedy signs, the Massachusetts delegates milled around the floor, pleading with other delegations to join the band wagon. But there was no band wagon to join. In fact, Kennedy had reached the peak of his strength on the second ballot. The Midwestern and Rocky Mountain states were sticking solidly with Kefauver, partly because Kennedy had voted against rigid, 90 per cent of parity farm props. Other states were breaking toward Kefauver and evening up the race. The next few minutes would tell the story. As confusion mounted, half a dozen delegations were waving their standards for recognition. What state would Sam Rayburn recognize? At this moment, McCormack was down on the floor.

"Sam! Sam! Missouri!" McCormack yelled up at the Texan. Did he think Missouri was shifting to Kennedy? Or did he see a chance to even scores?

Missouri had just caucused and by a narrow margin shifted its vote from Gore to Kefauver. There was a roar as Missouri announced its shift. Now the pendulum swung fast to Kefauver. In a few moments he went over the top.

Kennedy turned from the television screen. "That's it—let's go." He appeared as calm in defeat as in the prospect of victory. At the convention hall, he pushed his way to the rostrum: "Ladies and gentlemen of this convention. I want to take this opportunity to express my appreciation to Democrats from all parts of the country, North and South, East and West, who have been so kind to me this afternoon. . . ." He moved that Kefauver be nominated by acclamation. The crowd shouted its agreement. As Kennedy left the platform, the band swung into the "Tennessee Waltz."

Despite his grin, Kennedy looked wilted and disappointed. Yet, as things turned out, this was his great moment—the moment when he passed through a kind of political sound barrier to register on the nation's memory. The dramatic race had glued millions to their television sets. Kennedy's near-victory and sudden loss, the impression he gave of a clean-cut boy who had done his best and who was accepting defeat with a smile—all this struck at people's hearts in living rooms across the nation. In this moment of triumphant defeat, his campaign for the presidency was born.

11 ★ SENATOR FROM THE UNITED STATES

Kennedy's excursion into national politics in 1956 was a milestone in his political and intellectual development. It forced him into the midst of national forces far removed from the parochial influences of Boston. It was appropriate and perhaps symbolic that in this same year, Harvard, which had never seen fit to cite Joseph P. Kennedy as onetime ambassador to the Court of St. James's, awarded an honorary degree to his son. The citation read: "Brave officer, able Senator, son of Harvard; loyal to party, he remains steadfast to principle."

It was even more symbolic of the change in Kennedy that, in a speech that same June day to a Harvard audience, he paid tribute to the intellectual's role. Politicians, he said, needed to have their temperatures lowered "in the cooling waters of the scholastic pool"; they needed both the technical judgment and the disinterested viewpoint of the scholar, "to prevent us from becoming imprisoned by our own slogans."

But his speech was a defense of the politician, as well, and of the compromises he must make. The goal of education, he said, is the "advancement of knowledge and the dissemination of truth," but in politics, it is different: "Our political parties, our politicians, are interested, of necessity, in winning popular support—a majority; and only indirectly truth is the object of our controversy." Both the scholars and the politicians need each other and should call a truce in their misunderstandings, for both operate in the common framework of liberty; political and intellectual freedom are indivisible—". . . if the first blow for freedom in any subjugated land is struck by a political leader, the second is struck by a book, a newspaper, or a pamphlet."

After the convention, where his party failed to follow Harvard's lead with its own award, Kennedy left to join his father on the Riviera for a vacation, too tired to feel his disappointment keenly. Jacqueline, who was expecting a baby in the late fall, had chosen not to go with him to the Mediterranean; she had gone to Newport after attending the convention to stay with her mother and stepfather and await her child there.

Kennedy's staff had been amused by a letter that came in from a Haverhill Irishman shortly after word got out about the expected child, and during the fight with Burke:

"Dear John and Jackie," the letter began. "God love you both and good luck on the coming event. Now you kids will have one of your own. Whatever it is boy or girl you'll love it like you never loved anything in your life. Now Johnny boy what in H—— are they trying to do to you? Of course I am slightly on your side but this is just a little to rough. Gee, it must be tough to have money. Thank God John I never envied anyone for all they had. In my book Kennedys are the tops. But we know these Irish, particularly these tough ones. . . . I wrote all this stuff and my little Nova Scotia herring wife says 'watch your blood pressure.' . . ."

But now an urgent message caught up with Kennedy sailing on the peaceful Mediterranean with his brother Teddy: Jacqueline had lost her baby and was in serious condition. Kennedy flew home at once. Jacqueline had gone through an emergency operation at Newport Hospital. For a while she was in a critical condition, but by the time her husband reached her bedside she was recovering.

In their big house in Virginia, Jacqueline had spent many hours planning and setting up a nursery for their expected first child. Within a few months of the miscarriage, they sold their Virginia farm to the Senator's brother Bob and moved to Georgetown. (There, late in 1957, a daughter, Caroline, was born.)

After Jacqueline's convalescence, Kennedy turned to the presidential campaign. Eisenhower and Nixon had been renominated at San Francisco, so it was the battle of 1952 all over again, with the same results. Despite the general pessimism, which he shared, Kennedy threw himself into the struggle. He stumped through twenty-six states, campaigning harder than probably any Democrat other than Stevenson and Kefauver themselves. He also went out of his way to make speeches endorsing a host of local candidates.

While Stevenson and Kefauver went down to defeat in November, the Democrats held their majorities in both houses of Congress. It was vindication for the judgment of Kennedy's father; it is doubtful that even if Kennedy had been on the ticket Stevenson would have done much better outside Massachusetts and perhaps Rhode Island. The fruit that Kennedy had sought and narrowly missed turned out to be hollow. It was Kefauver who was to go into a political eclipse, while Kennedy's sun was rising.

Two weeks after the election, Stevenson wrote to Kennedy: "I should have thanked you long before this. I can think of no one to whom we should all be more grateful than to you. And I am only sorry that I did not better reward you for your gallantry in action. I have confident hopes for your future leadership in our party, and I am sure you will help immeasurably to keep it pointed in a positive direction. With my boundless gratitude, and affectionate regards. . . ."

A Democrat Looks at Foreign Policy

Ironically, Kennedy and Kefauver clashed again at the start of the new session in January 1957, but this time the Massachusetts man won. A vacancy had been left on the Senate Foreign Relations Committee by the retirement of Senator George. There was no committee assignment that Kennedy prized more highly. Kefauver wanted it, too, however, and he had four years' seniority over his rival. After a quiet undercover tug of war between the two, the Democratic steering committee, headed by Lyndon Johnson, gave the place to Kennedy. That the Democratic "insiders" would ignore the Tennesseean's seniority was a sign of Kennedy's popularity and Kefauver's unpopularity with the conservatives and moderates in the Senate's "inner club." As in the House, Kennedy had got along well with all factions of the Senate, and with the older members; Kefauver had not.

Kennedy wanted Foreign Relations not only for its obvious political advantages, but because he believed that he belonged there. His youthful experiences at his father's embassy, his interest in foreign policy while in the House, and his extensive travels equipped him, he felt, to shape foreign policy with other committee members like Fulbright, John Sparkman, and Morse. He saw no reason to act the part of a self-effacing freshman.

Later in the year, Acting Secretary of State Christian Herter appeared before the committee in the wake of a storm over the appointment of Maxwell Gluck and other Republican campaign contributors to ambassadorships. Gluck, it had turned out, knew nothing about the country, Ceylon, that he was headed for.

Wouldn't it be in the best interests of the United States to reassign Gluck? Kennedy asked the Acting Secretary bluntly.

"I'm very glad to have your views on that," Herter said. But it was a presidential appointment, and, anyway, the costs of an embassy were so high that people with means had to be sent. This led Kennedy into a denunciation of the social demands on ambassadors by Americans abroad.

"I really don't see any reason why United States Ambassadors should be obliged by custom to give a party for tourist Americans and visiting Americans, two or three thousand of them, who come and eat up in one day his whole representation allowance for the year," he told his fellow Bostonian. It was up to the department to prohibit it.

"I'm sure the ambassadors would be awfully glad," Herter said, "but the Congress would have to take the rap on that one."

"I think it is a most defensible rap that we could take," Kennedy said. Then, returning to Gluck, he made a formal request that Gluck's reassignment be considered.

A few months later, Kennedy took on John Foster Dulles himself during hearings on the Mutual Security Act of 1958. Citing the Secretary's own figures, Kennedy observed that Russia's ratio of economic aid to its military aid was far greater than America's.

"Don't you think," he asked Dulles, "that, while it is very important that we maintain our own national defense, particularly in the missile field, the Soviet Union may be using better judgment in concentrating on the economic, rather than the military, in contradistinction to ourselves?" This question of Kennedy's suggested a shift of emphasis in his own thinking since the days when he stressed military aid.

Dulles dwelt on the need for military aid to countries to combat internal communist subversion.

"Mr. Secretary," Kennedy persisted, "the point I want to make is that I think the economic assistance that is proposed in this bill is inadequate, in view of the very serious nature of the problems within those underdeveloped countries, the population increase and the effort that the Soviet Union is making." He went on to talk knowledgeably about the rate of interest of the Export-Import Bank, hard loans and soft, the record of Germany, and the special problem of India. The two ended up by agreeing, however, on the need to amend the Battle Act, which restricted aid to Soviet satellites like Poland.

Kennedy was not content merely to take potshots at Dulles's foreign policy. In July 1957, he made himself a target by speaking up on the Algerian question. Just as he had criticized French policy in Indochina in earlier years, now he delivered to the Senate a long and devastating indictment of the refusal of France to make needed concessions to the Algerians. The speech was carefully prepared, and advance copies were distributed to senators and the press and to opinion leaders throughout the country.

Kennedy's analysis offered little that was new; it was his concluding proposal that contained the bombshell. Tired of American "pieties" that had been addressed to France, he urged that the President try to achieve a solution through the North Atlantic Treaty Organization or through the good offices of the Prime Minister of Tunisia and the Sultan of Morocco—a solution, moreover, that would recognize the "independent personality of Algeria." If this attempt failed, he proposed that the United States support an effort to gain for Algeria straight independence. Kennedy's speech was "perhaps the most comprehensive and outspoken arraignment of Western policy toward Algeria yet presented by an American in public office," asserted a New York *Times* correspondent in a front-page story.

A small tempest ensued. Eisenhower said in a news conference that the United States must be fair to both sides and would jeopardize its role as peacemaker if it began to "shout about such things." Dulles said acidly that if the Senator wanted to tilt against colonialism, he ought to concentrate on the Communist variety. French officials charged that Kennedy's meddling would only prolong the struggle and cost more lives, and in Brest, civic groups pointedly boycotted the American Fourth of July celebration.

Senate liberals, including Humphrey and Mike Mansfield, rallied around Kennedy, but an unkind cut came from a fellow Democrat, Dean Acheson. The former Secretary of State, whom Kennedy had criticized in the past, attacked the Senator's position as a threat to vitally needed Western solidarity.

Disappointed, Kennedy telephoned his father and wondered aloud whether he had made a mistake. Replied Joseph P.: "You lucky mush. You don't know it and neither does anyone else, but within a few months everyone is going to know just how right you were on Algeria." It didn't quite work out that way. Two years later, with France still grimly holding on to Algeria, Kennedy regretted that so little attention had been given to his suggestions for negotiations for self-determination and so much to his reference to independence.

A few weeks after this venture into international politics, Kennedy sent to the scholarly quarterly *Foreign Affairs* for publication a piece that put the problem in wider perspective. Entitled "A Democrat Looks at Foreign Policy," the article was a sweeping statement of the philosophy that underlay Kennedy's approach to specific foreign-policy problems. Appropriately, it was printed in the journal directly after a defense of American policy by Dulles.

"To an observer in the opposition party," wrote Kennedy, "there appear two central weaknesses in our current foreign policy: first, a failure to appreciate how the forces of nationalism are rewriting the geopolitical map of the world—especially in North Africa, southeastern Europe and the Middle East; and second, a lack of decision and conviction in our leadership which has recoiled from clearly informing both the people and Congress, which seeks too often to substitute slogans for solutions, which at times has even taken pride in the timidity of its ideas.

"International events today are subject to a double pull—a search for political *identity* by the new states and the search for *unity* among the established states of the world. As Europe draws in upon itself toward a Common Market and greater political integration, Africa, its former colonial estate, is breaking apart into new and emergent states. Through the world today runs both a tide toward and away from sovereignty. . . .

"The task," Kennedy continued, "is to strike a realistic balance between the legitimate appeals to national self-determination which pulsate through the uncommitted world and the gravitational pulls toward unity which grow from the technological and economic interdependence of modern states. This is a very difficult exercise in political ballistics. Different parts of the world are at divergent points along the trajectory of political independence. Both democratic self-government and large supra-national mergers have preconditions—a capacity to govern and a communality of interests which cannot be created only out of military fear or idealistic impulse. Americans have always displayed a faith in self-enforcing moral principles and have hankered for apocalyptic solutions and fixed patterns; they must learn that most current issues in international politics do not encourage such unrealistic hopes. Many of the old conceptions of war and peace, friend and foe, victory and defeat, must be reshaped in the light of new realities."

Kennedy warned against rigidity of policy, against relying on "paper defenses" like the Baghdad Pact, against irresponsible promises such as "liberating" the satellites, against our unwillingness to accept partial gains, against getting "lashed too tightly" to a single man and party, such as Adenauer and his Christian Democrats, against the American tendency to seek absolutist solutions, against "old liberal bromides" that had no appeal to nations seeking a quick transition to industrialization and admiring "the disciplined attack which Communism seems to make upon the problems of economic modernization and redistribution." He attacked the use of foreign-policy bipartisanship to stifle dissent, the lack of presidential direction, the "mongrelization of clashing views" from agencies operating in a vacuum that led in time to central policy-making bodies becoming "mere vendors of compromise."

What, then, would Kennedy do? In the spirit of his criticism, he offered no sweeping programs or solutions. In the interstices of his article, though, was a series of specific proposals: amendment of the Battle Act and other acts in order to provide help to Communist satellites; the forging of closer ties with younger leaders and opposition parties such as the German Socialists; encouragement of independence for Algeria within a framework of economic interdependence with France; a broader-gauge and more sustained policy in the Middle East, embracing a multilateral regional-development fund, the Jordan River scheme, a food pool backed by our farm surpluses, and a program for Arab refugees; selective, long-term, better-planned economic aid; higher allowances for ambassadors so that the best career men could serve; and, above all, leadership and a "clear articulation of policy at the pinnacle."

The essay was stronger on criticism than positive proposals; and it had its inconsistencies, most notably in its upbraiding of Dulles for the "jagged" ups and downs of his Middle Eastern policies while offering no Kennedy alternative that would not prolong shifting policies of immediacy and expediency. Still, it was a signal achievement—meaty, informed, insightful, and candid. Our foreign-policy makers, Kennedy said, must avoid both the utopian moralism of Don Quixote and the doubt and vacillation of Hamlet. It was clear that he proposed, as a possible top foreign-policy maker, to be neither.

Moreover, the articles served as a kind of prologue to Kennedy's foreign-policy stands during 1957 and the next two years. Following a trip to Poland, he made some major speeches on the importance of re-establishing ties with that country to pull it out of Moscow's orbit through peaceful means, and he fought hard and successfully in the Senate for an amendment to the Battle Act that would permit United

States aid to Poland. Working closely with former Ambassador to India John Sherman Cooper, Republican Senator from Kentucky, he helped gain Senate approval of a resolution urging United States support of India's efforts to stabilize its economy, and during 1959 a plan for long-term and intensive aid to India was one of the key points in his foreign-policy program. He also introduced a bill to provide assistance to South Asia by encouraging the establishment of an international mission to co-ordinate aid programs of all Western countries to India and other South Asiatic nations. With Humphrey and Fulbright, he cosponsored a five-year Development Loan program that, in modified form, was incorporated in the Mutual Security Act. More recently, as chairman of the Africa Subcommittee of the Senate Foreign Relations Committee, he turned his attention to some of the acute problems of that turbulent continent.

Kennedy's heightened interest in aid programs, however, did not change his views on the need for a full-scale, modern weapons program for defense. In 1958, in a speech in the Senate on the widening arms gap, he warned that Soviet missile gains were shifting the world balance of power toward Russia, and he predicted that the gap between Russian and American missile strength would be largest—and most dangerous—during the early 1960's. The "deterrent ratio might well shift to the Soviet so heavily, during the years of the gap, as to open to them a new shortcut to world domination. A portion of their homeland would still almost inevitably be destroyed, no matter how great their defenses or how decimated our retaliatory power. And without doubt world opinion would not tolerate such an attack. But our experience with the illogical decisions of Adolf Hitler should have taught us that these considerations might not deter the leaders of a totalitarian state—particularly in a moment of recklessness, panic, irrationality, or even cool miscalculation. . . .

"In the years of the gap, every basic assumption by the American public with regard to our military and foreign policies will be called into question." One by one, Kennedy ticked them off: the assumption that peace is the normal relation between states, that "we should enter every military conflict as a moral crusade requiring the unconditional surrender of the enemy," and so on. He attacked the administration's willingness to "place fiscal security ahead of national security."

"We have been passing through a period aptly described by Stanley Baldwin . . . in 1936, as 'the years the locusts have eaten.' "

Senator Symington rose. Would his able friend from Massachusetts agree that the situation faced by America in the late 1950's was considerably comparable to that faced by the British in the late 1930's?

"The Senator is completely correct," Kennedy answered.

Civil Rights: A Profile in Cowardice?

On a midsummer day in 1957, a New Yorker who had long battled for civil rights wrote to Kennedy a letter bristling with indignation. He recounted how he had headed a civil-rights group working for Stevenson and Kefauver in the preceding year's campaign, how he had had to combat the Republican pitch that "a vote for any Democrat is a vote for Eastland," how he had worked hard to minimize the defection of Negro voters from the Democratic candidates.

"Your vote, and those of the other 'liberal' Democratic Senators came, therefore, as a distinct shock and surprise to me. The vote plainly and simply confirms . . . the previously mentioned charge of the Republican party and will without question force thousands of loyal Democrats, both Negro and white, into the ranks of the Republican party in future elections. Speaking for myself personally, I made the switch as soon as I saw your 'Profile in Cowardice' in my copy of this morning's *New York Times*.

"Since, Senator, you are a leading candidate for the Democratic presidential nomination in 1960, and even though I abhor Richard Nixon, I must in good conscience inform you that I will do all in my power to see that you lose not only in New York State but in New York City as well.

"P.S. I do so hope that your Administrative Assistant will pass this along to you for your personal attention."

The letter was passed along, and Kennedy replied that he thought the writer's interpretation of his actions entirely wrong and he hoped that he would see this after "more sober reflection." He added, "Frankly, I have never been impressed by threats, especially when the results of actions which I have taken after thorough and conscientious thought."

The exchange reflected the passion surrounding the Civil Rights Bill of 1957. The bill, in turn, issued from a tangle of conflicting ideologies, sectional strife, party maneuvering, and presidential ambitions. Eisenhower and Stevenson had stressed civil rights in their campaign talks, and now Nixon and Knowland, their eyes on the White House, were pressing for action. The Southerners, of course, were hostile; liberal Democrats wanted to push ahead of the administration, and

Lyndon Johnson was negotiating for a compromise that would help hold his shaky coalition together. For Kennedy, the bill posed a sharp political dilemma, for he had close ties with Southern political leaders and they had come through for him at Chicago; yet he had to prove his liberalism in the eyes of the Northern progressives.

Unluckily for Kennedy, the very first vote on the bill theatened to throw him into a political embrace with Senator James Eastland, of Mississippi, the hated symbol of Southern racism. Under the regular procedure, the civil-rights bill passed by the House would go to the Judiciary Committee, chaired by Eastland, before coming to the Senate floor. Knowing of the Mississippian's dexterity in bottling up such measures, liberals sought to invoke a little-used Senate rule that would let the bill bypass the committee.

Kennedy would have none of it. The temporary advantage to be gained by bypassing Eastland's committee, he felt, was not worth a dangerous precedent that might come back to haunt liberals. He argued, too, that a discharge petition could be used to pry the bill out of Eastland's pocket, and he promised to vote for such a petition if one was needed. Morse strongly supported this view, but most liberal Democrats, including Humphrey and Symington, favored the bypass, which barely carried the Senate.

"The most disgusting news I have read in a long time," a Long Island Negro wrote Kennedy on hearing of his position. Negroes would not forget, he added.

When it came to the substance of the bill, however, Kennedy was all militancy. The acid test was Section 3, which authorized the attorney general to use injunctive power to enforce school desegregation and other civil rights, hence allowing greater use of civil sanctions instead of cumbersome criminal prosecution. The implications of Section 3 were enormous; it might become the device by which a liberal President could push school integration, as well as voting rights, throughout the South. Well aware of these possibilities, the Southerners were seething, and the White House itself had misgivings. One might expect, then, that the "moderate" Kennedy would shy away from it. But no—Kennedy not only backed Section 3 but took the floor to make his views clear.

The debate over Section 3, he told the Senate, had persuaded the nation and the watchful world, whether correctly or not, that the vote on it would be a stand for or against the Supreme Court decision on school desegregation, "even though the Attorney General has recently given his assurance that it will not change in any way the deliberate pace at which this decision is to be implemented in the local courts.

"My own endorsement of that decision, and its support in the State I have the honor, in part, to represent, has been too clear to permit me to cast a vote that will be interpreted as a repudiation of it." Kennedy then voted with liberal Democrats and Republicans in an effort to salvage this part of the bill. But a conservative Democratic-Republican coalition knocked Section 3 out of the measure.

Shorn of its strongest section, the Civil Rights Bill still looked eminently desirable to the civil-rights bloc, because of its buttressing of the all-important right of Southern Negroes to vote. But now a new road block appeared. Many moderates and some liberals were disturbed by the lack of a requirement for jury trials in criminal contempt cases involving voting rights. Other liberals, however, feared that inserting such a requirement would put the enforcement of voting rights into the hands of white Southern juries who would invariably rule in favor of white election officials. Senator Joe O'Mahoney plumped strongly for a jury-trial amendment, and picked up more support when a provision was tacked on in effect requiring that juries in such voting-right cases include Negroes.

Now Kennedy was caught in probably the severest pressure he had known in the Senate. The civil-rights bloc of labor, NAACP, and ADA leaders was dead set against the O'Mahoney amendment. Southern senators threatened to filibuster the whole bill unless the amendment went through. Southern governors wired Kennedy urgent requests to vote for the amendment; one of them added, unsubtly, "Still hearing good things about you and your future." All factions were watching the Senator with a steely eye.

What should Kennedy do? In this dilemma he turned to several law professors who had concluded that the jury-trial amendment would probably not hurt the effectiveness of the amendment of the bill in a major way. One of these was Mark De Wolfe Howe, a noted civil libertarian and ADA leader who had urged Kennedy to take a strong stand against McCarthyism. Over the telephone, Howe advised Kennedy to support the O'Mahoney amendment. "The issue has aroused more legal fuss than it deserves," Howe said, "and is certainly not a question which permits of too much dogmatic stubbornness." Another leading authority, Paul Freund, of Harvard Law School, felt that the O'Mahoney amendment did not seriously weaken the bill. These arguments helped Kennedy take the position toward which he already leaned for political reasons.

As usual, he lost little time telling the Senate of his decision. The day of his telephone discussion with Howe, he declared on the floor that the major portion of the bill was still intact in that the civil-contempt power of federal judges could be used effectively in behalf of persons wishing to vote. Even in criminal-contempt cases, he went on, Southern juries, "mindful of the watching eyes of the nation," would convict; if they did not, Congress could always strengthen the legislation in the future. Moreover, the amendment actually would broaden civil rights by inducing Southern officials to put Negroes on juries in order to have jury trials. Finally, Kennedy said candidly, as a practical political matter the Southerners might filibuster the bill to death unless they got jury trials.

In the face of scorn from civil-rights groups, Kennedy stuck to this position during the ensuing debate. A few civil-rights leaders came over to the view that the bill with the jury-trial amendment was the best that could be had, but most Senate liberals, including Humphrey, Symington, and Morse, and liberal and pro-Eisenhower Republicans, including Saltonstall and Ives, voted against the amendment. Kennedy, a few liberal Democrats like John O. Pastore, of Rhode Island, and Henry Jackson, of Washington, and the solid phalanx of Southerners gave the amendment enough votes to put it over, 51 to 42. The whole civil-rights bill—or what was left of it—passed by a heavy majority a few days later.

Had Kennedy, then, shown a profile in cowardice? His outspoken support of Section 3 and his pledge to help vote the bill out of Eastland's embrace if necessary would indicate that the answer was no. Certainly, however, he showed a profile in caution and moderation. He walked a teetering tightrope; at the same time that he was telling liberals of the effectiveness of a bill that included the O'Mahoney provision, he was assuring worried Southerners that it was a moderate bill that would be enforced by *Southern* courts and *Southern* juries—Kennedy's italics.

For moderate liberals like Kennedy, the issue boiled down to the practical one of how strong a bill could be gained in the existing legislative situation. He insisted that he would not surrender principle for the sake of expediency; indeed, the main question he directed at his civil-libertarian friends was whether the O'Mahoney amendment did involve a "betrayal of principle," and he was assured by them that it did not.

Other liberals like Humphrey disagreed. They believed that more could be won from the Senate by all liberals and moderates sticking together, and if they failed to pass a bill, the issue could be taken to the country in an election. If the Southerners filibustered a bill to death, so much the worse, but at least the issue would have been dramatically sharpened. Kennedy preferred a somewhat crippled bill on the books to a lively issue for the platform. He played with compromise for the sake of moderate, immediate ends.

Kennedy has often defended the necessity for compromise in politics. He told a Harvard audience in 1956 that "compromises and majorities and procedural customs and rights affect the ultimate decision as to what is right or just or good." The politician, he said, resents the scholar "who can with dexterity slip from position to position without dragging the anchor of public opinion."

Both politicians and intellectuals can be, on occasion, insufficiently sensitive to important issues of principle, he said: "Politicians have questioned the discernment with which intellectuals have reacted to the siren call of the extreme left; and intellectuals have tended to accuse politicians of not always being aware, especially here at home, of the toxic effects of freedom restrained."

Kennedy's civil-rights beliefs were soon tested under fire. In the fall of 1957, he flew to Jackson, Mississippi, to deliver a campaign speech. He was told on arriving that the Republican state chairman had just challenged him to declare himself on the school-desegregation issue. The time was shortly after Little Rock.

"I have no hesitancy in telling the Republican chairman the same thing I said in my own city of Boston," Kennedy told the crowd. "That I accept the Supreme Court decision as the supreme law of the land. I know that we do not all agree on that issue, but I think most of us do agree on the necessity to uphold law and order in every part of the land."

There was no sound from the audience. "And now I challenge the Republican chairman to tell where he stands on Eisenhower and Nixon," Kennedy said. This time the crowd broke into cheers.

Hooverism and Housekeeping

While Joe McCarthy had been using his Government Operations Committee as a vehicle for exposing "subversives" in government, Kennedy had taken it seriously as an instrument of government reorganization. His father had served on the Hoover Commission, and since the start of his legislative career, Kennedy had shown a strong interest in the managerial and housekeeping side of government. In the House, he had supported Hoover Commission proposals and had berated the Truman administration for its "confused" and "muddling along" operation of foreign-aid programs. In the House, too, with considerable assistance from Reardon, he had made an exhaustive study of methods of selecting Annapolis and West Point cadets, and he had proposed a system for a "politics-proof Academy selection system" that won widespread notice.

Later, as chairman in the Senate of the Reorganization Subcommittee, Kennedy served as a kind of receiver general for Hoover Commission proposals. Under his leadership, the Government Operations Committee, now back under the chairmanship of Democrat John McClellan, had reported favorably on twelve reorganization measures incorporating Hoover Commission proposals, and most of these ultimately were passed by Congress. Among the Reorganization Subcommittee's proposals were those to centralize records management and disposal of surplus property in the General Services Administration, to expedite payments of certified claims where appropriations had lapsed, and to authorize donation of surplus property for civil defense.

Herbert Hoover watched admiringly. He wrote Kennedy from Palo Alto thanking him for "the way you have been carrying the ball" for the reports of the Hoover Commission. In a letter to his friend Joseph Kennedy, Hoover called his son "my favorite Democratic Senator."

A key Hoover Commission proposal was a drastic reorganization of budgeting, accounting, and appropriations procedures. Sponsored by thirty-two Republicans and Democrats in the Senate, the proposal would put the entire financial structure of the government on an annual accrued-expenditure basis by requiring that budgets be based upon actual costs, that agency accounts be maintained on an annual accrued basis, and that appropriations be related directly to expenditures each fiscal year.

"Thus we will no longer see," Kennedy remarked to the Senate, "the departments and agencies rushing to obligate their unused funds as the end of the fiscal year approaches." Senate economizer Harry Byrd estimated that the measure would eliminate or substantially reduce carry-overs of unexpended balances estimated to amount to $74 billions, over which Congress had little control once the appropriations were made.

Some proposals, even of Hoover himself, Kennedy viewed with a critical eye. Eisenhower's illnesses had focused interest on the organization of the White House, and the former President had suggested that Congress establish the position of administrative vice-president to relieve the President of some of his managerial burdens. After three days of hearings on the proposal, Kennedy rejected the idea. Not only were there enough officials in the White House to whom work could be delegated, but he was wary of making changes affecting the presidency. "The American Presidency," he told the Senate, "was not intended by its creators . . . as primarily a ceremonial or coordinating job, with its most essential responsibilities delegated to non-elected officials. The Congress, therefore, should not take the lead in diluting the President's responsibilities in order to lessen his burdens, unless such authority is actively sought by the President."

Most of the Hoover Commission proposals involved humdrum matters with little attraction for the public. Even Kennedy could squeeze little political sex appeal out of them. But this did not bother him. The problems, which were controversial enough to legislators and officials, challenged his cool and intellectual approach to government. Moreover, his painstaking work on the bills proved that he was not interested only in glamorous, front-page issues, but could do his homework and provide leadership on internal problems of government. Probably nothing brought Kennedy more respect from the moderates who ruled the Senate.

Two other projects that Kennedy took on during this period were of somewhat wider public interest. One was a proposal to create a National Library of Medicine. For years, the single greatest center of medical information, books, treatises, journals, periodicals, and unpublished research papers had been in the Armed Forces Medical Library, reportedly the greatest medical library in the world. But the library had long existed on a hand-to-mouth basis in the defense establishment, without an adequate physical plant. With the support of the American Medical Association and four other health groups, Kennedy secured passage of a bill that gave the new library independent, statutory power and a civilian as well as a defense role.

But nothing engrossed Kennedy more than the job he got of chairing a special Senate committee to choose the five all-time (and deceased) senators whose portraits would be placed in the Senate reception room. Acknowledged as the Senate's "historian in chief" because of *Profiles in Courage*, Kennedy turned what might have been a lackluster formality into a widely publicized historical sweepstakes. He polled senators and several hundred historians and political scientists for nominees for the honor. The five finalists endorsed by Kennedy, his committee, and the Senate were Henry Clay, Daniel Webster, John C. Calhoun, Robert M. La Follette, Sr., and Robert A Taft.

Picking the Big Five was no routine exercise. Since senators and scholars agreed that the immortal trio, Webster, Clay, and Calhoun, had to be included, only two other places were left. It was agreed that one of the two remaining posts should go to a conservative, one to a liberal. Choice of the former was not difficult; Kennedy went along with the conservative majority on his committee, who insisted on Taft. On the liberal side, the committee had to choose among Norris, La Follette, and Borah, and picked La Follette. Various senators and scholars grumbled that Taft was too partisan for the selection, Norris was head and shoulder above all those selected—and how come not one Democrat got chosen?

Kennedy stood his ground, citing scholarly support. Actually, he was glad from a political standpoint to support Taft. At a time when his voting was becoming increasingly down-the-line liberal, he still wanted to keep some ties with the conservative camp. Doubtless he had noted that many conservatives, if denied the substance of right-wing policies, will settle for symbolic recognition of the justice of their cause. The success of the first Hoover Commission, for example, showed that many conservatives were willing for the government to spend billions if the billions were spent in "businesslike" ways. Right-wingers like Basil Brewer forgave Kennedy many a liberal vote as long as the Senator paid tribute to Bob Taft's greatness.

Kennedy, in short, was acting as a kind of junior senator for all sections and major ideologies in the United States. His solicitude for Hooverism and governmental housekeeping was in part a result of conservative feeling, in part a political device to keep some ties with the right wing generally and with Southerners in his own party. Sometimes it was an awkward position; not surprisingly, Kennedy feels that in the Senate he was "so inhibited by all the pressures" that he was "not very much good to anybody," compared to the House years, when he was "independent" and even "brash." Still, even at this stage in the Senate, there was some direction to his policies and politics. Essentially, he was already sailing toward 1960 before winds of liberal doctrine; he had the helm fixed toward the port but he was still dragging a small anchor to starboard.

12 ★ SWINGING FOR THE FENCES

By 1958, Kennedy was becoming a national celebrity. Over one hundred speaking invitations a week streamed into his office; some came to him via friends, family, or even Catholic hierarchs in Boston. He accepted as many as he could of those that were politically profitable. He spoke to the National Conference of Christians and Jews on Middle East problems; to the Overseas Press Club on the need for closer relations with the satellites; to the American Jewish Committee on liberty; to the Citizens Committee for the Hoover Report, honoring Herbert Hoover. He addressed the Society of the Friendly Sons of St. Patrick in Baltimore, the American Gastro-Enterological Association in Colorado Springs, the Arkansas Bar Association at Hot Springs, Democratic functions in Kansas, Nevada, Mississippi, and Massachusetts. During 1957, he gave at least one hundred and fifty talks throughout the country, during the next year probably two hundred more.

Kennedy was saying nothing about his plans for 1960, but his admirers suffered no such inhibitions. At the Democratic dinner in Topeka, a huge homemade placard reading "Kennedy for President" was waved from a table directly in front of the Senator's rostrum. At Reno, a University of Minnesota coed told the Young Democrats' convention that she bore a message from her fifty-eight sorority sisters: "Every girl told me to give Senator Kennedy all her love and tell him they would all vote for him." One Midwestern group gave

199

him a plastic replica of the White House—"I'll take it home
to Caroline," the Senator said. It was a rare Democratic
chairman who could introduce Kennedy without allusions—
arch, humorous, or eloquent—to the "next President of the
United States." Autograph-hunting students mobbed him after
speeches. Gray-haired mothers gushed over him. Heads
turned as he and Jacqueline walked through air terminals.
A veteran campaigner by now, Kennedy took it all with
aplomb, but Jacqueline sometimes found the uproar disconcerting. A middle-aged woman in a Western city embraced
him on the sidewalk, murmuring, "God bless you, Joe." In
Ashland, Wisconsin, a teen-ager asked him to explain how he
had become a war hero. "It was involuntary," Kennedy said.
"They sank my boat."

The Kennedy family ambition and what one reporter had
referred to as "Kennedy togetherness" were gently ribbed at
a Gridiron press dinner in Washington in March of 1959.
Joseph Kennedy was pictured singing to a familiar tune:

> All of us
> Why not take all of us?
> Fabulous—
> You can't live without us.
> My son Jack
> Heads the procession.
> Then comes Bob,
> Groomed for succession. . . .

Publicity fed on publicity. As Kennedy stumped the country, magazine editors found that he was superb copy, with
his youth, war record, family, and money, and that he and
his wife made a wonderful front cover, especially in color.
During 1957, *Time* did a cover story on Kennedy, *McCall's*
and *Redbook* wrote him up in feature articles with plenty of
attention to Jacqueline, the *American Mercury* played him
as the "perfect politician." *U.S. News & World Report* and
Parade struck the theme of John and Robert Kennedy as
a governmental "brother act," and the *Saturday Evening Post*
and the *Catholic Digest* covered the whole Kennedy family.
Newspaper coverage was heavy, too, and soon news clips
were overflowing Kennedy's filing cases into cardboard
cartons.

Kennedy himself had contributed a remarkable number of
articles to a variety of publications. His favorite theme—
or the favorite theme requested by the magazines—was
still political courage; he applied the test to others besides the
heroes of *Profiles in Courage* and squeezed the last drop

out of this topic when he wrote a piece on three *women* of courage for *McCall's*. He did an article on his illness— "What My Illness Taught Me"—for the *American Weekly* and on brotherhood for *Parade*. Several of his favorite legislative problems he popularized in magazines; he urged in the *Saturday Evening Post* that the military academies be taken out of politics, and in the New York *Times Magazine* he wrote on lobbyists and on the challenge of political courage. Kennedy was not interested solely in mass-circulation magazines; he also appeared in the *Foreign Policy Bulletin*, the *National Education Association Journal*, and business and labor periodicals.

In earlier days, Kennedy had had to offer articles to journals like any other beginner, but after 1956, editors were dunning him for submissions. They had discovered that he could be depended on to send in a knowledgeable, well-argued piece, not eloquent or brilliant, perhaps, but highly satisfactory and likely to arouse further notice when newspapers quoted from the Senator's remarks. The award of the Pulitzer prize to *Profiles in Courage* in May 1957 made Kennedy's writings more prized than ever.

All in all, Kennedy got a magnificent build-up in 1957—a build-up that he mightily aided and abetted. Sometimes the Senator and his aides wondered whether all this was premature—the presidential election, after all, was three years off. But the matter was largely out of their control; there was no way to pace the publicity to fit their political needs. "If top magazines want cover stories, calling him 'hot copy,' we don't throw them out suggesting they come back next year," declared a staff member. They would take what they could get when they could get it, and hope that the morrow would bring new ideas and more headlines.

Room 362

Life in Kennedy's office had become more frenetic than ever. The sheer output of work was extraordinary. Secretaries toiled far into the evening over mountainous correspondence. Aides returned at night to work on speeches and legislation. The office was more jammed than ever; visitors could hardly find a place to sit, and an extra person coming in to help out had to play musical chairs, grabbing any desk that was momentarily unused. Reardon now supervised sixteen employees, some of whom worked in the basement office.

As the years had passed, this office had taken on the appearance of a museum and a library. On the right, as one entered in 1959, stood a large glass-faced bookcase housing volumes sent to Kennedy and arranged indiscriminately. Among the books there were Paul Blanshard's *American Freedom and Catholic Power*, a book by Billy Graham, several Bibles, and a biography of Al Smith. On top of the bookcase sat several models of World War II ships, and hanging over it a nine-foot eight-inch sailfish Kennedy caught in a two-hour struggle off Acapulco in 1953. Completing this nautical display was a huge harpoon section of a darting gun used in hunting whales, maps of the New Georgia Islands, and a telegram—THE NAVY IS PROUD OF YOU—that Kennedy received from James Forrestal after his election to Congress.

In the far right corner from the entrance door was the historical section of the office: old cartoons from *Harper's Weekly*, old prints, and more than fifty framed pictures of the Senator's friends, most of them inscribed to him. The pictures suggested the broad range of his friendships: Harry Truman, Herbert Hoover, Bishop Weldon of Springfield, Massachusetts, Senators Lyndon Johnson, Walter George, and Hubert Humphrey, the last inscribed to Kennedy, "a man of courage, brilliance and dedicated to public service, with admiration and friendship." In the center of the room, before a green marble fireplace and the flags of his state and nation, stood Kennedy's large desk. Within arm's length he had several books—at that time, Margaret Coit's *Mr. Baruch*, John Dos Passos' *The Men Who Made the Nation*, Walter Lippmann's *The Communist World and Ours*, the Alsop brothers' *The Reporter's Trade*, and the *Report of the United States Commission on Civil Rights, 1959*. On this desk, too, were some souvenirs: a gavel presented by Stevenson in 1956, a long pipe, and, the most valuable of all, the coconut shell on which Lieutenant Kennedy scratched the message that led to his rescue in the Pacific.

In a cubbyhole room surrounded by filing cases, Sorensen labored on campaign talks, magazine articles, speeches for the Senate floor, newspaper releases, correspondence with political leaders. Though he was incessantly interrupted by telephone calls and visitors, Sorensen never lost his composure; somehow he was able to supply Kennedy with the meaty articles and speeches he wanted, often just before the deadline. In the same cubbyhole, at a desk next to Sorensen's, sat Mike Feldman, a tall rangy Pennsylvanian and seasoned government lawyer who did legislative analyses and bill-drafting for the Senator. Fred Holborn, a Harvard-trained expert on international affairs, helped out on foreign-policy statements and a host of lesser matters. Ralph Dugan, of the staff of the Senate Education and Labor Committee, assisted Kennedy on a wide range of labor and social-welfare matters. Sitting just outside the Senator's door was his personal secretary, Mrs. Evelyn Lincoln, who, amid the hurly-burly of ringing phones, special messengers, gawking visitors, and chattering typewriters, seemed to know exactly where everybody and everything was located.

The door was still open: an election was coming up, and the office could not forget for a moment the power held by the people back home. Constituents came in to get admission cards for the Senate gallery from Pamela Turnure, a pretty New Yorker who sat by the door; some visitors tarried a bit hoping to get a look at the Senator. Reardon was on the phone to Boston, making arrangements for Kennedy appearances, smoothing over local frictions among the Kennedy forces, sending instructions to the state Democratic committee, and keeping a watchful eye on Massachusetts politicians.

An air of tense, bustling informality hung over the office. Kennedy was everywhere, darting out to talk with Reardon or Sorensen, stopping by Mrs. Lincoln's desk to take a telephone call or to dictate a letter, welcoming a visitor, closeting himself in his office for long conferences and phone talks, rushing off to the Senate floor at the sounding of a quorum call. As he talked with visitors in his office, Kennedy would sit back in his big chair, lean forward to make a point, fidget with a pencil, interrupt himself to pick up the phone. Mrs. Lincoln would show in more visitors—the Senator would look up with a smile, "Hi Bill! How're you doing?" At times the office seemed like a five-ring circus, as Kennedy simultaneously performed as senator, committee member, Massachusetts politician, author, and presidential candidate.

Producing a dozen major articles and speeches a month, the office devoured factual information and new ideas. Kennedy was the biggest senatorial user of the Legislative Reference Service in the Library of Congress. Help was found also in the nation's universities, especially Harvard. Kennedy went to historians for advice on the five outstanding senators, to political scientists for help on governmental problems such as lobbying and the Electoral College, to law professors for their views on civil liberties and civil-rights bills. A brilliant student of international politics at M.I.T., W. W. Rostow, had a major part in working up several of the Senator's foreign-policy statements. Other help came from Earl Latham at Amherst and John K. Galbraith at Harvard.

If Kennedy had access to brains in his big operation, he also had another requisite—money. Big-time politics was expensive. Giving a banquet at the Mayors' Conference at

Miami Beach cost Kennedy over $2,000. Every Christmas he sent out several thousand greeting cards. During the first seven months of 1956, when the Democratic convention and national campaign were in the offing, Kennedy spent $72,206 outside his regular allowance for his Washington office. Among the major items were $19,913 for his Washington house expenses, $1,697 for clubs and contributions, $18,647 for extra Washington office expenses, $2,791 for his Boston office, $11,061 for hotel, travel, and other business expenses. Some of Kennedy's bills were paid by him through his father's New York office, which served as a financial clearing-house for tax and accounting purposes and as a communication center for the whole family. At one point, the Senator feared that he had inadequate control of his own expenses and he had to request the New York office to send all bills and requests for essential expenditures to him for his approval.

By 1958, Senator and Mrs. John F. Kennedy and daughter Caroline were well settled in their Georgetown house. Jacqueline was happier here than out in Virginia. Fronting on a quiet, tree-lined street, the three-story brick house looked out in back on a walled garden with outdoor furniture and a play area for Caroline. Jacqueline hoped to make the house a restful, nonpolitical retreat for her husband, and furnished and decorated it to reflect her personality and interests rather than his. On the walls of the living room were old prints of French scenes; on the table were art books and folios; the furniture was dainty and elegant. It was clearly not a house for politicians' smoke-filled rooms.

But even in this tranquil setting, Kennedy was still his restless self. He hated to waste time; in the morning he would read a magazine while taking a bath and at the same time shave there, guiding his razor by glancing occasionally at a mirror set up on a bathtub tray. Often friends and politicians came in for breakfast, served on trays in the living room. The Senator took a few minutes to play with Caroline, but after that everything was on split-second timing. Sometimes he let John J. ("Muggsy") O'Leary, a genial Senate doorkeeper who helped out in the office, drive for him, but he usually preferred to take the wheel and race over to the Capitol. If he got to an airport ten minutes early, he rushed to a phone booth to shower Mrs. Lincoln with instructions or even squeeze in a couple of long-distance calls. No time was lost at lunch, either; Muggsy brought a hot meal from home. Kennedy rarely got back to his family before eight in the evening, too late to see his daughter.

He rushed to finish dinner to get to a meeting or to take Jacqueline to the movies. The Kennedys did little entertaining. The Senator's idea of the ideal way to spend an evening was with a book, especially history. When queried at one point during 1957 as to what he was reading, he listed John Buchan's *Oliver Cromwell*, Arthur Schlesinger, Jr.'s *Crisis of the Old Order*, and Arthur Link's *Road to the White House*.

"Young man in a hurry," one journalist called him. Sometimes his friends feared that he was too much in a hurry, that he was going too far too fast, that he should pace himself better, that he should learn to take a breather. But the dynamo would not or could not slow down. He was always in the process of going or coming. Friends noted with a smile that of the first six words Caroline had learned at a year and a half—Daddy, airplane, car, shoe, hat, and thank you—at least three had something to do with motion.

In his usual shrewd and gentle way, James Reston, of the New York *Times*, summed up Kennedy's position in Washington as the 1958 session ended. Kennedy, said Reston, had established himself as the rookie of the year when he first came to the Senate and this was about the way he was regarded until the Democratic convention of 1956.

"The pros, who are older and therefore allergic to rookies, thought he was too young—35 when he came in, 41 now —and some of them even thought he was too pretty. Also he read, and even wrote, books, and spoke to people at Harvard—all of which encouraged the professionals to wonder whether he was tough enough for the big time. . . ." Reston described Kennedy's successes in the 1956 convention and after.

"In short, Senator Kennedy is on the make; he makes no pretense about it, and he dismisses out of hand the suggestion that he is young enough to wait for some other presidential campaign . . . when newer and perhaps tougher competition will arrive. He is swinging for the fences now. . . ."

Home Run in Massachusetts

Kennedy's senatorial term expired at the end of 1958. As the fall campaign approached, hardly an informed Democrat—or even Republican—in Massachusetts saw any real possibility that he could be beaten. No Republican of any stature wanted to be the sacrificial lamb. It looked as though a Democratic trend was on generally, and Republican leaders forlornly surveyed their stable of younger candidates.

What discouraged the opposition most was the extent of the defection to the Senator from their own ranks. Rank-and-file Republicans did not hide their determination to vote for Kennedy. Despite his voting record, they simply refused to look on him as a Democrat or as a liberal: somehow he seemed above or outside the regular party battle. It was hard to think of this engaging young green blood as a politician—what with his money, his education, his prize-winning book and all.

Kennedy was, of course, very much a politician, but he had cultivated the feeling among the voters as a whole that he was a "different breed," with his moderate speeches, emphasis on economy, and standoffish attitude toward Boston polls. The remarkable thing was the number of conservative businessmen who were going to vote for him, not from any sentimental attachment to him or misunderstanding of his voting record, but because of concrete things that he had done for them. A Democratic candidate for Congress, campaigning in one of Massachusetts' districts in 1958, was amazed at the number of businessmen who said they had seen Kennedy two or three times on their tariff or tax or labor or regulatory problems. Somehow Senator Saltonstall had been too busy and their own Republican representative unavailable, but they had always been able to get in to see the junior Senator.

Kennedy was especially eager to help prominent Republicans, who might forgive him his Democratic votes as long as he attended to their problems with the federal government. For example, Robert Choate, the very Republican editor of the very Republican Boston *Herald,* for years had been trying to get a prized television channel in the Boston area but had run into difficulties. The rival paper, the Boston *Globe,* and others in Boston had opposed this grant on the grounds that control of mass media should be diversified rather than concentrated in one man's hands. Choate drew up an amendment that would bar the Federal Communications Commission from discriminating against applicants for TV licenses because of their other interests in mass media —in short, because of their newspaper ownership. Kennedy obligingly submitted to the chairman of the House Inter-state and Foreign Commerce Committee a long memorandum that argued against the discrimination policy and included Choate's amendment. Kennedy insisted both in his submission and in private correspondence that he was not necessarily endorsing the amendment; but certainly he had given Chaote good service.

Kennedy had also intervened in the scramble of airlines for routes allotted by the Civil Aeronautics Board. He and five other New England senators wrote the CAB in July 1956 in favor of the certification of a New England enterprise, Northeast Airlines, for a Florida route. In a separate letter to the CAB, Kennedy made clear that he supported Northeast's bid over Pan American's.

It was small wonder that Kennedy kept his reputation as a fighter for Massachusetts' interests. His office also toiled in behalf of the thousands of persons who wrote in for little favors. This help is, of course, routine for any congressional office—but again the remarkable thing was the sheer volume of Kennedy's "case load," as favor administration is called on the Hill. Frustrated by their labyrinthine state and local governments, Massachusetts people would write in to Kennedy concerning not only federal but all sorts of local problems—road construction, school difficulties, liquor licenses, housing, and so on—and as often as not the Senator's office would ask a Kennedy lieutenant back home to help out. Old Pat Kennedy would have admired the efficient processing of these requests. The main difference between Kennedy and his forebears was patronage; the Senator had few jobs to give out because of Republican control of the administration.

* * *

The political consequences of all this activity were simple: Kennedy had decisively won re-election long before the campaign. Still, he had some worries. One was complacency and apathy among his own forces. Another was the annoying tendency of the newspapers to set margins by which Kennedy would have to win in order to maintain his national prestige. Victory alone would not be enough; he must win by 200,000 or 250,000 votes. And as the campaign got under way, the newspapers kept raising the ante—to 300,000 or 400,000 votes. The faster Kennedy ran, the more he stood still.

But the thorniest problem for Kennedy was that of maintaining his nationwide momentum while devoting himself to a campaign back home. A smashing victory would, of course, enhance that prestige; the trouble was that Democratic candidates everywhere were appealing to him to come to their bailiwicks and help them out. The Kennedy name, it had long been known, could be depended on to pack a party rally or dinner. For his part, Kennedy prized these invitations, for they could lead to closer contacts with state party leaders, and also build up political debts to him on the part of candidates who might become senators and governors and congressmen and hence control delegates to the national convention.

But how could he campaign for the party nationally while building up a massive margin in Massachusetts? As usual, Kennedy decided to try to do both.

The Republicans had dug up an obscure blue blood to run against Kennedy, but a scrappy Italo-American from East Boston fired the Republican party convention with an impassioned speech pledging a fighting campaign. It was none other than Kennedy's old congressional foe of 1950, Vincent J. Celeste.

Nominated by acclamation, Celeste started on the warpath. "I'm running against that millionaire, Jack Kennedy," he would say on his handshaking tours. He charged that Kennedy had given aid and comfort to the Faubuses and the Eastlands by his civil-rights votes, that he had destroyed the Port of Boston by voting for the Seaway, that he had supported a labor bill dictated by Walter Reuther. But Celeste always came back to the Kennedy family and their money.

"What right do Kennedy and his brother Bobby have to sit in judgment on labor without ever doing a day's work in their whole lives?" demanded Celeste, who still lived on the top floor of a three-decker tenement. "Look how my opponent voted for the St. Lawrence Seaway—it starts right at the front door of the Merchandise Mart in Chicago, which is owned by old Joe Kennedy." The Senator's father, he added, was calling the signals.

Celeste, it was felt in the Kennedy camp, was about the weakest man the Republicans could have nominated. Still, he was worrisome in two ways. His pitch about the Kennedy money hit a sensitive chord; some people were still accusing Kennedy or his father of having "bought" the 1952 election. To counter this, Kennedy decided on a minimum-expense campaign, especially in regard to television and other media. Celeste also had an obvious appeal to the large Italo-American population in the state, and to Furcolo Democrats who felt that Kennedy had snubbed the Governor, who was running for re-election. Arrangements were made for the Senator to receive the "Man of the Year" award from the Sons of Italy, testimonials were obtained from Italo-American notables such as former heavyweight champion Rocky Marciano, of Brockton, and Kennedy and Furcolo presented a more or less united front during the campaign.

The netwwork of Kennedy secretaries did the campaign spadework. Old-fashioned campaign methods came to the fore again because of the diminished TV budget. Kennedy decided not to go in for big tea parties again because this campaign gimmick, it was felt, had been "used up." Making use of thousands of volunteers, the secretaries stressed house-to-house canvassing, distribution of a Kennedy newspaper, and gathering signatures—ultimately over 300,000—on cards pledging the signer to vote for Kennedy.

As usual, the Senator ran solo. On the stump he called for the election of his running mates but he kept his political operations as separate as possible from the other campaigns. He had his own elaborate campaign headquarters in Boston, with a window display of copies of *Profiles in Courage* and photostats of the handwritten manuscript. Every candidate in the state grabbed for the Kennedy coattails, but in most cases the Senator maintained his distance. He could be tough, too. When one politician proposed to put out a bumper sticker linking his name with Kennedy's, the Senator instructed an aide to tell him not to do so for either or both of two reasons: "We have refused Furcolo and several other candidates; we don't like ———— [the name of the beseeching politician] and don't want to be associated with him." Billboards suddenly appeared with Kennedy and Furcolo standing shoulder to shoulder, but this was the work of the Governor and was viewed as sheer political gamesmanship by the Kennedy people.

Kennedy campaigned with his usual skill and with greater presence than ever before. He toured the state on a tight campaign schedule that still allowed a few minutes for unplanned appearances at an Elks' picnic or a union convention. At times, he even played to the gallery. At a rally in Athol, he abruptly left the stage, strode over to the large high-school band that was blaring out a march, took the baton from the bandmaster's hand, and led the group through the rest of the piece, ending with a flourish—and on the beat.

Even during the last few weeks of the campaign, Kennedy took time out to stump for candidates in other states. Early in October, he spoke for Democrats in Delaware, New Jersey, West Virginia, and Maryland; a week later, he flew out to Des Moines. These forays had to be conducted unostentatiously, because Celeste was hitting the theme of Kennedy's interest in the presidency rather than in Massachusetts.

By the end of October, some Kennedy enthusiasts were predicting a margin of 500,000 or even 600,000. The Senator had tried to discourage this optimism. "In looking over past records," Sorensen had written a campaign aide, "he is *sincerely* convinced that it will be tough to beat Dever's old record of 250,000 in an off year. Can you see that everyone gets the word?" The highest margin in the state's history had been Saltonstall's victory of 1944 by 561,668 over a Democratic unknown.

The day before election, Kennedy campaigned for hours through factories and precincts in Boston. Finally, he and his party climbed wearily back into their car, sank into their seats, and started back to headquarters. The car slowed for an old woman plodding across the street.

"Stop the car," Kennedy ordered. He climbed out, shook hands with the woman, asked her for her vote, and climbed back in. Next day, the old woman, it can be assumed, and 1,362,925 others voted for Kennedy. His margin was 874,608 —the largest margin ever accorded a candidate for any office in either party in the state, the largest margin received by any senatorial candidate in the United States in 1958, and the largest percentage of the vote received in 1958 in any major senatorial contest in the country.

Kennedy had swung for the bleachers—and connected for a homer.

The Senate as Testing Ground?

When does a man decide to run for President? Usually there is no one climactic moment when he makes a clear irrevocable decision. Rather, he plays with the notion, pushes it away, ponders, temporizes, beckons toward it again, until time and circumstance help make the decision. But in Kennedy's case, if there was one moment when he decided to go for the big prize, it was the moment when he got the election returns late in the evening of November 4, 1958, in his father's hotel room.

Kennedy now had six more years in the Senate. As a student of American history, however, he knew that the upper chamber was not a good springboard to the presidency. Only Warren G. Harding had gone directly from the Senate to the White House, and he was not a very good advertisement for this kind of recruitment. As the spotlight again swung to Kennedy after his triumphal re-election, pundits were quick to explain why being a senator handicapped a candidate for the presidency. The main difficulty was that he had to take specific positions on a multitude of controversial issues at awkward times. Too, he was surrounded by several score politicians of both parties, including sharp-eyed rival presidential hopefuls who had him constantly under surveillance and who could unite against him at will. If he took the initiative on any bill and made it his project, his success or lack of it would become a test of his presidential quality, even though the fate of the bill might be largely outside his control. If he did nothing, he would be written off as a cipher.

Kennedy had good reason to coast on his Senate record and duck the tough assignments. On the other hand, one of his main problems, he realized, was a widespread feeling that he was a political playboy, bright but superficial, energetic but incapable of following through, a compromiser who avoided the tough issues. He had been compared to one of his PT boats, darting around, moving in to let loose a torpedo, taking evasive action, and disappearing in the night. He had to build a reputation on the strength of managing the prickly problems that had wrecked the presidential hopes of some senators; indeed, he had to show in the Senate the tactical judgment, political finesse, and bulldog determination expected of Presidents as chief legislators.

And waiting for him as the 1959 session opened was precisely the kind of issue that could make or break an ambitious young senator: labor legislation. Kennedy had good reason to know the pitfalls of an effective labor measure, for, in partnership with Republican Irving Ives of New York, he had piloted such a bill through the Senate in 1958. Drawn from recommendations by a group of labor experts headed by Professor Archibald Cox, of the Harvard Law School, the bill would have required union officials to file financial reports and union rules with the Secretary of Labor; to report financial transactions with employers or others that might involve conflicts of interest; and to report on union trusteeships. The bill also required regular elections by secret ballot and tried to control "shake down" picketing. Employers were compelled to report money spent to influence employees, and labor-relations consultants had to submit financial reports. The bill was pulled into the vortex of controversy over Taft-Hartley by proposed amendments to that act which would allow strikers who had been replaced to vote in representation elections; would permit prehire contracts, without a representation election, in the building trades; and would require the non-Communist affidavit of employers proposing to use the services of the National Labor Relations Board. Kennedy opposed this last amendment; indeed, he wanted no such affidavit requirement for either employer or employee.

It was one of those bills that, as a package, appealed to the vast majority of voters but whose provisions separately repelled a variety of business and labor groups. At a private meeting with George Meany early in 1958, Kennedy found the president of the American Federation of Labor and the Congress of Industrial Organizations unexpectedly hostile to even moderate legislation, and the labor leader was strongly backed by leaders of the old craft unions in the AFL-CIO. Other union leaders, such as Walter Reuther, of the Auto Workers, and David Dubinsky, of the Garment Workers, were less adamant. Hearings on the bill, presided over by Kennedy as chairman of the subcommittee on Labor, produced clashes between the Senator and Meany. At one point, after Kennedy had argued that his bill was not antilabor because the Cox Advisory Committee was made up of experts friendly to labor, Meany burst out, "God save us from our friends!"

Later on, however, Meany became more amenable to the Kennedy-Ives Bill when Knowland, campaigning for governor of California, began talking about sweeping labor legislation that would tighten the Taft-Hartley Act. On June 17, 1958, the Senate passed Kennedy's bill by the top-heavy vote of 88 to 1. But this near-unanimity was deceptive, for two months later, the bill was done to death in the House by an "unholy coalition" of labor and business groups, as Ives called it, and by "sabotage" on the part of Labor Secretary James P. Mitchell, as Kennedy put it. In a bitter statement, Kennedy charged that "only the Jimmy Hoffas and the Nathan Sheffermans can find satisfaction" in the bill's defeat.

"Constructive labor reform legislation will be brought forward again next year," Kennedy promised, and by New Year 1959 he was hard at work on a new measure and still busily picking the brains of the experts on the Cox Committee. Once again Kennedy decided on a bipartisan labor bill, because he felt that a straight Democratic bill could not pass. He even sent an emissary to Mitchell to find a basis of agreement, but the Labor Secretary rejected the overture—his views and Kennedy's, he said, were too far apart.

So once again Kennedy had to guide his bill through the labyrinthine legislative channels. He and Mitchell clashed repeatedly in subcommittee hearings as Kennedy sought to bring out the weaknesses in the administration's position and warned that an attempt to attach sweeping changes in the Taft-Hartley Act to the reform measure would kill it. But the main threat to Kennedy's bill came not from Republicans, but from a member of his own party, Senator McClellan, who had great prestige in the Senate as chairman of the Labor Rackets Committee, of which Kennedy was a member and Bob chief counsel. During a Senate debate on the labor-reform bill in April 1959, McClellan suddenly brought in an amendment to write in a strong "bill of rights" for union members. Anathema to almost all labor leaders, the amendment would have brought down in one stroke the extensive labor acceptance of his bill that Kennedy had built up during the past two years.

Even worse for Kennedy, at this point he stood almost alone. Ives had retired from the Senate; an effort to find another Republican cosponsor of the bill had failed; and Sam J. Ervin, Jr., a North Carolina Democrat who had agreed to cosponsor the reform bill, was deserting Kennedy on critical amendments. Two able liberals, Douglas and Humphrey, were out of town. With him on the floor, as he managed his bill, were Cox and Ralph Dungan of the Labor Committee, but these experts, confronted by scores of proposed amendments, were not especially well briefed on the McClellan proposal, and at this critical moment they could not supply much assistance.

So, all alone, except for occasional help from Morse, Kennedy stood up to senator after senator who pounded him with questions as to why the "bill of rights" was not a logical extension of his own reform measure. Many of his antagonists were lawyers who liked to cite legal chapter and verse. Kennedy was bone-tired, he was disconcerted by the quick turn of events, and most of his recent homework on labor reform had been sandwiched between exhausting campaign trips and legislative duties. Still, he had done that homework, and this, along with his twelve years of work on labor bills, enabled him to hold his own in the debate. His most telling argument was one that he, of all liberal Democrats, was in the best position to offer—that the "bill of rights" would involve a vast intrusion of federal regulation into areas reserved to state control. He threw the old jury-trial argument back into the faces of the Southerners.

But in the tense roll call that followed, the Southerners and Republicans beat Kennedy's forces by one vote; the deciding vote was cast by Vice-President Nixon to break a tie. Things were going badly for Kennedy, and the newspapers were making the labor bill a test of his presidential chances. It was a "grave defeat" for the Democratic hopeful, the New York *Times* correspondent reported. A night and a day of frantic conferring, redrafting, and maneuvering followed. Cox and Kennedy managed to come up with a less stringent bill of rights proposal that won strong support on the floor. Humphrey flew back from California, where he had been campaigning, to help gain reconsideration. On issue after issue, Kennedy was able to mobilize backing to outvote the McClellan and administration forces. He was even able to muster a strong majority for the amended bill of rights. By the week's end, he had regained control of the legislative situation, largely through his arguments on the floor and also with the help of Majority Leader Lyndon Johnson. Finally, the Kennedy Bill passed the Senate, 90 to 1.

But the battle was not over for Kennedy. The House of Representatives, under pressure from the administration, passed the Landrum-Griffin Bill, which was much stiffer than Kennedy's Senate bill. The conference committee, set up to reconcile the two bills, numbered seven men from each chamber, including Kennedy. Many doubted that the committee would come up with a compromise that would pass both houses. Both prolabor and conservative legislators preferred no bill at all to a weak bill, for then they—each of them—would have the "big issue" for 1960.

For two and a half weeks, the men labored over the multitudinous provisions of the two bills. Kennedy's aides had never seen him work so hard on a legislative matter. The focus was on Kennedy; would he compromise in order to get a bill out or would he cling to his Senate stand for a mild, internal labor reform and hence hang on to his labor support? He chose to compromise. There were some difficult moments. At one point, conferee Barden turned on Cox, who had advised Kennedy throughout the sessions, and said that he was tired of "these intellectual outsiders nitpicking and scratching for little holes." Kennedy replied: "And I'm sick and tired of sitting here and having to defend my aide time and again from your attacks." The conferees sat in stunned silence for a moment, and then the discussion went on. The final version was much closer to the House bill than to Kennedy's in its boycott and picketing provisions, but most of the internal union reform provisions came from Kennedy's original bill.

"Compromises are never happy experiences," Kennedy told reporters. "I think it's the best bill we can get—and get a bill." The measure easily cleared both chambers. How would its passage—with Kennedy's name taken off by his own request—affect his presidential chances? A few union chiefs felt that he had precipitated the whole problem by pressing for internal union reform and then losing control of the situation. A New York *Times* editorial the next day praised the work of the joint conference committee, which, it said, "has done a conspicuous service to the public—and to honest, democratic unionism—in sweating out a labor reform bill." The committee's work, it went on, called for "utmost skill in the art of compromise—which the committee Chairman, Senator Kennedy, outstandingly provided." Though some union leaders condemned the bill as worse than Taft-Hartley,

Kennedy won a standing ovation on September 11—in his first speech after the vote on the bill—from the Building and Construction Trades Department of the AFL-CIO at its annual convention (the building-trades unions fared better than others in the final bill). Cabell Phillips, of the New York *Times,* described Kennedy's presidential campaign position as "equivocal" after his sponsorship of labor reform and his work on the Labor Rackets Committee. *Something* had happened to Kennedy's standing with organized labor, said Phillips, but nobody seemed to know what it was. ". . . There is no reliable consensus on the matter. . . ."

The whole affair had been a tight squeeze, and once again observers raised the question why Kennedy had pitted his presidential hopes on guiding a controversial bill through a Senate dominated by conservatives and presidential rivals. Kennedy was well aware of the traps, but he felt he had to take the chance. While he knew he could have ducked the floor leadership of the bill, he knew also that his experience made him the logical man for the job. Then, too, the senator who sponsored the bill would be acting for the vast majority of the people, despite what some union leaders said. Labor reform would also give him a key issue for the campaign and would keep his name before the public.

But his main reason went deeper—back to the problem of his stature as a presidential candidate. Unlike a governor or Cabinet member, Kennedy had no state or federal agency through which he could establish a reputation for political management. It was not enough to win a state election; he had to show an able President's capacity for pulling together disparate politicians and groups behind a program in the national interest. He had done this in an even more difficult arena than the President's—without the presidential power of patronage and pressure. The final scores of 88 to 1 in 1958 and 90 to 1 a year later were impressive tests of political effectiveness in the Senate. And he was given considerable credit for final passage of the bill.

His fight for moderate labor reform also was an example of Kennedy's theory that in politics one must keep moving, must try for the breaks, must look for the openings, must not stand still. If you move ahead, he has said, you may get some luck otherwise denied. As it turned out, his setback by McClellan and the conference committee tussle dramatized the battle and the difficulties and made the final result all the sweeter. And by sheer luck the Senate tie forced Nixon to show his hand—in favor of a harsher labor-reform measure—and gave Kennedy a big issue for 1960.

"Victura"?

By mid-1959, even while Kennedy was still grappling with the labor-reform bill, his campaign for the presidency was accelerating into high gear. His candidacy was still unannounced but universally expected; the coy pretense about his waiting to make up his mind had all but disappeared. During the summer he acquired an airplane, a forty-passenger Convair, and hired a full-time crew to speed him around the country. The plane was named "Victura" after the sailboat Kennedy had as a child.

He was still leading the Democratic pack in the polls. George Gallup and Elmo Roper ran Kennedy against every likely rival for the Democratic nomination, and then against possible Republican opponents; Kennedy usually emerged on top, sometimes by a small margin, more often by a large one. Some of the local polls produced even more one-sided results. Joseph Alsop, after polling an area in Queens with Louis Harris, came up with figures so top-heavily for Kennedy that he published them with an almost apologetic air.

Polls were unreliable; the voters were fickle, many politicians said. And besides, Kennedy needed the votes of hardboiled delegates to the convention, some Democrats pointed out, not the well-wishes of moon-struck women interviewed by poll-takers while they were hanging out the wash. As Kefauver could testify, popularity polls do not make a man his party's choice. But even by the delegate test Kennedy was doing surprisingly well. A poll by the Chicago *Daily News* early in 1959 of delegates to the 1956 Democratic convention expecting to return as delegates four years later gave the Senator 409 votes on the first ballot in 1960, to 259½ for for Symington, 244 for Stevenson, 195½ for Johnson, and 120½ for Humphrey. Later in the year, a Democratic county chairman in New York State informally polled the twenty-two members of his executive committee; Kennedy won more straw votes than all the other candidates combined.

But was Kennedy fading as the election year neared? Some contended he was meeting this classic fate of those who run too hard too soon, and they felt that their predictions were vindicated when the New York *Times* in August 1959 published a statement to this effect by New York Democratic leaders, following their endorsement of Catholic Mayor Robert Wagner as vice-presidential favorite son. Here again the polls—though inadequate ways of testing opinion, so far the only ones—told a different story. During the same summer, Kennedy's campaign lost momentum while he was tied down in Washington by his legislative duties, especially the labor bill, but his popular strength remained high. A Gallup poll of Democratic voters showed him running neck and neck with Stevenson, and when the latter's votes were reallocated (on the grounds that the former nominee had insisted that he would not be a candidate again), Kennedy had picked up twice as many of them as any other candidate.

During the fall of 1959, Kennedy stepped up his campaign even further. While Congress was adjourning, he stumped for three days in Ohio, including an appearance before 60,000 at a steer roast, followed by three days in Wisconsin and another in Ohio. His schedule for October and November called for a four-day sortie into Indiana, a weekend in West Virginia and New York, a one-day trip to Nebraska, two days in Louisiana for the Rice Festival, a swing up to Milwaukee for the Pulaski Day banquet, three days on the West Coast—including two in vital Oregon—and then a transcontinental overnight trip to New York for an Al Smith dinner. Then were planned in rapid succession three days in Illinois, four in California, four in Oregon, two in Wisconsin, a day each in Oklahoma, Delaware, and Kansas, two in Iowa, two in Nebraska, three in Colorado and Oklahoma. One- or two-day breathing spaces were scheduled in between these trips, but this time, too, was rapidly yielding to campaign plans.

By now the trips were falling into a pattern: last minute briefings and checking of names as the plane circled low around the airport; the receiving party standing in little knots, some holding Kennedy signs; a flurry of introductions and handshaking amid grinning travelers from the terminal who had crashed the party; the fast drive into town behind wailing police cars; the confusion of bags, coats, brief cases at the hotel; interviews with local reporters and short TV appearances with the inevitable questions: "Do you think a Catholic can be elected President?" and "What is your present stand on McCarthy?" Then would come the real pay-off work: a speech to a local college assembly, followed by questions; a Democratic luncheon, followed by questions and a receiving line; a quick stop and short talk at a nearby business convention; a long drive through the country trailed by two or three cars full of reporters to a Democratic tea in a neighboring county with a brief talk, questions, and the receiving line; the drive back to the city through the early dusk, chatting with politicians en route; the hour reserved for relaxation before dinner but actually filled with telephone calls, conferences with politicians, a short interview with a reporter who missed the morning press conference, the hunt for evening clothes amid a welter of newspapers, suitcases, books, garment bags, mimeographed copies of speeches; the grand entrance into the grand ballroom below, the crowd rising and applauding; the long dinner interspersed with introductions, snatches of conversation, and scrawling of autographs; the long preliminaries and more introductions; the speech itself, over a statewide hookup and through a faulty ballroom microphone; another endless receiving line of delegates to the National Convention of Something-or-Other; the final conferences back in the room with Stephen Smith and Sorensen and local Kennedy leaders; a look at the next morning's newspapers, and then to bed—this repeated day after day, month after month, and all amid the tension of keeping on schedule, looking alert and confident, avoiding slips in the question period, giving enough attention and inside news to national reporters covering the swing, dealing tactfully with rival local groups who each wanted to be first on the Kennedy band wagon, appealing to rank-and-file Democratic leaders without alienating the top party men who guard their little satrapies against intruders.

Mrs. Kennedy often accompanied her husband on campaign trips. At first, she had felt bewildered and lost in the commotion, overwhelmed by the press of people, numbed by the endless make-talk and political chitchat. Politicians talked too long; her feet hurt; and the pace was so hectic that she hardly saw her husband except when he was on exhibit. But gradually she became a seasoned campaigner. Reporters debated how much of an asset she was on the tours. "She is an obvious asset to the eyes and well-being of her husband," one of them, Fletcher Knebel, decided, "but an old political maxim says that the candidate's wife should not be too young or too attractive. Women tend to be jealous of both." In any event, campaigning around the country was giving her some preparation for the White House, which she would enter as First Lady at the age of thirty-one if her husband should be elected President.

Behind all the campaigning in the field was Kennedy's usual careful organizing in headquarters. As his operations expanded during 1959, he rented a four-room suite in the Esso Building in Washington near the Capitol and put his brother-in-law Stephen Smith in charge. Four girls, each in charge of a quarter of the nation, handled correspondence from politicians and voters. Names were broken down state by state, then into three political types—political leaders like governors or state Democratic chairmen; rank-and-file leaders such as local committeemen; and grass-roots voters. Coded card files and invitation lists were used to prepare thousands of letters expressing Kennedy's pleasure at having met people on his trips. New gray filing cabinets were packed with polls and electoral studies, press releases, newspaper clippings, and other political intelligence. In a corner office overlooking the Capitol, Smith and an assistant were in almost continuous telephone talks with politicians across the country and with visitors. As they talked they could study wall maps broken down into congressional, county, and local political jurisdictions.

Much of the incoming mail was unsolicited. Most of the letters were friendly, ending perhaps with "God be with you." Some offered advice: "Never, never deny your *religion!*" or "Don't do it!—the odds are against you." Some were hostile: "How does it feel to be a pious four-flusher?" "Dear Saturn," another letter started. And some were mildly zany: "Just finished Life," a fifteen-year-old girl wrote. "You must be very proud of Jackie and yall's beautiful daughter. Please excuse the 'yalls' you must think I'm a hick but it slipped. . . ."

Behind all this organization and activity was a simple strategy: to campaign early, hard, and long, to win the backing of the men and women so neatly tabbed and ticketed in the gray filing cabinets. This strategy had worked in the Eleventh Congressional District and in the State of Massachusetts. Would it work for the whole nation?

There are three main routes to presidential nominations: quiet understandings and deals with top state officeholders and party leaders who control blocs of delegates; establishing friendly personal contact with the multitude of county and local party chiefs who themselves may be delegates; and appealing to rank-and-file party members who in turn might influence delegates. Most candidates stress one of these routes; Kennedy was working all three as hard as he could. His actual tactics varied considerably from state to state because of the varying extents of party leadership and centralization. In most states the party organization was weak and hence he had to deal with a multitude of factions and mavericks.

Sixteen states were quite different from the others, however, and would probably decide Kennedy's fate in the convention. These were the states with presidential primaries— Wisconsin, Ohio, Oregon, Nebraska, California, for example. And, as election year opened, it was clear that Kennedy was making the most intensive effort ever known to sweep those primaries and arrive at the convention in July with a commanding psychological and numerical lead.

Many politicians were skeptical of this approach. The Kefauver glad-handing technique would help Kennedy no more than it did the Tennesseean, they said. Many old-time professionals distrusted Kennedy's party independence and his reliance on political amateurs. One Democrat told a reporter: "Lyndon Johnson had F.D.R. and Sam Rayburn behind him. Stu Symington has Harry Truman. Kennedy has nobody but his father and he does not always listen to him. He stays away from the bosses, and the bosses don't like him." A Democrat in Congress told the same reporter: "Jack needs somebody who can sit down with Sam Rayburn over a glass of bourbon and talk with Rayburn in Rayburn's own language. Jack himself doesn't talk Rayburn's language. And Rayburn is the guy who will be banging that gavel at the convention."

To these strictures, Kennedy and his aides respond mildly. They emphasize first that they are not ignoring party bosses; they are cultivating every Democratic governor, senator, and state chairman they can reach. Any other course would be suicidal; even in states with presidential primaries, a direct appeal to Democrats voting in the primaries is not enough —many such voters can be reached only through their local or state leaders. But when they are rebuffed by the top leaders, the Kennedy aides ask, what else can they do but put their bets on the local leaders and the rank and file? Primaries, says Kennedy, were "put in for a purpose, to give the people a voice—a far more satisfactory system than picking somebody in a hotel room in Los Angeles."

When pressed, some Kennedy lieutenants confess that they are not overly impressed by many party leaders. Their experience in Massachusetts had convinced them that the prowess of the so-called professional is much exaggerated, that bright, competent, and personable young amateurs can bring as much shrewdness and more vigor to politics. As Kennedy wrote in 1957 in an article in *Life* headlined "A Democrat Says Party Must Lead—Or Get Left"; "With a new breed of respected, dynamic professional politicians coming into prominence, we [Democrats] can no longer afford to continue in official party positions tired or tarnished hold-overs from another era—men whose stature and activities inspire neither the enthusiasm of volunteer workers nor the respect of their communities—men who keep busy by attending meetings, filing gloomy forecasts and complaints, and fighting zealously to hold on to their position." Asked if he had someone in mind to fill the role that Farley filled for Roosevelt, Kennedy has said, "I don't know anybody who can handle this thing right now better than I can handle it myself." And if older, wiser heads are needed, Kennedy people prefer someone like Ribicoff, who is working hard for Kennedy, to the old-fashioned party leader who is expert in intraparty politics but not himself an experienced campaigner. If in the end the Kennedy forces pick a veteran figure of the Farley type, he is likely to be closer to a figurehead than a powerful manager.

Behind this skepticism of party "pros," however, is something deeper—skepticism of party organization. In part, this is a tactical matter; Kennedy, if nominated, knows that he would have to run as more than a partisan Democrat in a country where the independents hold the balance of power. In the main, however, this feeling stems from the quality of independence, detachment, and noncommitment that has run through his whole life. He is no more willing to be thrust into the role of organizational "Democrat" than into any other. Kennedy is independent not only of party, but of factions within the party. By no means a conservative, he is not a categorical liberal either. He has considerable support among labor but is not a "labor candidate." He has strength in all sections of the country but, aside from New England, solid support in none.

The impact of this organizational independence on the Democratic convention would do much to determine Kennedy's fate there. The delegates might see it as a demonstration of his middle-of-the-road views and hence might turn to him as a consensus candidate standing between the two extremes, as conventions have so often done in the past. Or the delegates might see his independence not as a reflection of moderation, and party consensus, but as a façade for neutrality and detachment toward the supreme traditions and ideas of a party that was rarely neutral when headed by twentieth-century heroes. In this sense, Kennedy's noncommitment to party might invite party noncommitment to him. Whether he could escape this fate might depend on his power in 1960 both to invoke the best of the Democratic heritage and to renovate its finest principles for the perilous journey through the decade to come.

13 ★ KENNEDY AND THE CATHOLICS

Kennedy likes to tell the story of a United States congressman who visited the House of Commons. When an usher told him that he must leave his seat, for he had taken a place in a gallery reserved for peers, an old peer sitting nearby interposed, "Let him stay, let him stay. He is a Peer in his own country." But the congressman stalked out, saying to the peer, "I am a Sovereign in my own country, Sir, and I shall lose caste if I associate with Peers."

By the start of his second term in the Senate, Kennedy himself had become a peer, and much more. A member of the Senate's "inner club," holder of a Harvard honorary degree and a Harvard overseer, equally at home in Palm Beach or Newport, the Senator was a long way from the Irish cottage and the Boston slum where Pat Kennedy had begun his long journey a hundred years before. All barriers had been overcome.

All but one. The supreme political prize, the highest social position in America, had never been held by a Catholic; only one Catholic had been seriously considered for the job. The old sign that Boston Catholics had hated so much— "Only Protestants Need Apply"—still seemed to be stuck on the White House door. As Kennedy became the Democratic front runner following his 1958 campaign, speculation turned more and more to the prospect that by 1960 the sign might be taken off.

That Kennedy should be the Catholic American of this

generation to be most directly involved in this historic situation was, in a way, rather ironic. For the religious barrier was something to which he had had little personal exposure. He cannot remember today any unpleasant episodes in his early schools or at Harvard.

"My roommate at Harvard was a Catholic but I had some close friends who were not," he says. "I don't think my experience was comparable to the usual one, such as someone growing up and going to school as an Irish Catholic in Boston, where the social barriers between racial groups—between Irish and Italian, or so-called Yankee and Irish—are extremely sharp. I had gone to private school, I came from New York instead of Boston, my father had some money and was well known. I may have had a little feeling of a barrier but not acute."

Now, in 1960, Kennedy was facing the biggest barrier of all amid the blaze of publicity and the din of argument. And he was plunging into one of the historic areas of conflict in America.

Render unto Caesar?

By the mid-twentieth century, Protestants throughout the country were facing much the same problem, although in subdued form, that Massachusetts Yankees had encountered generations before. These Yankees, like the fictional Late George Apley, had seen Irish Catholic immigrants flood into Boston, take control of its politics, push on over Beacon Hill and out into the suburbs, and invade business, education, medicine, and the law. Each side had grievances and felt, each in its own way, beleaguered and discriminated against. And now in the present century, vast social changes brought significant Catholic populations into virtually every state outside the South and the border area. The election of a host of Catholic senators and governors, particularly during the years since the end of World War II, reflected these changes. Even the formerly staunch Republican and Protestant state of Maine had elected a Polish Catholic Democrat, first as a governor, then as senator. And just as Boston Yankees had once looked at the immigrants and their churches and asked, "What will become of our Protestant land?" so the question was now asked by a nation that was still dominantly Protestant in church membership, social heritage, and ideology.

A few who asked this question were bigots who would resort to schemes of discrimination and repression that had no place in a free society. But most were thoughtful people who felt they were defending not only their own creed, but

the cherished traditions of freedom of religion and the separation of church and state. As Americans, they could not and
did not object to Catholics following rules of their own
church. What they did object to was the imposition on Catholics and non-Catholics alike of Catholic standards, through
legislation and economic and political pressure, on education, censorship, marriage and divorce, on medical practices
of contraception, legal abortion, and in other matters. And
they objected to Catholic-backed laws that would pierce the
wall separating church and state, laws that provided, for
example, for governmental aid to church schools.

Protestants, along with most leaders of the Jewish community and most of those who did not identify themselves
with any of the three major American faiths, subscribed to
the admonition of Jesus: "Render therefore unto Caesar
the things which are Caesar's; and unto God the things that
are God's." So did many Catholics. But here was the rub:
Catholic official doctrine, some Protestants contended, assumed papal infallibility even on temporal matters, at least
according to the Vatican Council of 1870. Given the authoritarian, centralized, hierachical nature of the Roman Catholic
Church and its power to discipline its communicants, including officeholders, the Church was able, some contended, to
expand Roman Catholic power by moving into areas like
education that were supposed to be in Caesar's domain.

At the heart of this position was the belief that the "American way" turned on the maintenance of an open, free, and
mixed society, on the maintenance, in short, of pluralism.
Roman Catholic power threatened such a society, many
Protestants said, because, in its official doctrine, at least, it set
no limits to the reach of papal power. And since the reach
was unlimited, Catholics could not be allowed to breach the
church-state wall "just a little," because one opening in the
dike would be followed by more and more breaches as Catholic power expanded. In education especially, Protestants
feared that government services such as bus transportation
and health services, claimed ostensibly for the child alone,
would be followed by demands for more services such as
textbooks, blackboards, the fireproofing of parochial schools,
and so on that would strengthen the institution—the Church
itself—within whose sphere the help was given. Protestants
cited other cases in point. Ultimately, they feared, American
freedom would give way to Catholic power.

For years, the tension between Catholic and Protestant had
simmered under the surface of national life, or erupted in
isolated struggles. In 1928, the conflict had—perhaps omi-

nously for Kennedy three decades later—flamed up during Al Smith's campaign for the presidency. Much of it was precipitated by Ku Klux Klan bigotry that encompassed Jews and others as well. But some of it took the form of a debate between Catholic and Protestant spokesmen. The April 1927 issue of the venerable Boston magazine the *Atlantic* had carried an "Open Letter to the Honorable Alfred E. Smith," by Charles C. Marshall, sharply challenging Smith's ability, if elected President, to govern under the Constitution rather than under papal dictates. Smith answered the challenge in the next issue of the magazine. "I recognize no power in the institutions of my Church to interfere with the operations of the Constitution of the United States or the enforcement of the law of the land. . . . I believe in the absolute separation of Church and State. . . . I believe in the support of the public school as one of the corner stones of American liberty."

Al Smith concluded, "In this spirit I join with fellow Americans of all creeds in a fervent prayer that never again in this land will any public servant be challenged because of the faith in which he has tried to walk humbly with his God."

A vain hope. Although his statement had been enthusiastically acclaimed, the "Happy Warrior's" nomination for President in 1928 set off a surge of anti-Catholicism. During his election campaign, he squarely faced the issue; in centers of Ku Klux Klan strength he spoke on immigration and assaulted the forces of bigotry. Here and now, he cried, I "drag them into the open and I denounce them as a treasonable attack upon the very foundations of American liberty." But nothing—argument, indignation, explanation, emphatic disclaimers—seemed to do much good. The reasoned, moderate, Protestant position was obscured by the flood of bigotry, as was the reasoned Catholic answer. The relation of religion and politics was not, in 1928, a subject for honest and rational debate.

Kennedy Takes His Stand

Three decades after Smith's defeat, another Catholic candidate for the presidency awaited questions from reporters following a talk to the Los Angeles Press Club.

"Do you think a Protestant can be elected President in 1960?" a reporter asked amid laughter.

Kennedy grinned: "If he's prepared to answer how he stands on the issue of the separation of church and state, I

see no reason why we should discriminate against him!"
There was a roar of applause.

For Kennedy it was a nice twist on the old religious
question that had been confronting him in one form or another
ever since his boyhood. His family was devout, close to
the Boston hierarchy, and a heavy contributor to Catholic
churches and charities. Joseph Kennedy gave millions to the
Church through the Joseph P. Kennedy, Jr. Foundation,
which was headed for a time by John Kennedy, and later by
his brother Bob.

Yet the Kennedy men, in contrast to the Kennedy women,
were not brought up entirely in a Catholic mold. Joseph,
Sr. attended parochial school only to the seventh grade,
when he switched to Boston Latin and later to Harvard. John
Kennedy spent only one year in a Catholic school—and even
that school was taught by laymen. He never made a display
of his religion, though he observed the formalities. He
never encountered anti-Catholic bias in school and hence
was not forced back into a tight, defensive embrace with
the Church.

It was not surprising, therefore, that Kennedy entered
Congress without strong convictions about the problem of
church and state. During his first years there he took the
position that under federal aid to education programs,
private- and parochial-school students should share in funds
for bus transportation, nonreligious textbooks, and health
services, and he introduced a bill to this effect that was lost
in the midst of the public controversy between Mrs. Roosevelt
and Cardinal Spellman. The next year, Kennedy retreated
from this position to support an amendment (which failed)
to a federal-aid-to-education bill, providing funds for bus
transportation alone, and more recently he has strongly
backed federal-aid bills that lacked any provision at all
for aid to parochial-school students.

He argued that his Church was not trying to extend its
authority over secular affairs and, in an address at Notre
Dame in January 1950, when he received an honorary degree,
he affirmed the allegiance of American Catholics to democracy:

"You have been taught," he told the graduating class,
"that each individual has an immortal soul, composed of an
intellect which can know truth and a will which is free.
Because of this every Catholic must believe in the essential
dignity of the human personality on which any democracy
must rest. Believing this, Catholics can never adhere to any
political theory which holds that the state is a separate,
distinct organization to which allegiance must be paid rather

than a representative institution which derives its powers from the consent of the governed.

"In addition, a Catholic's dual allegiance to the Kingdom of God on the one hand prohibits unquestioning obedience on the other to the state as an organic unit."

Six years later, just before the Democratic convention, when Kennedy had lost the vice-presidential spot in a close contest to Kefauver, a reporter asked him: "Conceivably there could be a situation in which the dictates of your church and the demands of your country would conflict. In such a case, where would your higher loyalty lie?"

"In the first place," Kennedy answered, "I can't think of any issue where such a conflict might arise. But suppose it did? Nobody in my church gives me orders. It doesn't work that way. I've been in Congress for ten years and it has never happened. People are afraid that Catholics take orders from a higher organization. They don't. Or at least I don't.

"Besides, I can't act as a private individual does; my responsibility is to my constituents and to the Constitution. So if it came to a conflict between the two, and not just a personal moral issue, I am bound to act for the interests of the many."

The liberals' concern about the issue of separation of church and state was reflected in a comment by Mrs. Roosevelt in a Detroit interview. When she was asked if she had made up her mind whom to support for the 1960 presidential spot, she said, no, but "I did not say I was not for Kennedy; what I said was that I hoped that the first President who was elected and who was a Roman Catholic would be one whom we felt certain had the character to separate church and state completely, and I have been simply worried because I had not been sure that Senator Kennedy could do that. . . ." She thought that 1960 was very different from 1928 and that a man's religion would not be the determining factor; "I think it will depend on the feeling that people have about the character of the man, his own qualifications." She had said much the same thing a few months earlier to *Look:* "If I approved of a candidate, I would have no qualms about him because of his religion. . . . I do not think a Catholic would be a handicap on the ticket."

The fullest statement of Kennedy's recent views came almost by accident late in 1958 when Fletcher Knebel, a *Look* reporter, asked Kennedy his views on the religious issue as a part of a general roundup story on Catholic candidates in 1960. Kennedy's answer was off the cuff:

"Whatever one's religion in his private life may be," he told Knebel, "for the officeholder nothing takes precedence over his oath to uphold the Constitution and all its parts —including the First Amendment and the strict separation of church and state. Without reference to the presidency, I believe as a senator that the separation of church and state is fundamental to our American concept and heritage and should remain so.

"I am flatly opposed to appointment of an ambassador to the Vatican," Kennedy went on. "Whatever advantages it might have in Rome—and I'm not convinced of these— they would be more than offset by the divisive effect at home.

"The First Amendment to the Constitution is an infinitely wise one. There can be no question of Federal funds being used for support of parochial or private schools. It's unconstitutional under the First Amendment as interpreted by the Supreme Court. I'm opposed to the Federal Government's extending support to sustain any church or its schools. As for such fringe matters as buses, lunches and other services, the issue is primarily social and economic and not religious. Each case must be judged on its merits within the law as interpreted by the courts."

A storm arose as soon as *Look* hit the newsstands, amid wide newspaper coverage. The main outcry came from Kennedy's coreligionists. *America*, the Jesuit weekly, expressed its impatience with "the earnest Senator's efforts to appease bigots." The editor flayed Kennedy for asserting that whatever one's religion in his private life nothing takes precedence over his oath. "Mr. Kennedy doesn't really believe that. No religious man, be he Catholic, Protestant or Jew, holds such an opinion. A man's conscience has a bearing on his public as well as his private life." In his statement, the Senator himself had, in effect, violated the Constitution, *America* implied, by submitting himself to a religious test.

Other Catholic journals were no less severe. The Senator was overeager and had overstated his case, asserted a Providence diocesan newspaper. Why should a Catholic candidate permit himself to be queried on his "Americanism" by the Blanshards [Paul Blanshard] and the Archers [Glenn Archer of Protestants and Other Americans United for the Separation of Church and State], demanded a writer in the *Catholic Messenger*. Why did Kennedy have to say anything? editors demanded. "We do not ask the Baptist President or the Presbyterian President or the Episcopalian President . . . to declare his stand on the Constitution," said the *Catholic Review*. Why had not Protestants requested a statement of loyalty from Secretary of Agriculture Ezra Taft Benson, a Mormon bishop?

Running through the Catholic reaction was a tinge of doubt over the desirability of having a Catholic candidate at all. "I would not be at all happy to have a Catholic as a candidate for President in the next election," wrote one Monsignor. While he granted that prejudice in America had melted to the extent that a Catholic perhaps could be elected, he said that "bigotry is still so strong that the average Catholic candidate would feel he had to underplay not just Catholic but generally Christian ideas in order to 'prove' himself a 'patriotic' American."

Kennedy was surprised by the vehemence of the Catholic criticism, as he might well have been; Al Smith's similar statements had not met this reaction. He was also annoyed; "academic toe-dancing," he called some of the editorial comments. "They ask whether I really mean that my oath of office comes above my conscience. Well, of course, there's no conflict. It's part of your conscience to meet your oath." In retrospect he was pleased, though, that the issue had been debated so early. "I can now say that at least I've answered any reasonable question," he has said. So critical were some Catholics of Kennedy's position that the old friend of his family Richard Cardinal Cushing of Boston came to his defense. ". . . From my personal knowledge of him I can say without hesitation that Senator Kennedy will always perform his public duties to the highest standards of conscience and his oath of office."

Protestant leaders cautiously approved Kennedy's views. "A courageous stand," said POAU's Associate Director C. Stanley Lowell. Commendably forthright, declared the *Christian Century*—but only a beginning. The main trouble, Protestant spokesmen asserted, lay in the claim of the Roman Catholic Church to be the one true church, and its refusal to accept the secular, pluralistic basis of American life and the separation of church and state in law. To be sure, the Church departed from its more rigid precepts as a matter of expediency to meet practical situations. But its cardinal position was its exclusive claim to the total spiritual allegiance of its members. How could questions of political conduct be cut apart from this allegiance? In short, would not the Catholic Church, given its basic doctrine, have some claim on a Catholic President no matter what his sincerity and his protestations?

To discuss such problems face to face, the fifty-one man Council of Methodist Bishops, convening in Washington in April 1959, invited Kennedy to meet with it. "Boy, that's

Daniel going into the lions' den!" a Washington reporter said, as Kennedy entered the Senate Office Building room where the bishops had gathered. Although the Council interviewed other presidential candidates, Kennedy was the only one asked about church-state matters.

"I am a strong Catholic and I come from a strong Catholic family," Kennedy told them. "But I regret the fact that some people get the idea that the Catholic Church favors a Church-State tie." What about the persecution of Protestants in Catholic Spain? he was asked. "I deplore a loss of liberty under any circumstances . . ." Kennedy said. "I am opposed to forced conversions." The bishops, it was reported, applauded him warmly at the end.

Some Catholics were vexed by what *Time* called the "odd inquisition." Protestants would have been "screaming bloody murder were the Catholic Bishops to do the same thing," John Cogley declared in *Commonweal*. But Kennedy has never objected to the raising of the religious question, or to the way in which it is raised. Once, when a reporter cautiously introduced the subject and said, "I feel it is an unpleasant one—," Kennedy interrupted him: "I don't think it is unpleasant at all."

What Kind of Catholic?

Not unpleasant—except when he is catalogued in terms of a religious stereotype. Kennedy hates being pigeonholed under any encasing label such as "liberal" or "conservative" —and this extends to the term "Catholic." Thus he denies that *his* Catholicism implies obligations that would make it impossible or difficult for him, as President, to enforce the Constitution as interpreted by the Supreme Court. He believes that the Catholic Church is not a monolithic organization, that there is room in that Church for many points of view, and that the Catholic public official is not a slave to ecclesiastical political views. The Senator has been criticized by Catholic officials for trying to relegate religion to "private life"; he answers that he is perfectly willing to admit the claims on him of broader Catholic (and Judeo-Christian) doctrines such as expressed in the Ten Commandments. Like anyone else, he has a conscience. But he denies that he would respond to any effort by Catholic Church authorities to control his public actions, or, indeed, that such efforts would be made.

"The Pope speaks as the head of the Catholic Church. My faith is a personal matter and it doesn't seem to be conceivable, in fact it is impossible, that my obligation as one sworn to defend and uphold the Constitution could be changed in any manner by anything the Pope could say or do. What church I go to on Sunday, what dogma of the Catholic Church I believe in is my business and whatever faith any other American has is his business."

Kennedy, indeed, is rather mystifed by arguments based on elaborate interpretations of Church law. When he told a committee witness in 1947 that "there is an old saying in Boston that 'we get our religion from Rome and our politics at home,'" he was saying politely what Al Smith had said indignantly on first reading the challenge in the *Atlantic:* "I've been a devout Catholic all my life and I never heard of these bulls and encyclicals and books." Kennedy has no wish to be burdened by tomes of papal utterances on the hard climb toward the White House.

"It would be foolish to deny," Kennedy wrote to one Protestant critic in 1957, "that groups of Catholics bring pressure to bear at every level of government as do other religious groups. But I would deny your implied premise that a Catholic official is any more prone to the acceptance of a given position, if it is not in the public interest, than is a person who subscribes to the tenets of another creed or to no creed at all. . . . I quite sincerely do not believe that tensions between Catholics and Protestants are as serious as you believe and I certainly could not subscribe from my own experience to the thesis that the 'administration of a Catholic president would be marked by a savage running fight between Catholic and Protestant'."

"I can honestly say," Kennedy wrote to another worried Protestant, "that never in my public life have I been approached by a representative of the Catholic Church or for that matter any other church to perform an official act which was not consistent with the public interest as I saw it."

Kennedy's basic position, then, is that the overwhelming majority of Catholics in public office as well as members of the Catholic clergy and hierarchy do not act according to an old stereotype. He acknowledges that there have been Catholic officeholders and prelates who have violated the proper autonomy of the political order. He feels, however, that in general the Catholic hierarchy and most Catholic officeholders adhere to both the letter and the spirit of the statement made in 1948 by Archbishop McNicholas, at that time chairman of the Conference of Catholic Bishops in the United States: "We deny absolutely and without qualification that the Catholic Bishops of the United States are seeking a union of Church and State by any endeavors whatsoever, either proximately or remotely. If tomorrow Catholics constituted a majority in our country, they would not seek a union of Church and State. They would, then as now, uphold the Constitution and all its Amendments, recognizing the moral obligation imposed upon all Catholics to observe and defend the Constitution and its Amendments."

The issue, it is said in the Senator's camp, involves the particular Catholic who is running for office. It also involves the nature of the office itself, and on this score Kennedy's supporters contend that there is a further measure of reassurance for non-Catholics. The presidency, according to their argument, despite its huge scope and influence, touches directly on few matters of essentially religious concern, while the Constitution leaves the sensitive social issues—education, divorce, birth control, gambling, medicine, censorship, liquor —almost wholly in the hands of the states and their governors, state legislators, boards of education, and the like. Even Smith's worst detractors in 1928 could not point to biased actions of his in four terms as New York Governor. Catholic influence, like other special influences, finds its main expression in localities where Catholic majorities gain control of policy, for example, through referendums. In wider areas—so runs this argument—factions have less play. They quote James Madison on the subject: "Extend the sphere" from state to confederation, he urged in *Federalist* paper number 10, "and you take in a greater variety of parties and interests; you make it less probable that a majority of the whole will have a common motive to invade the rights of other citizens. . . . A religious sect may degenerate into a political faction in a part of the confederacy; but the variety of sects dispersed over the entire face of it must secure the national councils, against any danger from that source."

Kennedy himself prefers to pose the whole issue in terms of what he would do as President. On this score, he had moved by 1960 to a position more acceptable to non-Catholics than was the case several years earlier. For example, in April 1954, he had written a Cambridge voter that, Roosevelt and Truman having favored representation at the Vatican, he would vote in favor of an ambassador if an appointment were submitted to the Senate. Five years later, the Senator flatly opposed such an appointment. On "moral" issues such as birth control, his position is sometimes contrary to what is, correctly or incorrectly, understood to be the "Catholic position." When asked recently about his position on birth control, he said: "There is considerable difference among Catholics with respect to the application of general principles to specific fact situations. It is for this reason that one finds Catholics who subscribe to the same basic moral principles taking different positions on various issues of public policy. Public issues certainly are not divested of moral implication when they emerge in the political arena, but the responsibility of the officeholder is to make decisions on these questions on the basis of the general welfare *as he sees it,* even if such a decision is not in accord with the prevailing Catholic opinion. . . ."

Kennedy's views on church and state stem from his belief in diversity, in heterogeneity, in pluralism. "I have always been impressed in my study of American history," he says, "by the fact that this country has been singularly blessed in its ability to take the best of all religions and cultures—not merely tolerating differences but building a new and richer life upon them. I firmly believe that our religious and cultural pluralism has been over the years one of our principal sources of strength. . . ." To Kennedy, pluralism means neither a society of sharply segmented and isolated parts nor a dull, homogenized mass, but a mixed society in which every group, without surrendering its identity and uniqueness, makes its distinctive contribution to the whole.

He wrote to a Colorado woman in the spring of 1959: "As a public official, sworn to uphold the Constitution, I have no obligation to any private institution, religious or otherwise. My obligation is to the good of all.

"In sum, it is my firm belief that there should be separation of church and state as we understand it in the United States—that is, that both church and state should be free to operate, without interference from each other, in their respective areas of jurisdiction. We live in a liberal, democratic society which embraces wide varieties of belief and disbelief. There is no doubt in my mind that the pluralism which has developed under our Constitution, providing as it does a framework within which diverse opinions can exist side by side and by their interaction enrich the whole, is the most ideal system yet devised by man. I cannot conceive of a set of circumstances which would lead me to a different conclusion."

This belief in pluralism is common to a great number of Catholic, Protestant, and Jewish leaders who are emphasizing today the valuable contributions that diverse creeds can make to American thought. Those believing in such pluralism argue that one way to impair pluralism is to continue to deny the presidency to otherwise qualified Catholics. According to the pluralistic argument, the main historical source of Catholic exclusiveness and intolerance in America has been the sense of being discriminated against and excluded from some of the rewards of American life, while as discrimination has declined and economic and social opportunities have widened, Catholic insularity and solidarity have declined. Commenting on Paul Blanshard's view that "Boston is aggressively Catholic largely because it is aggressively Irish, and it is aggressively Irish because its people have not quite overcome their sense of being strangers in a hostile land," the Protestant scholar Dr. John C. Bennett, of New York's Union Theological Seminary, has remarked, "If this is the case, is it not natural to wonder if some of the aggressiveness will be lost as the Irish cease to have this sense of being strangers, when John Kennedy rather than James Curley becomes a symbol of the Irish leader in politics?"

The implications for 1960 are important, according to this argument. The image of the White House as "For Protestants only" is, they feel, one of the few remaining, but perhaps most conspicuous, and certainly most symbolic, barriers maintaining Catholic apartness. Shatter that image and a pillar of Catholic resentment and resulting intolerance would be torn down. And in that event, perhaps the day would come sooner when the White House would be accessible, in modern times, to a Jew or a freethinker or an agnostic as well.

"No Catholics Need Apply"?

So much for the merits or demerits of the case. What about the politics of a Catholic candidacy for President?

Politics permits few laboratory experiments. Only once had Americans tried running a Catholic for President. The outcome of that one experiment seemed so emphatic that it had left a pall over the prospects of other Catholics and members of other religious minorities. But does the Al Smith case prove anything? Kennedy supporters insist strongly that it does not. Their reasoning runs as follows:

Smith was many things besides a Catholic. He was a slum boy, a city boy, a salty, wisecracking New Yorker whose face, personality, and even clothes were stamped with the Bowery imprint. And Al was proud of his background. Even in 1928, when as a presidential candidate he had good reason to broaden his appeal, he refused to compromise with those who wished him to camouflage his urban, immigrant, Catholic background. It was a gallant gesture, Kennedy's supporters admit, but a self-defeating one. The people were simply not in a mood to take to a man who seemed so alien. In a way, Smith was too honest—or, from another point of view, too impractical. "It was as if he feared," says Oscar

Handlin, "that in concealing the accents of the Bowery he would be turning his back upon the people among whom he had grown up, be untrue to himself and to them." He would campaign as Al Smith and as nothing more.

The year 1928, moreover, was an unfair test for a Catholic candidate, Kennedy supporters contend, for it would have been a hard time for any Democrat to win the presidency. Calvin Coolidge was presiding over a "safe and sane" administration that offered few openings for attack. The Republican candidate, Herbert Hoover, was considered a somewhat liberal Republican. Most of the country was enjoying boom conditions. The Democratic party was still deeply split over Prohibition, religion, and other issues. In such circumstances, Smith did not come off so badly. He won 15 million votes, almost twice the Democratic total of four years before (when, to be sure, the Progressives captured some Democratic support). For a candidate who was supposed to have little appeal to the farm vote, he did remarkably well in some rural areas outside the South.

To Kennedy people, then, the lesson of Al Smith for presidential politics in the 1960's is that Al Smith is no lesson. The last thing anyone could call Kennedy is provincial. With his wealth, Harvard education, intellectual attainments, Brahmin accent, and cosmopolitan background and outlook, he stands culturally at the opposite pole from Smith. He has made precisely the transition that Smith refused to make—from the lower middle class of Beals Street to a place among the social elite.

The times, too, have altered, it is argued, by almost any test. America by 1960 had changed a good deal from the America of the 1920's. By 1958, Catholics had been elected governor or United States senator in states where Catholic voters were a minority, including California, Ohio, Pennsylvania, and even Minnesota. Twelve Democratic members of the Senate were Catholics. The success of these candidates doubtless reflected not only increased religious tolerance, but the increased Catholic population and the migration of Catholics across state boundaries so that the Catholic vote has become less localized.

Still these developments were suggestive rather than definitive. The ultimate test of a Catholic's chances for the presidency could be only the test itself—the capacity of a specific Catholic in a specific year to win the grand prize. As 1960 approached, some of those opposed to Kennedy held that polls and voting analyses proved that a Catholic could not win. They pointed to a Gallup poll that asked: "If your party nominated a generally well qualified man for President this year,

and he happened to be a Catholic, would you vote for him?"
The question, asked of almost 2,000 voters considered to be
a cross section of the national electorate a few weeks before
the presidential nominating conventions of 1956, produced
the following results:

Yes	72%
No	22%
Don't know	5%
Reject	1%

No candidate could win the presidency if he would auto-
matically lose a quarter of his own party's vote as a result of
his religion.

Kennedy's strategists deny this. Of those who would not
vote for their own party's nominee if Catholic, they point out,
a large number live in the South, where a Democratic candidate—especially one otherwise popular in the South, like
Kennedy—enjoys such a large margin of support that he
could afford to drop some voters. Most of the others are Republicans, who would not vote Democratic anyway. A number of persons who have said they would not vote for a
Catholic candidate for President, have also announced that
they *would* vote for Kennedy even though they knew his
religion. Though the Gallup poll reported in May 1959 that
only 47 per cent of the persons they had polled nationally
(30 per cent in the South) were aware that Kennedy is a
Catholic, Kennedy's strategists were betting that the knowledge would not deter the numbers who were already pro-
Kennedy. The real question, Kennedy backers say, is one
that the pollsters have *not* asked—how many persons who
ordinarily vote Republican, or at least voted for Eisenhower,
will support a Catholic candidate because he is a Catholic?

According to this view, in short, there *is* a Catholic vote,
however much some may deplore it, along with the Protestant vote. But the crucial aspect of the Catholic vote—
and this is not brought out in the polls—is its location. And
this is where the Electoral College—the system Kennedy
fought so hard to maintain intact—becomes so important.
Some Kennedy backers reason as follows:

The Catholic vote is far more important than its number—
about one out of every four voters who actually turn out to
vote—because it is concentrated in the key Northern states.
A dozen states are decisive because they have many electoral
votes and tend to switch back and forth. They are New
York, Pennsylvania, Illinois, New Jersey, Massachusetts,
Connecticut, California, Michigan, Minnesota, Ohio, Wis-

consin, and Maryland. The Kennedy camp estimates, based on studies of voting turnout, that the proportion of the two-party vote in these states made up of Catholic voters is 57 per cent in Massachusetts, 55 per cent in Connecticut, 47 per cent in New Jersey, 40 per cent in New York, and so on down a descending scale to the lowest, 25 per cent in Ohio. These dozen states have a total of 253 votes, with 269 needed to win. The Democrats won the presidency in 1940, 1944, and 1948 because most of the states went for Roosevelt and Truman. They lost in 1952 and 1956 because they all went for Eisenhower.

The key to the 1960 election, according to the Kennedy strategy, was the city vote. In New York, Philadelphia, Chicago, Los Angeles, and a host of other cities, the Catholic voters can usually determine the size of the Democratic margin in those cities; the size of the Democratic margin in those cities usually determines whether these states go Democratic; and whether these states go Democratic usually determines whether the Democrats win the presidency. This analysis lay back of a major premise of some Kennedy supporters—that the Senator's great problem was not the election but the nomination. The problem was less that of winning a majority of the electoral votes in November than winning a majority of the delegate votes in July.

It has long been a maxim of American politics that presidential candidates are chosen by a handful of powerful party bosses meeting in a smoke-filled room. This maxim was never wholly true, and in 1960, with a variety of willing candidates on tap, the prospects of a boss-controlled convention seemed dimmer than usual. Most state delegations, after a bow perhaps to favorite sons on the first ballot, seemed likely to split on the next ballots as factions moved toward their real candidates. Still, some state leaders would have considerable influence over their state delegations. Ironically for Kennedy—but reassuring to Protestants fearful of a "Catholic bloc" at the convention—most of the strongest state leaders outside New England were Catholics cool to his cause, at least as the campaign year opened.

In California, Governor Edmund G. ("Pat") Brown, a Catholic, was planning to head a delegation pledged to himself as favorite son, thus dampening Kennedy's hopes of entering the California presidential primary; no candidate wants to take the double risk of losing such a primary or, in the event of victory, of alienating the state's party leader. In Pennsylvania, Governor David Lawrence, a Catholic, flatly

came out for Stevenson. In Ohio, Governor Michael V. Di-
Salle, a Catholic, was maneuvering for a favorite son endorsement. Two leaders in New York, Mayor Robert Wagner and Tammany boss Carmine De Sapio, both Catholics,
were noncommittal to Kennedy. Sentiment for Kennedy
seemed stronger among the few Protestant county leaders
in New York State than among the Catholic.

Why were these Catholics cool politically to the leading
Catholic candidate? In part, they may have feared that if
nominated Kennedy might lose the election and that the
effect of his losing would be to reverse for years the present
tendency toward more acceptance by all religious groups of
Catholic candidates for office. Their main reason may well
have been political in a more personal sense. Party leaders
like Lawrence and De Sapio were well aware of Kennedy's
party independence in Massachusetts and in Congress. Would
he be equally independent as national standard bearer and
President, working with political amateurs and his own personal organization? Some Catholic politicians were simply
playing dog-in-the-manger; they themselves would lose any
chance they might have for a place on the ticket in 1960 or
1964. Or—a far simpler explanation—they may merely have
preferred some other candidate.

Perhaps it was only fair that Kennedy, who had denied the
monolithic nature of the Catholic Church, should find most
Catholic political leaders behaving like American politicians
rather than like Roman Catholics. Perhaps it was symbolic,
too, for Kennedy had deliberately moved to a position within
the Democratic party that brought him ties with all major
groups but identified him wholly with none of them. Despite his Catholicism, he had won considerable support from
the South, largely as a result of his moderate political views.
But his backing there was by no means solid. And not only
were leading Catholic politicians supporting other candidates,
but among the Roman Catholic clergy itself, there were some
who feared that Kennedy's stated acceptance of the separation of church and state might have roots in political expediency, and that if elected President he would lean far—too
far—toward keeping himself free of the suspicion of being
pro-Catholic. Clearly, if commitment had its dangers, so did
non-commitment.

The solution to some professional politicians and some
amateur ones also seemed to be to nominate Kennedy for
the Vice-Presidency, thereby having their cake and eating it,
too, since even militant Protestants were assumed not to
mind a Catholic Vice-President, while Catholics who had de-

fected to the Republican standard might be won back by the award of second prize.

Some of Kennedy's followers held that his moderate Catholicism, which had none of the crusading spirit of some in the American hierarchy, would temper and soften the religious arguments that 1960 was bound to bring. There were signs, however, that some of the old bitterness had not died. When Governor John Patterson, of Alabama, a Methodist, endorsed Kennedy for President, the Baptist organization in his own county chastized him, stating that they did not want a President "whose first allegiance is to the Vatican State, a foreign power." Governor Patterson would discover "to his horror," declared the *Methodist Christian Advocate,* official journal for the state's Methodists, that "the people of Alabama do not intend to jeopardize their democratic liberties by opening the doors of the White House to the political machinations of a determined power-hungry Romanist hierarchy."

In Massachusetts, the same concerns were evident, though touched with more subtlety and humor. After New England Methodist Bishop John Wesley Lord publicized a number of test questions for Catholic candidates for President, the *Pilot,* a weekly newspaper of the Catholic archdiocese of Boston, retaliated in an editorial with a series of questions for Methodist candidates, "Sauce for the Goose." In light of the "traditional racial segregation long practiced and still mightily supported in Methodist churches," asked the *Pilot,* "can you be relied upon to carry through the Supreme Court decisions recently made on this topic? Can you serve with Negroes in your cabinet . . . ?" "Moral," added the *Pilot:* "Anyone can play this game if he doesn't mind getting his hands dirty!"

"Dirty" or not, the game was evidently going to be in the minds of many voters in 1960 if a Catholic should be nominated. Certainly it was on the minds of many moderates; for example, Bishop Lord said in the fall of 1959 that it would be a "sin" to vote against a presidential candidate merely because he was a Catholic. And certainly the problem was on the minds of the Kennedy strategists, who were trying to be philosophical about it. "All of this religious discussion now means it will not be a mysterious unknown at convention time," one of them has said, "but a boring subject thoroughly surveyed and resurveyed—with some votes to be picked up and some to be lost, just as other candidates have handicaps which may lose them votes." One of Kennedy's closest supporters notes that Pat Brown was elected governor of California as a Democrat and not as a Catholic, and Ribicoff, governor of Connecticut as a Democrat and not as a Jew. Kennedy feels much the same way: "I am not sure I would vote for the 'Catholic' candidate for President —I hope I am not running as the 'Catholic' candidate."

14 ★ A PROFILE IN LEADERSHIP

For months before the coming of a critical election year, the acknowledged front runner was one who met none of the accepted tests of presidential timber. He was not a governor of a large state or a cabinet officer or a general. He was not a Protestant. He was not a longtime party leader. He did not personify any great national issue. He was not the champion of any one group or philosophy. He was not in his fifties or sixties, the supposed age for coming into the fullness of one's political powers. He was a senator hardly past his first term, Catholic, independent Democrat, barely into his forties.

"Unless the opinion polls are totally misleading, millions of Americans are eager to elect this still young, still incompletely tested man to the Presidency," Joseph Alsop has said. "But why?" How was it that Americans, facing what would be perhaps the most difficult decade in this century, were willing to turn to a man who seemed to stand for so little? a historian asked. And columnist Marquis Childs wrote, "At 42, with his unruly shock of hair, Kennedy still looks like a Harvard graduate student out to get his Ph.D. in political science." Yet Kennedy was a formidable contender for the most important position in the free world. Why?

Kennedy's political career provides some answers. In his early legislative life he had won the support of a wide array of political leaders and groups by establishing an image of moderation. Secondly, he had been, in effect, campaigning

241

for fellow Democrats and for President over a period of four years in every state in the Union (including Alaska and Hawaii), and in Puerto Rico and the Virgin Islands, which also send delegates to presidential conventions. He had probably appeared before more Democrats than any other Democratic candidate except Stevenson. Third, his candidacy always carried an extra quality of excitement and newsworthiness because of the controversy over a Catholic for President. On the otherwise rather flat and dreary political terrain, he was the one Democrat, aside from Stevenson, whose political image had been projected into the minds of millions of nonpolitical Americans. This was not simply to the credit of Kennedy; it was mainly a combination of his youthful, arresting appearance and the capacity of television and picture magazines to project that image into thirty million or more living rooms across the country.

What was this image? It was not just a physical picture of white teeth against a tanned face under a mop of hair. It was, at least superficially, a sense of the man's personality. When asked by pollsters in the summer of 1959 to describe, in their own words, what kind of person they thought Kennedy was, voters answered in such terms as "energetic . . . intelligent . . . good-looking . . . strong character . . . good family . . . aggressive . . . dynamic . . . outspoken." Though some Republicans considered him something of a "smart aleck" and a headline-hunter, most had a favorable image of him; their main grievance seemed to be that he was in the wrong party. Independent voters mentioned his honesty, impartiality, good background. The image of Kennedy expressed in these polls emerged as almost entirely favorable. In one poll, toward the end of 1957, voters were asked to evaluate Kennedy on a ten-point scale—from plus five for the most favorable rating to minus five for the lowest. Ten times as many people rated him on the plus side as on the low; most of those who rated him high rated him very high, but most of those who rated him low rated him just a bit low.

There were those who disliked Kennedy, too. One senses, however, that the dislike turned on the same impression of surface charm that accounts for the vote of those who did like him. For some, his youth and eager and attractive appearance did not match their image of the country's President. To many of his critics he seemed opportunistic, pragmatic, forever shifting with the political breezes. He has, indeed, been described as a "Democratic Nixon," an ambitious, hard-working politician, acting in terms of the immediate situation rather than on general and deeply rooted principles, and hence operating in a moral vacuum. "Where is the heart in the man—what makes it tick?" asked a close observer on Capitol Hill.

The more one studies the popular image of Kennedy, indeed, the more one is struck by its superficial, one-dimensional quality. The mass media, in their quick, kaleidoscopic way, have projected the characteristics that go only skin deep. The feeling about Kennedy, if it could be summed up in one phrase, is that he is "a nice guy who would like to be President"; indeed, this phrase often crops up in everyday political talk. It was with this same kind of phrase thirty years ago that Walter Lippmann dismissed, in words that historians will not let him forget, another presidential aspirant as an "amiable man with many philanthropic impulses but . . . not the dangerous enemy of anything," as a "pleasant man who, without any important qualifications for the office, would very much like to be President." This was Franklin D. Roosevelt. It does not follow, of course, that all hasty political judgments are equally doomed to be proven wrong. Still, it does remind us of our human fallibility and of the dangers of prophecy.

What Sort of Man?

Many people think of Kennedy as a sunny, gregarious type who likes nothing more than stumping the country, or as a glamorous matinee idol who would be a Hollywood star if he were not a Washington politician, or as a casual, happy-go-lucky kind of person. Actually, he is a serious, driven man, about as casual as a cash register, who enjoys the organizational, technical part of politics but not the stumping, which he considers simply grinding hard work, and whose resemblance to a matinee idol is purely on the surface. Nobody knows all this better than his wife. Talk of Kennedy as a glamour boy annoys her. "It's nonsense," she says. "Jack has almost no time any more for sailboats and silly things. He has this curious, inquiring mind that is always at work." She has said more than once that if she were drawing him, she would make a picture of a tiny body and an enormous head. Kennedy evidently shares this view of himself. When his wife once asked him what he considered his best and his worst qualities, his answer to the former was "curiosity." (She says she has forgotten his answer to the second part of the question.)

Kennedy, in short, has many qualities of the intellectual. It is not a press agent's pitch, but a solid fact, that he loves to read, to ruminate, to analyze. He is happiest not in social gatherings but sitting in bed, bespectacled, going through a recent biography, just as he prefers to spend his time with a small group of intelligent people (especially if it includes members of his family) rather than with crowds. Political life he calls a "treadmill." He never gives the impression of throwing himself into a campaign and loving the noise and confusion as Roosevelt and Truman did, or as Kefauver and Humphrey do now. Campaigning to him is hard but necessary work.

He has the intellectual's type of absent-mindedness. His friends never tire of telling how he leaves clothes behind in hotels, cannot find things, wear socks that don't match, breaks off a conversation with a staff aide, perhaps in the middle of his own sentence, to reflect for long moments on a different subject—or how, in an earlier day, he was once found after a wedding reception making off with the groom's extra shirt and cuff links. He forgets the little things around him because he is preoccupied with what seem to him bigger ones. And he has an excellent memory when he wants to use it, recalling details of something he read months back, and sometimes disconcerting his assistants by asking about a matter that he had mentioned long before and supposedly forgotten.

But if Kennedy is an intellectual, it is of a very special type. His mind is more analytical than creative, more curious and penetrating than wide-ranging or philosophically speculative, more skeptical than confident, more catalytic than original or imaginative. He shuns doctrinaire solutions and dogmatic talk. He is uneasy with slogans—and sometimes with statements of principle. He would prefer to present a dozen assorted reasons for a position than a single, over-arching one that to most intellectuals might seem compelling. He is surprisingly literal-minded; once when asked at a student convocation what he would do about Little Rock if he were President, he went through a step-by-step description of precisely what legal procedures were open to the Chief Executive. He considers the Eisenhower administration's favorite phrases tired substitutes for hard thought and action. If there is anything he dislikes more than the liberal stereotypes, it is the conservative ones.

One word describes Kennedy more exactly than any other —self-possession. He has never been seen—even by his mother—in raging anger or uncontrollable tears. He does not lose himself in laughter; the only humor he displays, aside from the contrived jokes of a political speech, is a light, needling, slightly ironic banter, such as one often meets in war or in other times of stress. He dislikes emotional scenes, at home or at work. His driving ambition to win out in politics seems to rise less from an emotional compulsion—though emotional drive manifests itself in his restless, hard-working, single-minded will—than from a calm evaluation of what he can do if he puts everything he has into it. He has apparently never lost himself in a passionate, unrestrained love affair; "I'm not the tragic lover type," he said once when pressed about whether he had ever gone through youthful agonies of love.

Where does this quality of detachment, of restraint, of moderation, of self-protection come from? The easy answer is from his glands, or his psyche, just as Hubert Humphrey says with a laugh that it is in *his* glands to throw himself into what he is doing, whether a marathon talk with Khrushchev or a liberal cause. But in Kennedy's case the roots of his dispassionate attitude toward personal and political matters can be traced in part to his background, as can the origin of his competitive will power; in his family the price of acceptance was effort and success. He grew up in a family that was moving from Boston to New York to Palm Beach and Hyannisport, that was rising from lower-middle-class environs to the financial and social pinnacle, that swung away from its lace-curtain Irish ties but did not forge new ones with any social or economic or ideological group. Kennedy, while friendly to all groups, has found a place for himself in none.

This fear of making too much of a commitment, of going off the intellectual deep end, is locked in Kennedy's character. To him, to be emotionally or ideologically committed is to be captive. On the few occasions when he has acted immoderately, he later regrets it. It was characteristic of him, for example, that long after he told the House of Representatives that the Legion leadership had not had a single new idea for years, he wondered if he had not overstated his case, for the Legion *had* had one or two new ideas, and if he overstated his case very much, Kennedy went on, "people would feel that I was not thoughtful or rational and I think that's terribly important."

What Sort of Democrat?

This refusal of Kennedy's to make commitments has alienated many liberals and intellectuals who feel that even a reasonable man, and certainly a presidential candidate, must "stand for something." It has alienated some professional Democrats, too. Where does he fit into the party spectrum? Kennedy is proud of his friendships in the Senate, stretching from Paul Douglas to Barry Goldwater, just as he used to boast of getting along personally with everybody in the House, from racist John Rankin to radical Vito Marcantonio. This is all right for a congressman, Democrats grant, but what kind of Democrat would he be as President?

"Win ye see two men with white neckties, set in opposite corners while wan mutthers 'thraiter' an' the other hisses 'miscreent,' ye can bet they're two dimmycratic leaders thryin' to reunite th' . . . party," said Finley Peter Dunne's Mr. Dooley. Kennedy is fond of this observation, which is as apt today as a half-century ago. But to some Democrats, the fights within the party are not just a joking matter—they are the way that the party finds out where a man stands. The question is not merely who is *for* him. The question is also who is *against* him. In Roosevelt's time, Democrats stretched a banner around Madison Square Garden: "We love him for the enemies he's made." What enemies would Kennedy make? Would they be the right ones?

Certainly Kennedy has made unusual efforts to get along with all factions of the party. Always conscious of the convention situation, he knows that the solid opposition of any one of the major Democratic groups—Southerners, union leaders, civil-rights blocs, farm leaders—would probably be enough to stop him. But his wish to get along with all party groups is a result of temperamental as well as political considerations. Kennedy doubtless believed that he was paying the ultimate tribute when he described Stevenson once as "beholden to no group or section, belonging neither to a left wing or a right wing."

Democratic chieftains in Kennedy's camp contend that too much is made of his appeal to all sections. That appeal, they say, is based on personal friendships, especially with Southern senators, and on a lag in understanding of Kennedy's congressional record. He has not catered to the South or the conservatives in his recent votes, they contend. He has simply stayed a bit to the right of Humphrey without losing his franchise as a Northern Democrat. They quote one Southern state chairman as calling Kennedy only "the best of a sorry lot."

Behind some of the liberal suspicion of Kennedy is not so much distaste for his views as worry over his temperament. They sense that emotionally and temperamentally Kennedy is moderate, and they are right. He has often mentioned his admiration for John Buchan's *Pilgrim's Way*, and no wonder, for Buchan admired men like Burke and Balfour who would not destroy what many generations had built "merely because some of the plasterwork was shaky." In Buchan, too, Kennedy found the line by Lord Falkland that he likes so much to quote: "When it is not necessary to change it is necessary not to change." He puts it a different way, but with the same meaning when he quotes Robert Frost: "Don't take down a fence until you know why it was put up."

The main suspicion of Kennedy among the Democratic pros stems less from doubts over his Democratic creed than from fears over his attitude toward them if elected President. They know of his critical attitude toward decrepit party organizations; of his independence of the party in Massachusetts, at least up to 1956; of his tendency to award patronage plums—the few he has had to give out—to leaders in his own organization rather than to "deserving Democrats"; and of his expressed hostility to some old party practices, such as awarding the best embassies to big contributors to the party. How much would this man upset the *status quo* in the party?

Mixed in with this worry is concern over Kennedy's age. Party leaders, like other careerists, work their way up the organizational ladder and usually come into their own by their fifties and sixties. When they look at a man a whole generation behind them, they wonder if, intentionally or not, he will shunt them aside and bring into power and recognition a host of his contemporaries. It is all very well for the Democratic orators to proclaim that America must make its own "leap forward" by changing from the tired Republican administration of men in their sixties to a vigorous government by younger men. Those leapt over have their misgivings.

Most Democrats care little about such party problems. To them only one question is important: Is Kennedy a liberal in the Wilson-Roosevelt-Truman tradition?

This question often is raised about Kennedy, partly because of his mixed voting record in the past, partly because he dislikes labels and hence cannot be easily typed. Moreover, he believes that much of the liberalism of the New Deal and the Fair Deal either has become properly entrenched in our way of life, and hence no longer a disputed political issue, or in a few cases has become outmoded or irrelevant. Liberalism itself, Kennedy feels, must be rethought and renewed—for example, in farm and business policy. In such a program of liberal renovation he believes that he could effectively take leadership as an "idealist without illusions," as his wife likes to call him.

"What we need now in this nation most of all is a constant flow of new ideas," he has said. ". . . We cannot obtain new ideas until we have a government and a public opinion which respect new ideas and the people who have them. . . . Our country has surmounted great crises in the past, not because of our wealth, not because of our rhetoric, not because we had longer cars and whiter ice boxes and bigger television screens than anyone else, but because our ideas were more compelling, and more penetrating, and more wise and more enduring." He has recognized the new challenges to liberalism, and hence its changing content, by dwelling in many speeches on the "ten peaceful revolutions" that "are rocking our nation and our world, reshaping our lives and remaking our destinies. These are the revolutions in our cities, on the farm, in the birth rate, in life expectancy, in technology (especially automation), in energy, in our standard of living, in weapons development, in the underdeveloped nations, and in nationalism."

Since none of the usual labels seems to fit Kennedy, his friends have gone to some trouble to devise a new one. One has come up with the term "humanism," meaning, in its nonphilosophical sense, a group of policies emphasizing social welfare and economic security and centering in the family—higher minimum wages, expanded health services, better housing, more protection for the aged, perhaps family benefits like those adopted in Canada.

But a new term is not necessary. Scrutiny of Kennedy's positions in the last several years shows that he does stand in the center of the Wilson-Roosevelt-Truman tradition, defined as embracing both economic welfare and civil liberties. Some contended that this was a shift mainly for political expediency as he came nearer to a national campaign. Possibly, but it seemed more likely that his shift went deeper, to a change in the pressures within him, and not merely those upon him. These pressures were reflected in the nature of Kennedy's political associates; he was working more closely than ever with men like Paul Douglas, Joseph S. Clark, John Sherman Cooper, Pat McNamara, Henry Jackson, and other liberal senators. At the same time, his father was saying, uncomplainingly, "Fifty per cent of what Jack thinks these days I am opposed to—and that's true entirely of foreign policy. We discuss it—but I don't expect to convert him." It was significant that by 1958 and 1959 Kennedy was consistently supporting the liberal Democratic party position both on welfare issues and on civil liberties and civil rights. He backed comprehensive housing legislation; introduced a ten-point "bill of rights" for improved living conditions for older people; introduced the first Senate bill to outlaw the bombing of homes, churches, schools, and community centers; continued to advocate statehood for Alaska and Hawaii (considered a civil-rights matter by many Southerners); worked for an antilynching bill and an anti-poll-tax bill. It was also significant that the two pieces of legislation he worked on hardest in 1959, aside from labor reform, were an increase of the federal minimum wage to $1.25 and the repeal of the federal defense education act requiring students to sign loyalty oaths if they wanted loans. He still strongly opposed the noncommunist affidavit requirement in the Taft-Hartley Act. Kennedy had come to grasp firmly the cardinal fact that the liberal Democratic tradition calls for *both* groceries and liberty. As he said in May 1959:

"It is the enduring faith of the American tradition that there is no real conflict between freedom and security—between liberty and abundance. Through centuries of crises, the American tradition has demonstrated, on the contrary, that freedom is the ally of security—that liberty is the architect of abundance—and that the truth will make us free."

What Sort of President?

"I am no Whig!" Kennedy says when asked about his conception of presidential power. He believes, unlike the Whigs in the early days of the Republic, whose distrust of the people led them to distrust presidential power, that the presidency must be the energizing and unifying force to make our divided governmental system work. Under him, the White House could be expected to generate a steady flow of policies and directives to the sprawling federal bureaucracy. Kennedy would agree that the American presidency's supreme role is to provide the "steady focus of leadership." His attitude has changed since his earlier days in the House of Representatives, when he himself seemed to distrust presidential power.

His would probably be a no-nonsense type of administration, run by men young, dedicated, tough-minded, hard-working, informed, alert, and passionless. The place would be quiet, taut, efficient—sometimes, perhaps, even dull. There would be little of the automatic delegation of power and responsibility to inter-departmental committees, as in Eisenhower's time, little of the boisterous relaxation of Truman's incumbency, or of the genial, creative disarray of Roosevelt's. The men with dreams—but no discernible plan—who could get in to see FDR, would not get past the White House door to see Kennedy, but those with an outline for a program would be welcomed, and the men in the White House would have no difficulty in deciding which visitor was which. But even the ablest man with the most ingenious ideas might find Kennedy a hard customer.

Such an administration would be composed of talented and expert people. Kennedy would look for men—regardless of whether they were labeled Democrats or Republicans, businessmen or professors or labor leaders, liberals, or conservatives—who were most likely to carry out his policies in a forceful, competent manner. He would make his Cabinet a "ministry of all the talents," composed of moderate men "a little left of center." Administering foreign policy would be men of the caliber, perhaps, of Adlai Stevenson and Chester Bowles; on the domestic side, of the background and temper of Abraham Ribicoff and Albert Gore. (These names are merely suggestive and do not represent any statements made by Kennedy or his assistants. This is also true of the ensuing discussion of likely policies, except where Senator Kennedy is directly quoted.)

The administration would be unusually sensitive to criticism. Newspaper editorials, Republican speeches, congressional attacks would bring quick answers from the White House or from someone down the line. There would be a never-ending process of self-appraisal. Incompetents would probably be politely but firmly replaced.

What would such an administration do? In some respects, its policies would not represent an abrupt break with those of the outgoing Republican administration. The sharpest immediate shift would come in federal social-welfare policies. Depending on the degree of congressional co-operation, minimum wages would be raised and exemptions narrowed, social security extended, the new labor policy of 1959 revised where in practice it unduly hurt democratic and honest trade unionism, federal housing and urban renewal subsidies expanded, big federal aid to school construction passed. The most striking change might be in the field of family allowances, with a small federal allotment to families for each child, and in medical care, perhaps in the direction of the successful British health program.

The budget would probably be balanced, at least in a time of full employment, not by cutting federal spending—an impossibility under the likely policies of a Kennedy administration—but by raising taxes, especially income and corporation taxes, and by plugging tax loopholes. Getting such a tax program through Congress would be the hardest legislative test of such a new administration.

"If you were elected President, what kind of foreign

policies would you pursue? Can you offer any new approaches? Would you try, while maintaining the nation's military and economic security, to set in motion forces that in the long run, at least, might ease East-West hostility and end the cold war? What hope can you hold out of breaking through the current impasse—or at least of releasing forces that might do so over the next decade or two?"

These questions were asked the Senator not long ago during a rare moment of relaxation between legislative activities and campaign tours. The occasion was a tranquil one; campaigns and cold wars seemed far away. Attired in shorts and sun glasses, Kennedy was lying back on a beach chair in the hot sun on the front porch of his Hyannisport home, a daub of sunburn lotion on his nose. His wife sat by reading; his daughter, Caroline, teetered up and down the porch steps.

"Well, in the first place," he said, "it takes two to make peace. I think it would be misleading to suggest that there are some magic formulas hitherto untried which would ease the relations between the free world and the communistic world, or which would shift the balance of power in our favor. When Khrushchev talks of peaceful coexistence, he makes it quite clear that he means to 'bury' us by means other than war. If our military power remains paramount— and I would include the traditional weapons as well as the nuclear weapons, for brush-fire wars remain our great military problem—then it might be possible to encourage the Russians and the Chinese to say a farewell to arms. We can then expect the competition would shift to nonmilitary spheres. It will then be a struggle between the two systems, then a test as to which system travels better, which system of political, economic, and social organization can more effectively transform the lives of the people in the newly emerging countries.

"There are many things we must do to win this struggle. We must recognize that free Africa will hold a balance of power in the General Assembly and in the world and will control some twenty-five per cent of the votes in the General Assembly. These are new countries with staggering problems which need assistance from the West both economically and educationally, and perhaps most importantly a sympathetic hand.

"A new Democratic administration, as the legatee of Franklin Roosevelt, would have a great opportunity to rebuild close relations with Latin America, if it supports a common market, the stabilization of raw materials, et cetera, demonstrating in other ways recognition of the real interdependence of North and South America, and supporting freedom as the goal of all countries North and South.

"We have a great opportunity also in India, which contains within its borders nearly forty per cent of all the people in the underdeveloped world and which has had the advantage of highly skilled economic planning. If India's third five-year plan fails, then India and Asia fail. It's for that reason that Senator John Cooper and I have been interested for the last two years in sending a high-level Western economic mission to India and surrounding countries in order to let both Europe and the United States—acting together—participate in reaching an economic break-through there. If China succeeds and India fails, the economic-development balance of power will shift against us.

"We should also take advantage of the present potential thaw to develop more intimate relations with Poland and those countries behind the Iron Curtain. It is because I believe that this represents the Achilles' heel of the Soviet Empire that I have been attempting (with George Aiken) to change the Battle Act to permit a freer flow of trade in many areas between these countries and ours. Also, George Kennan suggested an opportunity a year or so ago in Germany for discussing some kind of disengagement. The opportunity today has passed, but it might come again.

"We must rethink all of our policies in the Middle East— the Baghdad Pact, the Eisenhower Doctrine, the refusal to go ahead with the Aswan Dam—all mistakes. They were all based on concepts of the Middle East that were no longer valid.

"We should make decisions now about vacating Quemoy and Matsu, which are indefensible and which provide a needless irritant that could drag us into a struggle with Red China, a struggle in which we would be isolated by world opinion. If we are going to have difficulty with the Chinese, and we well may, then we should make sure that it involves basic principles of national independence and survival so that we may expect the good will of our allies and the neutrals. While the Red Chinese do not now indicate their willingness to relax their external and internal pressures in order to meet the standards which should precede our recognition and their admission to the United Nations, nevertheless we should indicate our willingness to talk with them when they desire to do so, and to set forth conditions of recognition which seem responsible to a watching world.

"In the final analysis, our foreign policy, our relations with other countries, will be most affected by what we do here in the United States. If we have a strong and well-distributed military strength, if our productivity is moving ahead, if we are devoting a reasonable share of our resources to assist the underdeveloped areas to make their economic break-throughs, if we are first in scientific achievements—in making fresh water out of salt water at a competitive rate, for example—if our educational system is being strengthened, and there is equality of opportunity for all Americans—*then* we will have demonstrated that freedom rather than Communism represents the wave of the future. It was Franklin Roosevelt's compassionate actions here at home that built his great reputation abroad. What we are speaks much louder than what we say."

"But is all this enough? Obviously as President you would try to be effective and resourceful in strengthening the unity of the Free World and maintaining a durable power balance against the communists. But in the long run balances of power have a tendency to topple, do they not?"

Kennedy answered: "In the long run there are many changes in power ratios. But I believe if we can hold out for the long run there will be sufficient evolutionary changes in the communistic system in Russia as well as in China to give us some hope of success. The 'magic power' on our side is the desire of every person to be free, of every nation to be independent. That is the really strong force on our side. That is the weapon and elementary principle for the destruction of the Communist Empire in eastern Europe. It is because I believe our system is more in keeping with the fundamentals of human nature that I believe we are ultimately going to be successful, provided we have sufficient self-discipline and perseverance to maintain our own strength through a long testing period."

"Since at least Polk's time not one of the great presidential leaders, Wilson possibly excepted, gave clear evidence before entering the White House of a capacity to shape a program, arouse public opinion behind it, control Congress, and dominate the bureaucracy. Today the presidential office holds vast legal power and moral influence, but how that power and influence are marshalled and focused depends on the occupant and the nature of the times. What is your estimate of the job of the President during the next decade?"

"The 1960's will be a terribly difficult time. I think Eisenhower is going to get home relatively free—at the end of his term there will probably be full employment, a level price index, the drop in food prices may equal any increase in industrial costs, there will probably be a deal on Berlin for eighteen months or so, and the now-independent countries will have survived.

"But it will be like Calvin Coolidge giving way to Herbert Hoover—all the pigeons coming home to roost will be circling over the head of the man coming in. In 1961 or '62 all the problems—changes in weapons' structure, changes in NATO, desperate inflation and economic problems in the southern half of the globe—will be coming to a head. The job of the next President will be the hardest since Roosevelt, and I think Roosevelt had the hardest of all except Lincoln and perhaps Washington. The job will be tremendous, and a great responsibility will center on the President. The real dilemma we face is whether a free society in which each of us follows our own self-interest can compete over a long period of time with a totalitarian society in which both the carrot and the stick are used to force all human and material resources into the service of the state.

"There are many short-term advantages which a totalitarian possesses in that kind of competition. The struggle between Sparta and Athens furnishes a classic case. The responsibility of the President, therefore, is especially great. He must serve as a catalyst, an energizer, the defender of the public good and the public interest against all the narrow private interests which operate in our society. Only the President can do this, and only a President who recognizes the true nature of this hard challenge can fulfill this historic function."

"In the Senate, you have been something of a traditionalist. You have opposed bypassing the Eastland committee; you have favored the seniority system for choosing committee chairmen, or at least seen no hopeful alternative; you have defended the American system of divided power seemingly down to the last check and balance. How does this position fit in with your concept of presidential leadership?"

"Even in the Senate today," Kennedy said, "I'm not, in a sense, a traditionalist. For example, I supported strongly the Fulbright development loan program putting the development fund on a long-term basis through direct borrowing from the Treasury rather than annual appropriations, thus bypassing the Appropriations Committee. I'm willing to follow the traditional procedure if we're going to get action, even if it means a delay of a week or two, but I won't follow the procedures if it means diluting or destroying action.

"It's going to be a hell of a revolutionary time—the increase of population here and abroad, changes in the underdeveloped world, changes in weapon strategy, and all the rest. The best the President can do is to track down the best talent he can get—people with ideas which are actionable, because the problems are quite sophisticated now—and then try, by his political management, by his mobilization of public opinion, by his hard work almost day by day in Congress and the nation, to bring along that more conservative and localized body.

"How far would I go? I believe that our system of checks and balances, our whole constitutional system, can only operate under a strong President. The Constitution is a very wise document. It permits the President to assume just about as much power as he is capable of handling. If he fails, it is his fault, not the system's. I believe that the President should use whatever power is necessary to do the job unless it is expressly forbidden by the Constitution.

"Congress is quite obviously not equipped to make basic policy, to conduct foreign relations, to speak for the national interest in the way that a President can and must. I am a traditionalist in that I believe in the procedural as well as substantive rights. I do, however, believe that in the next two or three decades there will be greater demands upon the President than ever before—and the powers are there, if the man will use them."

"To what extent would congressional problems boil down to the conflict between North and South in the Democratic party?"

"Of course there are conflicts within the Democratic party —it is inevitable that there will be when you have a national party which takes in varying regions which have been the scene of great historical struggles. But I believe that the Democratic party on the whole is progressive and will support a vigorous and progressive President. I think having had Congressional experience, which Eisenhower never had, could mean a good deal toward success in the job.

"Roosevelt maintained intimate relations with the Congress; and while he was never able to remake it in the way he wanted, nevertheless he was able to get through almost his entire program, at least initially. My judgment is that with the industrialization of the South you are going to find greater uniformity in the Democratic party than you had in the past.

"In the final analysis, this phase of the work comes down to how good a politican the President is or wants to be. You remember Eisenhower, when early in his first term a questioner asked him how he liked the game of politics, replied with a frown that his questioner was using a 'derogatory' phrase. 'Being President,' he said, 'is a very fascinating experience—but the word "politics"—I have no great liking for that.'

"I do have a great liking for the word 'politics.' "

A Place of Moral Leadership?

Kennedy as President would mobilize traditional tools of presidential power and use them with force, astuteness, and tenacity. He would show a flair for personal influence and manipulation, perhaps some of the flair Roosevelt had. He would drive hard bargains, forming alliances with Republicans when necessary, but compromising, too, when he lacked the votes.

But would all this be enough? The presidency "is preeminently a place of moral leadership," Franklin D. Roosevelt once said in a now-famous quotation. "All our great Presidents were leaders of thought at times when certain historic ideas in the life of the nation had to be clarified." It is precisely in this respect that Kennedy's critics, especially in the liberal wing, have trouble imagining him in the White House. What great idea does Kennedy personify? In what way is he a leader of thought? How could he supply moral leadership at a time when new paths before the nation need discovering?

To these questions Kennedy's friends offer no certain answer. They do point out that Kennedy is not unique in this respect—that few other candidates in recent years, except for Taft and perhaps Stevenson, and few recent Presidents, displayed strong leadership in behalf of a solid program. They argue, too, that something besides high-toned moral leadership may be needed for the 1960's—for example, adroitness and tenacity in getting through Congress measures to meet the accumulating needs of the nation. Roosevelt, they point out, had gone on in that same quotation to say something a little different—that the presidential office was also a "superb opportunity for reapplying, applying under new conditions, the simple rules of conduct to which we always go back. Without leadership alert and sensitive to change, we are all bogged up or lose our way." It is precisely this alert leadership sensitive to change, Kennedy's friends assert, that the Senator is ideally equipped to provide.

One of Kennedy's aides, who has worked and campaigned with him for years, feels that people exaggerate his moderation and restraint. He is able "coolly to keep prejudices, whims, and unreliable emotions out of the way when making a hard, tough decision," this aide says, but he does believe deeply in what he says and will fight fiercely for what he believes. While far from a fatalist, he accepts difficult assignments because, as he wrote in the last chapter of *Profiles in Courage*, a man does what he must, in spite of personal consequences or obstacles or dangers, and that is the basis of all human morality. "Kennedy should be judged by his times and his contemporaries—and it should be obvious from the crowds he attracts, the applause he stimulates, the devotion of his followers, and the electricity he has created across the country that he combines extraordinary qualities of strong leadership and intellectual brilliance with an uncanny sense of public relations and the public mood."

Obviously, much depends on the demands of the times. If the 1960's call simply for consolidation, continuation, and expansion of the New Deal–Fair Deal policies, Kennedy's political skill and liberal convictions would be enough for the presidential job. But what if the 1960's are a time of radical change, of unprecedented new crises? What if problems arise for whose solutions guideposts do not exist?

Such times would call for two types of leadership, and each would demand something of Kennedy that he might have difficulty supplying. One type is creative leadership. Instead of responding to political pressures and gusts of public opinion, the President seeks positively to change the shape of public opinion. He has many tools for this—speeches, press conferences, whistle-stop trips, fireside chats, and the like. But his most powerful tool is not persuasion but action, not the propaganda of the word but the fact of the deed. By boldly taking a position, without regard to Gallup polls, newspaper editorials, or congressional timidity, the Chief Executive can alter the whole constellation of political forces—at least until the next election.

During one of his presidential campaign tours, Kennedy spoke to the United Negro College Convocation in Indianapolis. His remarks were intelligent, liberal, eloquent, and unimpassioned. The audience applauded warmly. Afterward a long line formed the length of the big hall to shake Kennedy's hand. But hardly anyone in the line talked about the speech; they seemed interested only in meeting the attractive young man who had delivered it. He had satisfied them intellectually and attracted them visually—but he had not aroused them spiritually. Watching Kennedy campaign in Wisconsin in October 1959, Cabell Phillips of the New York *Times* noted the same quality. Kennedy radiated a gentle, honest warmth when among small groups, and people were instinctively at ease with him. "He tightens up noticeably, however, on a platform, facing larger audiences. He is more the advocate than the orator, and lines out his speech in a flat, hurried monotone. His talks are liberally sprinkled with apt, and often erudite, quotations and bits of verse, but he rarely reaches for a laugh or builds a climax or plucks at the heartstrings—nor, inevitably, has he often to wait for the applause to die down."

Kennedy is a rationalist and an intellectual. He wants political campaigns to be conducted like debates—"courteous but candid, friendly but frank, incisive without becoming inflammatory. . . ." He has denounced the "horrible weapons of modern internecine warfare, the barbed thrust, the acid pen, and most sinister of all, the rhetorical blast." But it was in part with rhetorical blasts that Wilson and Roosevelt moved their party and their country—and the world.

Could Kennedy supply creative leadership of this sort? In his studies of why Britain slept, he placed the chief blame on the failings of the people as a whole and little on the leaders who might at least have tried to arouse them. In *Profiles in Courage*, the heroes seemed simply to face the choice of giving in to public opinion or of defying it and becoming martyrs. But is there not a third alternative—especially for Presidents: consciously shaping public attitudes by positive leadership?

The other type of leadership that the 1960's may demand is charismatic leadership—the capacity to inspire, to lift the hearts, to exalt, to make people lose themselves in a cause they may not fully comprehend. Such leadership calls for magical qualities of heart and spirit, of joy and earnestness, indeed of rhetoric and passion, that are bequeathed to few men. It calls for faith in leadership on the part of the people, and the capacity of the leader to invoke and deserve that faith. "In the midst of doubt, in the collapse of creeds," Oliver Wendell Holmes, Jr., said, "there is one thing I do not doubt . . . and that is that the faith is true and adorable which leads a soldier to throw away his life in obedience to a blindly accepted duty, in a cause which he little understands. . . ." Charismatic leadership can be dangerous, too, for it may demand too much trust, blind faith, and dependence on a father image. But at its best—and assuming always the safeguards of free speech and fair elections—that leadership may be essential to guide a democracy through perilous times.

It is illuminating, indeed, to compare Kennedy's potential with that of Roosevelt. In some respects the two resemble each other. Like Roosevelt, Kennedy forged his own liberalism out of day-to-day experience rather than abstract dogmas; was caught between different classes and traditions and lingered between different worlds; became a pragmatist, a realist, a hardheaded political tactician willing to compromise— sometimes to the despair of his supporters—in order to gain some progress. Like Roosevelt, he can stand up under tremendous pressure, but a seemingly trivial thing—in Kennedy's case usually the antics of certain Massachusetts politicians—can lead to sharp irritation and some blowing off of steam. Like Roosevelt, he can be courageous, actutely intelligent, quick, responsive. Kennedy, like Roosevelt, is a moderate in his behavior as well as in ideas. He has a gentleman's distaste for lack of self-discipline, and self-restraint, for displays of emotion, for personal brawls and scenes. The bright charm is only skin deep; underneath there is a core of steel —metallic, sometimes cold, sometimes unbending, unusually durable.

But there are differences, too—and these relate to Roosevelt's special qualities of leadership. Kennedy lacks Roosevelt's humor and joyousness, his superb acting ability, his magnetism with crowds, his power of oral expression. He lacks also Roosevelt's blarney and exaggerations and deviousness. Clinton Rossiter has said that if Roosevelt was "as busy as Rabbit and as bouncy as Tigger, he was too often, I fear, as big a bluffer as Owl." But in a time of danger and evil, Roosevelt was able to use his less attractive qualities—as well as his superb imagination and daring—against democracy's foes.

Would Kennedy show similar imagination and daring under crisis conditions? A final answer to the question must take into account the role of the Presidency itself. The office has shown an almost magical power, as in the case of Truman, to elevate men, to bring out the best in them, to convert able politicians into great political leaders. Throughout his life, Kennedy has had the capacity to move into an office, exhaust its possibilities, and move beyond it. He is too young, curious, and flexible not to continue to grow. His life seems to show a steady growth into commitment from a position of detachment.

If the Presidency has an impact on its occupants, however, the times have an impact on the Presidency. It may be that the 1960's will be less demanding than the decade over which Roosevelt, or even Eisenhower, ruled. But Kennedy believes that they will be far more demanding and dangerous. "For now the age of consolidation is over and once again the age of change and challenge has come upon us," he has said. "The next year, the next decade, in all likelihood the next generation, will require more bravery and wisdom on our part than any period in our history. We will be face to face, every day, in every part of our lives and times, with the real issue of our age—the issue of survival." To that battle for survival, Kennedy could bring bravery and wisdom; whether he would bring passion and power would depend on his making a commitment not only of mind, but of heart, that until now he has never been required to make.

BIBLIOGRAPHICAL NOTE

Aside from published matter, the material for this book was drawn from two main sources: records in Senator John F. Kennedy's Washington office and interviews with Senator Kennedy, members of his family, aides, friends, opponents, and others. Each of these main sources requires a further note.

The records in the Kennedy office are located in two main places: in a screened-off room under the eaves on the fifth floor—actually the attic—of the old Senate Office Building, and in the Senator's regular suite of offices on the third floor of the same building. In the following notes the former is referred to as "Attic Office," the latter as "Main Office." As of this writing, files on the years prior to 1958 are located in the Attic Office, the others in the Main Office. The most important files for my purposes were the Legislative Files, grouped by year, and broken down by alphabetical order of names of legislative subject matter, such as "Agriculture" or "Foreign Policy." I have gone through all these files in both offices. Another set of files consists of carbons of letters from Kennedy to correspondents grouped by years, and then alphabetically according to name of recipient of letters. I have used this file as a guide to, and check on, the Legislative Files. A third file is a "case" file composed of correspondence involving individual matters, favors, requests for pictures, etc.; I have only sampled this file for its flavor. The

Attic Office also contains some files from the House of Representatives period, but regrettably incomplete, unorganized, and located in old cabinets and cardboard cartons. These I have gone through completely. Finally, the Attic Office contains a plethora of plaques, awards, souvenirs, and bric-a-brac that were of marginal usefulness to this study, and four-foot stacks of stationery, mimeographed speeches, and handouts, which were impediments.

The files in the Main Office are organized in the same fashion as in the Attic, minus the impediments. There are also special collections of political and campaign materials and other specialized materials located in cabinet files and other places in the Main Office, and miscellaneous collections such as manuscript material for *Profiles in Courage*. I have had unrestricted access to all the above sources, and no restriction has been placed on my use of materials gained from them.

Interviews were conducted with most members of the Kennedy family, including Mr. and Mrs. Joseph P. Kennedy, and I have corresponded with other members. I interviewed Senator Kennedy on several occasions at some length during 1959, and the quotations in the text not otherwise attributed are from these interviews. The interviews with the Senator were tape-recorded and transcribed. I have also had access to a collection of letters written by Senator Kennedy during his childhood and youth, cited below as Kennedy family papers.

Writing of a contemporary figure imposes special responsibilities of protecting the names of sources. Consequently, I have generalized the source of information received from particular members of the Kennedy family through use of the term "Kennedy family interview," and I have not specified the names of other persons interviewed. I have also omitted the names of persons corresponding with Senator Kennedy, but I have tried to indicate the kind of person making the remark I have quoted by a descriptive phrase, for example, a "priest in Pennsylvania" or an "ADA housewife."

CHAPTER NOTES

I. *Room at the Top*

On Lismore Castle see Encyclopaedia Britannica, 11th ed., 1911. The account of the New Ross visit is based on Kennedy family interviews. *To the Land of the Shanties:* On immigration from Ireland, see W. F. Adams, *Ireland and Irish Immigration to the New World* (New Haven: Yale University Press, 1932); Oscar Handlin, *Boston's Immigrants* (Cambridge: Harvard University Press, 1941, and revised edition 1959), and works cited therein. Information on the first Pat Kennedy is from interviews and correspondence with members of the Kennedy family; there seem to be no records. For the journey of the Irish to Boston, see M. L. Hansen, *The Atlantic Migration* (Cambridge: Harvard University Press, 1940). Chief source on immigrant life in Boston is Handlin, cited above, a painstaking and perceptive study; see also W. S. Rossiter, ed., *Days and Ways in Old Boston* (Boston: R. H. Stearns, 1915); G. E. Ellis, *Bacon's Dictionary of Boston* (Boston: Houghton Mifflin, 1886); Nathaniel Dearborn, *Boston Notions* (Boston, 1848); R. A. Woods, ed., *Americans in Process* (Boston, 1902). The quotation beginning "Unable to participate . . ." is from Handlin, *op. cit.* (1959 ed.), p. 176. The quotations by John Kennedy beginning "Each wave . . ." are from a speech to the Washington chapter of the American Jewish Committee, June 4, 1957, reprinted in the *Congressional Record,* Vol. 103, Part 12, Aug. 29, 1957, p. 16,492.

Behind the Lace Curtain: My sources on Patrick Kennedy and John F. Fitzgerald are chiefly newspaper clippings in the reference libraries of the Boston *Herald* and the Boston *Globe,* aside from Kennedy family interviews. The "Irish switch" story is from *Time,* December 2, 1957, p. 19; the story of the baseball game from a witness, Charles F. Ely, of Westfield, Mass. On the skills of Irish politicians acquired in Ireland, see D. W. Brogan, *Politics in America* (New York: Harper, 1954). On the politics of Boston during this period, I have relied mainly on M. E. Hennessey, *Twenty-Five Years of Massachusetts Politics* (Boston: Practical Politics, Inc., 1917); J. A. Garraty, *Henry Cabot Lodge* (New York: Alfred A. Knopf, 1953); J. J. Huthmacher, *Massachusetts People and Politics* (Cambridge: Harvard University Press, 1959); Duane Lockard, *New England State Politics* (Princeton: Princeton University Press, 1959); and J. F. Dinneen, *The Purple*

Shamrock (New York: W. W. Norton, 1949). For Curley's description of the socially aspiring Irish, see J. M. Curley, *I'd Do It Again* (Englewood Cliffs, N. J.: Prentice Hall, 1957), pp. 13-14, and for his relations with Cardinal O'Connell, see the same, p. 113. The quotation on the "inrushing immigrant masses" is from Brogan, *op. cit.*, p. 97. Dinneen's novel *Ward Eight* is an evocative picture of old-time Irish politics in Boston. On the attitudes in the Catholic Church toward liberal reformism, see the admirable treatment in Handlin, *op. cit.*, Chapter 5. The Fitzgerald exchange with the banker is from Kennedy family interview.

Upward Bound: The fullest account of Joseph P. Kennedy's business career is in *Fortune*, September 1937, and the quotations are from that source; see also *Time*, July 22, 1935; *The New Republic*, July 11, 1934, and July 18, 1934. I have also used Kennedy family interviews. Kennedy's book, *I'm for Roosevelt*, was published by Reynal and Hitchcock, New York, 1936. Roosevelt's comment on *I'm for Roosevelt* is from Elliott Roosevelt, ed., *F.D.R.: His Personal Letters* (New York: Duell, Sloan and Pearce, 1950), Vol. I, p. 595. His remark "I was born here . . ." is quoted in Cleveland Amory, *The Proper Bostonians* (New York: E. P. Dutton, 1947), p. 346.

No Terrors at Home: The "Home holds no terrors" quotation is from *Fortune*, cited above. The story of Joseph Kennedy in the Waldorf Astoria is from Joe McCarthy, "Jack Kennedy: Heir to Power," *Look*, Oct. 27, 1959, p. 92. The story of Joe, Jr. toppling off the sled is from H. H. Martin, "The Amazing Kennedys," *The Saturday Evening Post*, Sept. 7, 1957, p. 44. The reference to the children's thinking of problems in terms of how their father would approach them is from Eleanor Harris, "The Senator Is in a Hurry," *McCall's*, August 1957, p. 119, as is the father's statement that he never discussed money at the table. Information on Rose Kennedy is from Kennedy family interviews and interviews with acquaintances in Boston.

II. *The Green Bloods*

The plea for the raise is in Kennedy family papers, undated.

Canterbury and Choate: Information on Kennedy's early and school years is from teachers, family friends, Kennedy family interviews, and Kennedy family papers. The record of the year at Canterbury is especially full because the students there were evidently required to write letters home at least once a week. Kennedy's grades at Choate are from a transcript of his record at Choate, April 21, 1959. On Kennedy's relations with his father, see Kennedy family papers, especially Kennedy to Joseph P. Kennedy, undated (received December 4, 1934); Joseph P. Kennedy to Kennedy, December 5, 1934. Jean's letter protesting about the mistletoe kiss is from her letter to Joseph P. Kennedy, January 8 (no year indicated), Kennedy family papers.

Harvard: The best source—and one with more objectivity than might be expected—on Joseph P. Kennedy, Jr., is J. F. Kennedy, ed., *As We Remember Joe*, a memorial volume privately printed in 1945, which includes the quoted statement from Laski on Joe. A useful source on Kennedy at Harvard is Irwin Ross in the New York *Post*, July 31, 1956, p. 21. Kennedy's grades at Harvard are based on Transcript of Record, Office of the Registrar, Harvard University, April 21, 1959; the list of his activities, on 1940 Class Book, Harvard University, 1940. Kennedy's letters from Europe during 1937 trip are in Kennedy family papers; see especially, Kennedy to Joseph P. Kennedy, July 25, 1937, and August 11, 1937; letter to Mr. and Mrs. Joseph P. Kennedy, undated.

Alone at the Top: On Joseph P. Kennedy's trusts for his children see Martin's article in *The Saturday Evening Post,* cited above.

III. *War and Peace*

Kennedy's letter to his father on the latter's Navy League speech is undated, but probably November 1938, in Kennedy family papers; for his letter on the Danzig situation, see Kennedy family papers, Kennedy to his father undated but received June 7, 1939. On the *Athenia* incident, see Memo, "Telephone Call from Mr. William Hillman," Sept. 7, 1939, Kennedy family papers; and New York *Times,* Sept. 8, 1939, p. 14.

"Why England Slept": The letter from Kennedy to Joseph P. Kennedy is undated (penciled notation states "spring 1940" but internal evidence suggests fall 1939), Kennedy family papers. Information on Kennedy's stockmarket activities is from same letter. The thesis, "Appeasement at Munich," is dated 1940, and the copy I have used is deposited in Widener Library; quotations are from this manuscript and from *Why England Slept* (New York: Wilfred Funk, 1940). My chief source on Joseph Kennedy, Sr.'s views on the situation in Europe is W. L. Langer and S. E. Gleason, *The Challenge to Isolationism* (New York: Harper, 1952). For Joseph Kennedy, Jr.'s views on nonintervention, see the New York *Times,* Jan. 7, 1941, p. 7. Other quotations and analysis of Joseph Kennedy's stand during the war years are from several sources, mainly from the hearings of the Committee on Foreign Affairs, U.S. Congress, on H.R. 1776 (Lend Lease), January 21, 1941, pp. 229-30, 246-48, 250, 254, 258, and 259 ff. (Joseph Kennedy). For Joseph Kennedy's standing with America First, see W. S. Cole, *America First* (Madison: University of Wisconsin Press, 1953), p. 17. On commencement activities, the Class Day and Commencement programs are in Kennedy family papers, as is Joseph Kennedy's telegram of congratulations. These family papers include an extensive file of correspondence between Kennedy and his father in regard to publication of *Why England Slept;* the letter of his father that Kennedy used for his concluding remarks is dated May 20, 1940. The Roosevelt-Fitzgerald exchange is from Kennedy interview. On Joseph Kennedy's volunteering for service, see Elliott Roosevelt, *op. cit.,* Vol. II, pp. 1289-90. His instructors' estimates of Kennedy's abilities in the Navy are from a file of Navy Fitness Reports on Kennedy, Kennedy Main Office.

"Jesus Loves Me": The account of events on the Japanese destroyer is from K. Hanami to Kennedy, undated, 1952 Campaign Files, Main Office; K. Hanami to author, July 1, 1959; and T. Chichida (Hanami's translater) to author, July 7, 1959. The remainder of this section, aside from Kennedy interviews, is drawn entirely from John Hersey, "Survival," *The New Yorker,* June 17, 1944, pp. 31-43.

War's End: The Navy Fitness Reports also cover the period following active service. The New York *Times,* May 7, 1944, p. 43, refers to the first Duke of Devonshire's Protestantism. Kennedy's article on peace, with covering letter dated February 8, 1945, is in Kennedy family papers. For Kennedy's articles on the San Francisco Conference, see the New York *Journal-American*, April 28, 30, May 2, 3, 4, 5, 7, 9, 10, 14, 16, 18, 19, 21, 23, 28, 1945. The London coverage is in *ibid.*, June 24, July 10, 27, 1945.

IV. *The Poor Little Rich Kid*

Kennedy's indecision of 1945 is based on Kennedy and Kennedy family interviews. Description of Massachusetts politics is drawn mainly from Huthmacher, *op. cit.;* see also review of this book by John F. Kennedy, the New York *Times Book Review*, Sept. 20, 1959, p. 42.

Political Baptism: On Curley's situation in 1946, see J. M. Curley, *op. cit.*, and Dinneen, *op. cit.* Billings' participation in the campaign is described in *McCall's*, August 1957, p. 123.

Free-for-All: Account of the 1946 primary battle is based mainly on Kennedy and Kennedy family interviews and on interviews with six of the nine primary opponents and with Kennedy campaign workers. Newspaper coverage is rather scanty. Election totals are from *Election Statistics 1946*, Public Document No. 43, Commonwealth of Massachusetts, Boston, 1946, p. 70. Fletcher Knebel, "Pulitzer Prize Entry," in Eric Sevareid, ed., *Candidates 1960* (New York: Basic Books, 1959), p. 196, relates Fitzgerald's victory celebration.

Safe Seat: The 1948 and 1950 election results are in *Election Statistics 1948*, *op. cit.*, pp. 248, 341; *1950*, pp. 70, 270; interviews were also conducted with Kennedy's 1950 primary opponents still available, and with his 1950 Republican opponent. Kennedy could not remember in 1959 how he had become a member of the House Committee on Education and Labor.

V. *The Gentleman from Boston*

O'Neal's testimony is in *Proceedings* of Committee on Education and Labor, House of Representatives, 80th Cong., 1st Sess., pp. 1836, 1838. Material on Kennedy's personal life during the House of Representatives period is from interviews with representatives and others who worked with him during that period. The story of the football practice at the high school is from the New York *Times*, Nov. 9, 1949, p. 3.

Bread-and-Butter Liberal: The account of Kennedy's experience with veterans' housing politics and legislation is drawn mainly from interviews and from occasional newspaper clippings, House of Representatives material, Attic Office; copy of Kennedy's speech to the veterans' housing conference is in this file. His statement before the House of Representatives on the Legion is in the *Congressional Record*, Vol. 95, Part 3, March 22, 1949, p. 2950. His quoted remark on the Taft-Hartley Bill is *ibid.*, Vol. 93, Part 3, April 16, 1947, pp. 3512-13; for his views on this bill more generally, see *ibid.*, Vol. 95, Part 4, April 27, 1949, pp. 5147-48.

Defying the White House: Kennedy's statement on the Chinese situation is in *Congressional Record*, Vol. 95, Part 1, Jan. 25, 1949, pp. 532-33; the speech at Salem was reprinted in the same document, Appendix, Vol. 95, Part 12, Feb. 21, 1949, p. A993. Kennedy's notes on his European trip of 1951 are in an envelope marked "European Trip—January—February 1951," Attic Office. For Kennedy's stand on sending troops to Europe, see *Hearings* before the Committee on Foreign Relations and Committee on Armed Services, United States Senate, "Assignment of Ground Forces of the United States to Duty in the European Area," Senate Concurrent Resolution 8, February 1951, 82nd Cong., 1st Sess., pp. 424-44. For Senator George's interrogation and Kennedy's answers, see *Hearings* cited above, "Assignment of Ground Forces . . .," pp. 432-33.

A Subject of the Pope?: For the exchange between Rogers and Kennedy, see *Hearings* before Subcommittee No. 1 of the Committee on Education and Labor, House of Representatives, 80th Cong., 1st Sess., Vol. 1, pp. 332-57. Cardinal Spellman's statement was reported in the New York *Times*, July 23, 1949, p. 1, and Mrs. Roosevelt's answers on July 28, p. 16. Cardinal Spellman's statement on fringe benefits for parochial schools is in the New York *Times*, Aug. 6, 1949, p. 1, and Bishop Oxnam's answer in the *Times*, Aug. 8, p. 13. Kennedy's bill is summarized in the *Times*, March 16, 1950, p. 29. This description of Kennedy's amendment to the federal school bill is based on his statement of his position in biographical statement for the 1952 campaign (p. 5); this document is cited more fully in notes for Chapter 6. The New York *Times* editorial appeared on March 16, 1950, p. 30; and the remarks of Representative Barden on Cardinal Spellman, and Mrs. Roosevelt on the Kennedy amendment, in the *Times*, March 7 and 8, 1950, p. 1 and p. 28. The reasons for the fate of the bill are discussed by Benjamin Fine in the New York *Times*, March 19, 1950, Sec. 4, 6. E9. The *Pilot* quotation is from the issue of March 18, 1950. Kennedy's position on budget-balancing is reflected in speeches in the House of Representatives and also in correspondence with constituents in House of Representatives material, Attic Office.

Kennedy as a Congressman: Joseph Kennedy's remarks, beginning "Our policy today . . .," are from a speech to the Virginia Law School Forum, Dec. 12, 1950, reprinted in the *Congressional Record*, Vol. 96, Part 18, Dec. 15, 1950, p. A7723; and the Republican congressman is Representative Paul W. Shafer of Michigan, whose remarks are in the *Congressional Record*, Vol. 97, Part 12, April 16, 1951, p. A2207. Kennedy's comment on "Uncle Sugar" was in his speech to the Boston Chamber of Commerce, Nov. 19, 1951, reprinted in the 1952 campaign statement, p. 24. McCormack on "Where's Johnny?" is from an auditor. The Kennedy-McCormack dialogue on the Curley petition is as Kennedy remembers it; Curley, *op. cit.*, pp. 331-34, has an account of the petition episode from Curley's viewpoint. The comment on Kennedy's talking only about New England is in the *Congressional Record*, Vol. 98, Part 3, April 1, 1952, p. 3329; I have altered the quotation very slightly. On Kennedy's appearance before the Harvard seminar, see J. P. Mallan, "Massachusetts: Liberal and Corrupt," *The New Republic*, Oct. 13, 1952, pp. 10-12; see this same journal, Nov. 3, 1952, p. 2, for a rejoinder by the professor in charge of this seminar; I have interviewed and corresponded with witnesses in connection with this controversial episode. The Boston *Post*, April 22, 1951, reported Kennedy's opposition to negative anticommunism. The Handlin quotation is from *op. cit.*, p. 142.

VI. *Green Blood versus Blue Blood*

The two reporters whose descriptions of Kennedy are mentioned are Fletcher Knebel in *Candidates 1960, op. cit.*, p. 198, and Ralph M. Blagden, "Cabot Lodge's Toughest Fight," *The Reporter*, Vol. 7, No. 7, Sept.

30, 1952, pp. 10-11. Morrissey's statement on the campaign handshaking is quoted in *McCall's, op. cit.,* p. 118. I have also used interviews with Morrissey and Kennedy and other participants in the early campaigning.

The Battle Joined: Text of Kennedy's announcement, mimeographed, April 7, 1952, is in Senatorial Campaign File, Attic Office. Material in Kennedy's office on the 1952 campaign is rather disorganized; some of it is in the Attic Office and some in the Main Office. Some of the staff studies arguing in favor of flanking Lodge on the right are in the collection, but undated and unsigned. Material includes an eight-page, single-spaced typewritten document, "What They Said and Did—Kennedy—Taft—Lodge" purporting to show Kennedy's frequent support of the Taft position as compared with Lodge's. Chief source on Kennedy's positions on campaign issues is a 178-page mimeographed compilation, well organized by subject, prepared by T. J. Reardon, and including biographical data and comparisons of Kennedy's and Lodge's voting records, Attic Office.

By the Left—or Right?: The fullest published source on Kennedy's campaign financing is H. D. Price, "Campaign Finance in Massachusetts in 1952," in C. J. Friedrich and J. K. Galbraith, eds., *Public Policy* (Cambridge: Graduate School of Public Administration, 1955), pp. 36-8. On the Brewer-Kennedy relationship, copies of messages between Brewer and Kennedy campaign aides are in the campaign collection. Ralph M. Blagden, in *The Reporter,* cited above, provides excellent coverage of the work of Taft supporters for Kennedy; he quotes from a letter sent out by Taylor. My account of the encounter in Kennedy's living room between Jackson and Joseph Kennedy is based on interviews with participants. On the Kennedy, Sr.-Fox episode, see "Investigation of Regulatory Commissions and Agencies," *Hearings* before a subcommittee of the Committee on Interstate and Foreign Commerce, House of Representatives, 85th Cong., 2nd Sess., Part 11, June 27, 1958, pp. 4126-4132.

Battle of the Teacups: There are a few campaign posters in the 1952 campaign collection. The billboard episode is drawn from an interview with an eyewitness. Kennedy's campaigning on his own, apart from the party, was observed by the author and was well established also in interviews. The best description of a Kennedy campaign tea party is Cabell Phillips, "Case History of a Senate Race," the New York *Times Magazine,* Oct. 26, 1952, p. 10. The speech by Robert Kennedy is reported in Paul F. Healy, "The Senate's Gay Young Bachelor," *The Saturday Evening Post,* June 13, 1953, p. 27. Kennedy's television schedule is in the 1952 Campaign Collection, as are suggested speeches for Mrs. Kennedy. On Lodge's campaign finance, see Price, *op. cit.,* p. 36. For a somewhat different evaluation of the 1952 voting returns, see Elmo Roper, "The Myth of the Catholic Vote," *The Saturday Review,* Oct. 31, 1959, p. 22.

VII. *The Senator from New England*

The episode of Kennedy's being warned back by the guard is from *The Saturday Evening Post,* June 13, 1953, p. 26, and the remarks of William S. White on the Senate are from his *Citadel* (New York: Harper, 1956), p. 2.

The Open Door: Kennedy's office allowance is estimated from the regulations thereon; see George B. Galloway, *The Legislative Process in Congress* (New York: Thomas Y. Crowell, 1953), pp. 416 ff. The list of Kennedy achievements is from a far longer compilation, "Memorandum from John F. Kennedy to his Constituents," January 1955, in Attic Office. The Burke quotation is from Galloway, *op. cit.*, p. 209.

What's the Matter with New England?: Kennedy's three speeches on the New England economy may be found in *Congressional Record*, Vol. 99, Part 4, May 18, 1953, pp. 5054-70; May 20, 1953, pp. 5227-40; and May 25, 1953, pp. 5455-66. For the claimed results of the New England program, see "Progress Report December 1953," 8 pp. (mimeographed), in 1953-54 Legislative Files, Attic Office. Kennedy's position on the Seaway is explained by him in *Congressional Record*, Vol. 100, Part 1, Jan. 14, 1954, p. 238. On the tariff problem, see Kennedy's Memorandum to Constituents, January 1955, cited above.

The Girl from Newport: The *Post* article is that by Healy, cited above, and the asparagus episode from *Time*, Dec. 2, 1957, p. 20. Mrs. Kennedy's comment on the courtship is from Eleanor Harris, "The Senator Is in a Hurry," *McCall's*, August 1957, p. 123 (an article, incidentally, that presents an interesting interpretation of Kennedy). The New York *Times*, Sept. 13, 1953, p. 1, offered full coverage of the wedding. The "Rules for Visiting the Kennedys" was published in the *Post*, Sept. 7, 1957, cited above. Source of Mrs. Kennedy's comment on sabotaging Monopoly is André Fontaine, "Senator Kennedy's Crisis," *Redbook Magazine*, November 1957, p. 119. Most of this section is drawn from Kennedy family interviews.

VIII. *McCarthyism*:
The Issue That Would Not Die

The main general sources on McCarthy that I have used are Jack Anderson and R. W. May, *McCarthy: The Man, the Senator, the "Ism,"* (Boston: Beacon, 1952); W. F. Buckley, Jr., and L. Brent Bozell, *McCarthy and His Enemies* (Chicago: Henry Regnery, 1954); and Richard H. Rovere *Senator Joe McCarthy* (New York: Harcourt, Brace, 1959).

Kennedy and the Liberals: On the Christoffel episode, see *Hearings* before Subcommittee No. 1 of the Committee on Education and Labor, House of Representatives, 80th Cong., 2nd Sess., pp. 2131 ff; and *Congressional Record*, Vol. 95, Part 14, June 29, 1949, pp. A4169-70. On the Harvard seminar episode, see Mallan, cited in notes for Chapter 5 above. The political scientists quoted prefer to remain anonymous. The Healy quote is from *The Saturday Evening Post, op. cit.,* p. 127; I am satisfied from other evidence that Healy quoted Kennedy accurately. Letter from ADA housewife to Kennedy is dated June 25, 1953, and his reply to her, July 13, 1953; both of these are in 1953 General Files, Attic Office. Kennedy to Boston insurance man opposed to ADA is in 1953-55 Legislative Files, February 11, 1954, Attic Office.

On The Fence: The Lodge-Dever exchange is from Rovere, *op. cit.,* p. 13. Letter to Kennedy from Western Massachusetts woman is in 1953 Legislative File, McCarthy Folder, letter dated Feb. 6, 1953; letter from Harvard law professor to Kennedy, Jan. 23, 1954, is in 1953-55 Legislative Files, Subversive Activity (Congressional Investigation) Folder. Kennedy letter to Boston newspaperman, March 23, 1954, is in 1953-55 Legislative Files, Communism Folder; his letter to Fitchburg woman, May 4, 1954, is in same file, Foreign Policy General Folder. Kennedy's answer to the Harvard Law School professor, Feb. 10, 1954, is in same file as letter from him to Kennedy, cited above. The other correspondence referred to in this section is also in the 1953-55 Legislative Files.

"The Honor and Dignity of the Senate": The Rovere quotation is in *op. cit.*, pp. 35-36. Conant's confirmation was by voice vote and hence votes were not recorded; my sources are Kennedy and Irwin Ross, in the New York *Post*, July 30, 1956, p. 21; Ross states that he was with Kennedy when McCarthy, by telephone, requested Kennedy to vote against confirming Conant, and Kennedy refused. Kennedy's comment on McCarthy is also from Ross, *op. cit.* On the Bohlen nomination, see the *Congressional Record*, Vol. 99, Part 2, March 27, 1953, p. 2392; on the Lee nomination, see *ibid.*, Vol. 100, Part 1, Jan. 25, 1954, p. 698; and on the Brewster appointment, see the New York *Times*, Aug. 4, 1954, p. 8. In answer to queries on Kennedy's stand on McCarthyism, his office issued in June 1959 a mimeographed statement, "Notes on the Record of Senator John F. Kennedy on McCarthyism and Civil Liberties." For Humphrey's statement on not being soft toward communism, see the *Congressional Record*, Vol. 100, Part 11, Aug. 12, 1954, p. 14210; for McCarthy's statement about the skunks, see *ibid.*, Vol. 100, Part 11, Aug. 16, 1954, p. 14569; and for Kennedy on the Annie Lee Moss case, see *ibid.*, Vol. 100, Part 10, Aug. 2, 1954, p. 12962. A photostat copy of the "undelivered speech," which had been misplaced in the Main Office, was made available to the author on June 23, 1959, by the Kennedy office. The speech is undated but presumed by the Kennedy office to have been scheduled for July 31, 1954. Ross refers to this speech in his *Post* story of July 30, 1956, p. 21.

"A Reasonable Indictment"?: I have interviewed several participants in the television episode. Quotations of Kennedy, including his "reasonable indictment," are from author's interview with him, July 17, 1959. Quotations of Mrs. Roosevelt are from Fletcher Knebel, in *Candidates 1960, op. cit.*, p. 204; her article "Of Stevenson, Truman and Kennedy," *The Saturday Evening Post*, March 8, 1958, pp. 72-73; and her book *On My Own* (New York: Harper, 1958), pp. 163-64. Kennedy's review of Rovere's book appeared in the Washington *Post and Times-Herald*, June 28, 1959, p. E4, and his critic's letter (with a brief reply from Kennedy) in the Brooklyn *Tablet*, Aug. 8, 1959.

IX. *The Anatomy of Courage*

My source on Kennedy's hospitalization is chiefly Kennedy family interviews.

Grace in a Vacuum: The Addison's disease rumor was taken up in an interview of Kennedy by Fletcher Knebel; I have used a copy of the press statement issued by the Kennedy office and the study by Knebel; a more recent statement by the Kennedy office based on report by his endocrinologist; and other sources. The report of Kennedy's doctor is dated July 21, 1959; the doctor prefers to remain anonymous.

"Profiles in Courage": There is an extensive file of material and drafts for *Profiles in Courage* in Kennedy's Main Office; I have studied these and also the original manuscript material. Canham's review is in the *Christian Science Monitor*, Jan. 5, 1956, p. 7. The statistics on Kennedy's increase in poll popularity shortly after the award of the Pulitzer prize is from the Roper Public Opinion Center at Williams College.

The Meaning of Courage: Quotations are from *Profiles in Courage* (New York: Harper, 1956). The priest's letter on McCarthy is in the McCarthy Folder, 1957 Legislative File, Attic Office.

X. Vice-Presidential Politics

On Kennedy's return to duty, see accounts in the Boston *Herald*, the Boston *Post*, and the New York *Times*, all reprinted in the *Congressional Record*, Vol. 101, Part 5, May 25, 1955, pp. 6965-66.

Fight for the Electoral College: For list of sponsors of the Daniel-Mundt resolution see the *Congressional Record*, Vol. 102, Part 4, March 15, 1956, p. 4749. Douglas's letter to Kennedy is dated April 10, 1956, 1956 Legislative File (Electoral College); see also Boston *Traveller*, April 5, 1956.

Melee in Massachusetts: This section is based in small part on personal observation and participation by the author as candidate for delegate and later as delegate to the Democratic national convention of 1956. The Kennedy-McCormack contest was well covered in Boston and other Massachusetts newspapers. On Kennedy's and McCormack's early plans and activities, see letter and telegram, Kennedy to Stevenson, March 23, 1956; letter, Kennedy aide to Adlai E. Stevenson, Jan. 12, 1956, Kennedy Personal File, 1956, Attic Office; I have used also McCormack to author, Dec. 8, 1955. Kennedy to James Finnegan, May 2, 1956, Attic Office files, described Kennedy's plans at that point. The Attic Office files contain a copy of a list of Kennedy's contacts for the Democratic state committee chairmanship contest, and the "scenario" for the anticipated committee meeting, both undated. My account of the actual committee meeting is drawn from several of those present and from Boston newspapers.

Who but Kennedy?: The account of the early stage of convention planning is based on interviews with Kennedy aides, on Kennedy family interviews, and on mimeographed copies of both the documents referred to (the report on the religious aspect and the report on the availability of various men for the vice-presidential nomination), entitled "The Democratic Nominee for Vice President in 1956" (11 pp.), both in Main Office files, undated. Shriver's interview with Stevenson is described in Shriver to Joseph P. Kennedy, July 18, 1956, Main Office files.

The First Hurrah: There are good accounts of Kennedy's convention campaign for the vice-presidential nomination, especially for the period after the nomination was thrown open, in *Time, Newsweek,* and the New York *Times;* I have also made extensive use of Knebel, *op. cit.*, pp. 184-85, based on Tom Winship's eyewitness accounts in the Boston *Globe*. Eleanor Roosevelt describes her meeting with Kennedy in her *On My Own, op. cit.*, pp. 163-64. My account of McCormack's role in the floor fight is taken from *Time;* however, there is considerable question as to what did happen because of the confusion on the floor at that time. Kennedy today says that he does not know if McCormack had the role that *Time* and other periodicals imputed to him. Probably McCormack did not; it seems likely that the "conspiracy theory of history" should yield to the "confusion theory" here.

XI. Senator from the United States

Kennedy's speech to the Harvard alumni at the June 14 commencement exercises was reprinted in the *Congressional Record*, Vol. 102, Part 8, June 22, 1956, pp. 10800-801. The letter from the Haverhill man is in 1956 Personal Files, Attic Office. Stevenson's letter to Kennedy was dated Nov. 18, 1956; the original hangs on the wall of Kennedy's office in Washington.

A Democrat Looks at Foreign Policy: Source of the exchange between Kennedy and Herter is "Ambassadorial Appointments," *Hearings* before the Committee on Foreign Relations, U.S. Senate, 85th Cong., 1st Sess., Aug. 1, 1957, pp. 26-29; and between Kennedy and Dulles is "Mutual Security Act of 1958," same committee, 85th Cong., 2nd Sess., March 24, 1958, pp. 179-84. The New York *Times,* July 3, 1957, p. 5, reported the reaction in France to Kennedy's speech on Algeria. The account of Kennedy's telephone conversation with his father is in *Time,* Dec. 2, 1957, p. 20. Citation for Kennedy's article is "A Democrat Looks at Foreign Policy," *Foreign Affairs,* Vol. 36, No. 1, October 1957, pp. 44-59. The speech on the arms gap was delivered in the Senate Aug. 14, 1958; see *Congressional Record,* Vol. 104, Part 14, pp. 17569-575.

Civil Rights: A Profile in Cowardice?: The indignant New Yorker's letter to Kennedy is dated Aug. 2, 1957, and Kennedy's reply, Aug. 10, 1957, 1957 Legislative File, Civil Rights Folder, Main Office. For the legislative and parliamentary background of the 1957 civil-rights battle, see H. E. Shuman, "Senate Rules and the Civil Rights Bill," *The American Political Science Review,* Vol. 51, No. 4, December 1957, pp. 955-75. For Kennedy's position on bypassing the Eastland Committee, see *Congressional Record,* Vol. 103, Part 7, June 20, 1957, pp. 9793, 9805, 9815; Long Island resident to Kennedy, June 26, 1957, and Kennedy's answer, July 3, 1957, 1957 Legislative File, Civil Rights Folder, Main Office. Senator Morse set forth his position in letter to the Washington *Post and Times-Herald,* July 1, 1957. Kennedy's speech endorsing Section 3 is in the *Congressional Record,* Vol. 103, Part 9, July 23, 1957, pp. 12467-468; the vote is recorded in *ibid.,* p. 12565. For the legislative history of the Civil Rights Bill, see the two excellent articles in *The Reporter* by Douglass Cater, "The Senate Debate on Civil Rights," Aug. 8, 1957, pp. 37-40, and "How the Senate Passed the Civil-Rights Bill," Sept. 5, 1957, pp. 9-13. Telegrams to Kennedy from the Southern governors are in 1957 Legislative File, Civil Rights Folder, Main Office. Kennedy's defense of his position on the jury-trial amendment is in *Congressional Record,* Vol. 103, Part 10, Aug. 1, 1957, pp. 13305-307; see also, correspondence in Civil Rights Folder cited above. Example of Kennedy's mollifying of Southerners is Kennedy to Birmingham, Alabama, woman, Aug. 1, 1957, in Civil Rights Folder cited above.

Hooverism and Housekeeping: Hoover's tribute to Kennedy is in letter to Joseph P. Kennedy, Aug. 20, 1956, Kennedy Personal Files, Attic Office. Kennedy stated his position on the accrued-expenditure bill in *Congressional Record,* Vol. 102, Part 6, May 21, 1956, p. 8524; for his stand on the proposal for an administrative vice-president, see *ibid.,* Vol. 102, Part 6, May 9, 1956, p. 7744; and for his defense of his committee's choices of the five senatorial greats, see *ibid.,* Vol. 103, Part 5, May 1, 1957, pp. 6206-16.

XII. *Swinging for the Fences*

These anecdotes are from interviews and from reports by newspapermen covering the affairs; Kennedy's exchange with the teen-ager was reported in the New York *Times,* Oct. 12, 1959, Kennedy's negotiations with publishers are in miscellaneous files in both t' e Senate offices.

Room 362: This account of life in Kennedy's office is based mainly on extensive observation and work by the author in this office during 1959. Some of Kennedy's financial memoranda are in 1956 Personal File, Attic Office; see also, Thomas J. Walsh to Kennedy, July 18, 1956, and Aug. 17, 1956, same file. Kennedy's current reading was reported in the New York *Times,* July 21, 1957, Sect. 7, p. 6. Reston's comments on Kennedy were reprinted in the *Congressional Record,* Vol. 104, Part 15, Aug. 21, 1958, pp. 18979-980.

Home Run in Massachusetts: The candidate for Congress observing the extent of Kennedy's personal support among businessmen was the author. On the television-channel case, see Kennedy correspondence with Robert Choate and others in Federal Communications Act File, Attic Office, 1956 Legislative File; and for Kennedy's memorandum, see *Hearings* before a subcommittee of the Committee on Interstate and Foreign Commerce, House of Representatives, 84th Cong., 2nd Sess., pp. 345-48. The Civil Aeronautics Board information is based on Kennedy, *et al.* to Chairman, CAB, July 12, 1956; Kennedy to *ibid.,* July 13, 1956, 1956-57 Legislative Files, Attic Office. The quotation of Celeste is from the New York *Times,* Oct. 19, 1958, p. 57. Kennedy's memorandum to aide in regard to the coattail-seeking candidate is in 1958 Election Files, Main Office. The baton-seizing episode was witnessed by the author. The memo about lowering campaign predictions is in 1958 Campaign Files, Main Office. Voting returns are from *Congressional Directory,* 86th Cong., 1st Sess. (Washington: Government Printing Office, 1959), p. 325.

The Senate as Testing Ground?: My account of the labor measure is drawn from interviews, the *Congressional Record,* congressional hearings, and John Van Camp, "What Happened to the Labor Reform Bill?," *The Reporter,* Oct. 2, 1958, pp. 24-28. Kennedy's statement on the defeat of the labor bill in the House was issued in mimeographed form, undated, Main Office. On the 1959 labor bill, see especially *Congressional Record,* Vol. 105 (unbound), April 22, 1959, pp. 5795-827; 1959 Labor Legislation File, Main Office, correspondence between Kennedy and Labor Committee staff and advisers; and accounts in the New York *Times.* Cabell Phillips's comments appear in the New York *Times,* Sept. 13, 1959, Sect. IV, p. E7.

"Victura"?: The description of a typical Kennedy campaign trip is drawn from the author's observations after accompanying Kennedy on a Midwestern trip in the spring of 1959. Description of the campaign office is from author's observation. Fletcher Knebel's comment on Mrs. Kennedy as a campaigner is from *Candidates 1960, op. cit.,* p. 200. The Chicago *Daily News* poll was published in a series of articles in April 1959. The convention first-ballot estimate was based on answers from about half the 1956 delegates who responded to the questionnaire; these answers were then projected as gauges of the whole delegation vote in 1960. The Gallup poll of Democratic voters is from Press Release of the Public Opinion News Service, Princeton, N. J., Aug. 13, 1959. Quotations from Democratic leaders on Kennedy's strategy are from Joe McCarthy, "The Remarkable Kennedys," *Look,* Oct. 13, 1959, pp. 27-33. Kennedy's *Life* article was in the issue of March 11, 1957, pp. 164-66.

XIII. *Kennedy and the Catholics*

The story of the visiting congressman is told in *Profiles in Courage,* pp. 123-24.

Sources on Catholicism and Protestantism that I have used are John A. Ryan and Francis J. Boland, *Catholic Principles of Politics* (New

York: Macmillan, 1950), the revised edition of *The State and the Church;* Leo Pfeffer, *Church, State, and Freedom* (Boston: Beacon, 1953); John C. Bennett, *Christians and the State* (New York: Scribner, 1958); *Catholic Mind,* Vol. LVII, No. 1143, May, June 1959 (articles and addresses by John Courtney Murray, S.J.).

Render unto Caesar?: A recent reference to the Vatican Council of 1870 is Gerald W. Johnson, *The New Republic,* March 5, 1959, p. 10. Mrs. Roosevelt's comments on the church-state problem and a Catholic candidacy are in *Look,* March 3, 1959, and the New York *Times,* Feb. 17, 1959, pp. 1, 19. Her Detroit remarks were made in an interview with Lou Gordon of "Detroit Headline." The article challenging Al Smith appeared in *The Atlantic,* Vol. 139, April 1927, pp. 540-49; and his reply, *ibid.,* May 1927, pp. 721-28.

Kennedy Takes His Stand: Kennedy's address at Notre Dame was delivered Jan. 29, 1950; a copy of the speech is in the Kennedy office. His statement appeared in Fletcher Knebel, "A Catholic in 1960," *Look,* March 3, 1959, p. 17. The Catholic doubt over the advisability of a Catholic President is reflected in *The Catholic Observer,* Vol. 5, No. 17, March 6, 1959, pp. 1, 3; see especially, the roundup of Catholic editorial opinion in this journal on p. 3. Cardinal Cushing's defense of Kennedy is in the New York *Times,* March 10, 1959, p. 19. Lowell's statement on POAU's reaction to Kennedy's comments in *Look* was given to the press.

What Kind of Catholic?: Kennedy's statement "The Pope speaks . . ." was made to Martin Agronsky, NBC interview, December 1957. Source of his statement to the Council of Methodist Bishops is *Time,* April 27, 1959, p. 16. The Cogley statement is in *Commonweal,* May 8, 1959, p. 152. Smith's remark is quoted in Oscar Handlin, *Al Smith and His America* (Boston: Little, Brown, 1958). Kennedy's answers to Protestant critics and interrogators are in 1957 Legislative File, Religion Folder; see especially, Kennedy's answers dated June 17, 1957, and July 2, 1957. On the Vatican question, see Kennedy letter to Cambridge man, April 12, 1954, 1953-55 Legislative Files, Foreign Policy—General Folder, Attic Office. One letter sent out from Kennedy's office over Kennedy's name, and dated June 5, 1959 (Main Office), stated his position on the question of birth control as follows: "Without minimizing the moral implications which many people see in the so-called birth control issue or minimizing the relevance of these considerations to political decisions, I nevertheless agree with you that consideration of legislation is essentially a political issue. I believe also that those who have no religious or moral scruples concerning the use of contraceptives should not be hampered in their freedom of choice." However, the Kennedy office stated recently that this letter does not represent Kennedy's personal viewpoint. For Kennedy's belief in pluralism, see his letter dated July 31, 1957, Religion Folder, Main Office. The Bennett quotation is from *Christians and the State, op. cit.,* p. 263.

"No Catholics Need Apply"?: Handlin's quote is from *Al Smith and His America,* pp. 130-31. See the perceptive columns on the Al Smith precedent by William Shannon, "The Lesson of Al Smith," New York *Post,* March 31 and April 1, 1958. The position of some Kennedy campaign strategists on the effect of his Catholicism on the vote was summed up in the study cited in Chapter 10, "The Catholic Vote in 1952 and 1956"; I have supplemented this with interviews. For the report on Governor Patterson's support of Kennedy and Methodist reaction in Alabama, see the New York *Times,* June 17, 1959, p. 38; June 25, 1959, p. 16. The Baptist rebuke was quoted in a dispatch in the *Berkshire Eagle,* July 1, 1959, p. 4. The exchange between the *Pilot* and Bishop Lord is reported in the New York *Times,* Aug. 1, 1959, p. 14. Bishop Lord's statement against voting anti-Catholic is from the New York *Times,* Oct. 10, 1959, p. 6. Kennedy's statement on not voting "Catholic" is a quotation from a friend.

XIV. *A Profile in Leadership*

Joseph Alsop's comment is from his column, the *Berkshire Eagle*, April 13, 1959. The quotation of Marquis Childs is from his "Washington Calling," the *Berkshire Eagle*, July 8, 1959. The Gallup poll on Kennedy's characteristics is from the above source, same press release. The plus-minus rating of Kennedy is drawn from Gallup Survey No. 591-K prepared by the Roper Public Opinion Research Center, Williams College. Kennedy's aggregate score (rating times number of people so rating) was plus 3135 to minus 220. Lippmann's comments on Roosevelt are quoted in A. M. Schlesinger, Jr., *The Crisis of the Old Order* (Boston: Houghton Mifflin, 1957), p. 291.

What Sort of Man?: Mrs. Kennedy's comments on her husband are from *Life*, Aug. 24, 1959, p. 80, and from Kennedy family interviews. For a good example of Kennedy's attitude toward the "New Republicanism" and some of its tenets, see his review of Arthur Larson's *What We Are For* in the New York *Times Book Review*, Feb. 8, 1959, p. 1.

What Sort of Democrat?: Mr. Dooley on the Democratic party is quoted by Kennedy in *Life*, March 11, 1957, also inserted in the *Congressional Record*, Vol. 103, Part 3, March 8, 1957, p. 3356. Kennedy's quote on Stevenson is from the *Congressional Record*, Vol. 102, Part 4, March 8, 1956, p. 4352. The phrase "the best of a sorry lot" is from Joe McCarthy, "Front Man for a Dynasty," *Look*, Oct. 13, 1959, p. 31. The book by John Buchan (Lord Tweedsmuir), *Pilgrim's Way*, is published by Houghton Mifflin (Boston, 1940). The Kennedy quotes beginning "What we need now . . ." and ending with ". . . and in nationalism" are from his speech at the Jefferson-Jackson Day dinner at Detroit, Mich., on May 23, 1959. So also is the paragraph beginning "It is the enduring faith. . . ."

What Sort of President?: The presidency as serving as a "steady focus of leadership" is from Clinton Rossiter, *The American Presidency* (New York: Harcourt, Brace, 1956). The interview with Kennedy quoted here was conducted by the author at Hyannisport, Mass., July 17, 1959. By previous agreement, Kennedy later (October 1959) edited and expanded these remarks.

A Place of Moral Leadership?: The New York *Times*, Nov. 13, 1932, Sect. 8, p. 1, is the source of the quotation of Roosevelt on presidential leadership. Cabell Phillips's description of Kennedy's speaking style is in New York *Times Magazine*, Oct. 25, 1959, pp. 24 and 48. The Kennedy quotation beginning "courteous but candid" is from the Detroit address of May 23, 1959, cited above; and on "internecine warfare" from his remarks to the Harvard alumni, cited in notes to Chapter 11. The quotation from Holmes is taken from Max Lerner, ed., *The Mind and Faith of Justice Holmes* (Boston: Little, Brown, 1943), p. 20. Rossiter on Roosevelt as "owl" is from his volume cited above (Mentor Book ed., p. 114). The final quotation from Kennedy is from his speech in Milwaukee, March 11, 1959.

INDEX